Alternative models of elementary education

A BLAISDELL BOOK IN EDUCATION

CONSULTING EDITOR **John I. Goodlad**
University of California at Los Angeles

Alternative models of elementary education

BRUCE R. JOYCE

Teachers College, Columbia University

Blaisdell Publishing Company
A Division of Ginn and Company

Waltham, Massachusetts • Toronto • London

372
J 89

*To John and Dorothy Headly and their grandchildren,
Cynthia, Lisa, Kevin, and Brendan, with a fond hope that all
grandchildren may enjoy a richer education and a more
meaningful and delightful life.*

Foreword

Professor Joyce's book is about schools, places where education (planned and unplanned) takes place. He assumes that schools can and should be consciously shaped. Although he has his own preferences with respect to ends and means, these are subordinated to his concern for the development of alternative models. "I fervently hope," he says, "that diversity will replace the remarkable similarity of our schools, and I believe that a more interesting world will result."

Professor Joyce is guided throughout by assumptions about learning and teaching, only some of which are made explicit at first. But his assumptions tend to open up rather than narrow the range of viable models for schooling. For example, the entire social system of a school, rather than just a formal curricular structure, determines how children behave and what they learn. Learning need not be dependent on teachers. A model of elementary education can include individual children teaching themselves or small groups of children teaching one another. Teachers need not teach alone in their individual classroom cells; they can and should group and regroup as purposes and demands change. Subject-matter need not and should not be laid out as the diet for all; there is nothing sacred about age as the criterion for what is to be learned. Joyce insists that the customs and habits of schooling be subjected to critical analysis — that the school, in mission and means, be a product of selection.

To me, the most exciting implication of Professor Joyce's book is the prospect of a school community selecting its own destiny, so to speak. We in the United States make much of local control of education, but there is more myth than fact here. What schools do and become is largely the product of certification requirements for teachers, state-prescribed textbooks, legal codes, and so on. If this were not so, surely schools would be much more varied than they are. But what would happen if at least some schools were freed experimentally from these and other restrictions? Many decisions would be made as they are now prescribed; we are not accustomed to exercising freedom in truly basic realms of educational practice. Some people would do foolish things; there is nothing unusual about people acting foolishly. On the other side of the coin, however, some unusually exciting schools would undoubtedly emerge.

Join, then, the Responsible Parties (one member of the Board of Education, three citizens from the neighborhood, the directors of curriculum and elementary education of the school district, three teachers and the principal of the school-to-be, and a technologist from the state department of education) brought into being by Professor Joyce to plan the mission of a mythical school. And let us hope that such Responsible Parties will come together in communities of the United States to plan the mission of real schools.

Bruce Joyce's book on elementary education is a fitting companion to Lawrence Downey's *The Secondary Phase of Education,* 1965. Like Downey, Joyce identifies necessary realms of educational decision-making, suggests alternative stances in each realm, and illustrates the practical consequences of assuming a stance.

Professor Joyce brings highly relevant credentials to his manuscript. His early teaching experience was in elementary education, as was extensive later consultation. After securing his doctorate and teaching at Wayne State University, he taught at the University of Delaware and later joined the faculty of the University of Chicago where he directed the program for the preparation of elementary school teachers. Currently, he is at Teachers College, Columbia University. He writes extensively and insightfully on elementary education, curriculum, and teaching.

We take pleasure in adding *Alternative Models of Elementary Education* to the growing list of Blaisdell Books in Education.

JOHN I. GOODLAD

Contents

1
Decisions that create schools   1

2
The press of events: motives for decision   11

3
A sense of purpose: the mission of the school   51

4
The means of education, 1: the social system of the school   95

5
The means of education, 2: the technical support systems of the school   121

6
The means of education, 3: the curricular systems of the school   137

7

The means of education, 4: the concept of curricular modes   *195*

8

The regeneration of education: a multiple-modes approach   *215*

9

Postscript: alternative models   *237*

Bibliography   *239*

Index   *245*

Decisions that create schools

*The only reason that a teacher should be a person, alive to the things that are, is that he must encourage speculation and lead it. To help a student learn about an unknown and vastly different country requires a medium, a metaphor in which the known and the unknown can meet, each taking meaning from the other, and such a medium is the essence of music, of poetry, or art. Students taught by a real humanist will become real humanists, readers, listeners, men of intellectual and emotional delight, ready for a kind of intimacy with the world which will breed not contempt, but freedom of mind, a way out of the slavery of mere conformism to society.**

1

Our need to learn to think creatively about education is very great. Our society is changing rapidly and our schools are struggling to reshape themselves. The purpose of this book is to present a framework for analyzing educational ends and means — a framework that can help us see the alternative functions the school can serve and the alternative means that are available to achieve them. In its whole, it is a model that can be used for generating new models of education.

Hence, the tone is analytical. I have attempted to develop a rational system for analyzing education. Yet, education is an emotional *thing* — it happens to humans who feel and value and become attached to their own ideas. Therefore, we will begin with a caution.

A personal view

Even when we attempt to write about education from a "neutral" or analytic stance, most of us find that what we say is suffused with our own personal views about what makes a driving, exciting place in which children can learn.

---

* Ole Sand, from remarks made before the Tanglewood Symposium, Music Educators National Conference, Lenox, Massachusetts, July 24, 1967.

I am no exception to this, and I would like to try to express my biases here, where the reader can identify them before he "tries on" the body of the book.

I feel strongly that, in education, we have depended far too much on a few, simple educational methods, mostly mediated through personal, face-to-face encounters between teachers and students. The means of education seem to me to be far less "curricular" than we have assumed. When most of us think about schools, we think of the "standard" curriculum areas: reading, arithmetic, and so forth. Actually, I believe the social system of the school is as powerful as the curricular systems, because the social system provides us with values, ways of thinking, and views of ourselves, to mention only a few of its effects. The influence of the social system on the student has received much too little attention in educational theory as well as in practice. Very few teachers and administrators know as much about the social system they are creating as they do about the curricular systems they develop. Nor can they create an effective social system as readily as they can make a curriculum in science or in social studies or any other curriculum area. In fact, the social system of the school actually can undermine the curricular and instructional effects of the faculty.[1] Hence, the reader will find, in Chapter Four, that the means of education are described not simply as curricular systems, but as social and technological systems as well — the environment of education is seen as a many-sided one.

Another of my beliefs that has affected this book is that too much education today is mediated through the teacher. We should learn to think, not just in terms of teachers leading groups of children, but in terms of many kinds of educational agents. Some of these should be man-machine systems, using computers or other devices and "live" teachers. Some should be tutorial systems in which teacher and child relate together on a one-to-one basis. Some should be composed of inquiring groups of children who operate with and without teacher leadership. In Chapter Five, the section dealing with multiple-systems approaches to teaching is close to my heart.

---

[1] James S. Coleman, *The Adolescent Society* (Glencoe, Illinois: The Free Press, 1963) is a vivid account of just such a phenomenon.

My third bias is that the schools of America (and actually, the world) are far too homogeneous. Considering the possible goals and means of education — the possible combinations of ends and means that we could employ, the educational models we use are few and uninspiring. I fervently hope that diversity will replace the remarkable similarity of our schools, and I believe a more interesting world will result.

Last, it is in the schools that the young learn whether and how to debate the future. In our concern with the teaching of skills and "essential" knowledge, we have neglected the personal, reflective functions of education. We have gone only a short way toward learning how to build an education that helps children discover and expand themselves and learn to act to create their world. While I have expressed in other places my acute concern that we make the dialogue on human events a central part of general education,[2] it will be evident that I have not yet finished unburdening myself on that subject.

No doubt many other biases affect this work. No apology is offered for them nor should we dwell longer on them. The task of analyzing education is more important and deserves our chief attention.

The creation of schools: reason and non-reason

The world presses on us; even in the most benign circumstances we are not wholly free. When there is no pressure to move in any particular direction, there are still constraints imposed by our lack of vision and resources — our sense of what is possible. In every important human activity it takes an enormous effort to back off from our present stance and try to achieve a philosophical awareness of where we are going and where we *might* be going.

In the case of a social institution such as education, the basic processes of the society continually shape the function and character of the school. In a primitive society, the resulting institution would

---

[2] For example, see Bruce R. Joyce, *Strategies for Elementary Social Science Education* (Chicago: Science Research Associates, 1965).

rarely be questioned — probably only if it became severely out of step with the rest of the society due to a period of rapid social change. In a highly-developed society, however, we are able, by dint of a mighty force of will, to be sure, to step back and observe ourselves, our society, and our school. Once we gain some perspective, we can attempt to create a school that will have deliberately-selected goals — a school that will not only be produced by the society but which will, perforce, return the favor and have a beneficial effect on the future course of civilization.

The purpose of this book is to identify the crucial decision areas that bring a school program into existence, the alternative courses of action that are possible in each decision area, and how various combinations of decisions can bring into being schools that reflect certain beliefs about the ends and means of education.

Our approach assumes that it is possible to make effective analyses of the educational process, that the various aspects of educational process can be coordinated one with the other, and that schools *should* be produced by conscious decision wherever possible, rather than shaped by the force of events.

However, to build schools rationally — on a model, in a manner of speaking — requires that we make explicit the factors that can be put together to create the education of children. We have to agree on terms and on a frame of reference for analyzing education. We will find that our frame of reference will change over a period of time as we test it against reality, but it is essential that we begin with one that promises to give us an intellectual structure with which we can think about schooling. Much of the present volume will be devoted to the development of one analytic frame of reference and a specific language that enables us to use this frame of reference to analyze existing school programs and to set out the decisions that need to be made to build fresh approaches to elementary education.

The frame of reference we will use in this book hypothesizes that schools are created through three realms of decisions:

(1) Decisions in the first realm answer the question: "What will be the mission of the school?" This question can also be phrased: "How will the school serve the individual and his society?"

(2) Decisions in the second realm answer the question: "What means will the school employ?" This question can also be re-phrased: "How will the dimensions of the environment be shaped to carry out the mission of the school?" or "What social, technological, and curricular systems will be developed to enter effectively into the life of the student?"

(3) Decisions in the third realm create environmental structures that organize people and materials. Questions in this area include: "Who shall teach whom?" "How will children and instructional materials be brought together?" "What kind of plan will be used to communicate purposes and means to teacher and students?" "What system will assess growth and communicate it to those concerned?"

Listing these three realms in order does not mean that they occur, or should occur, in that order. At times, people think about ends by creating means and then looking at their goals. In recent years, for example, school buildings have been designed to facilitate "Team-Teaching," which is a structural arrangement. Then, after the school has opened, its functions and means gradually developed. It is also not unusual to find a school faculty struggling to develop a "non-graded" structure before they have defined mission and means.[3]

However, it is important to recognize that decisions are made in each of these realms, even when they are not made consciously. *Every* school will serve certain functions for the individual and society (and will *not* serve others). Every school will use some means and not others. Every school will have some organizational forms and may not have several other possible forms.

As decisions are made, functions selected, means matched to function, and structures developed to bring the educational system into being, many combinations of function, means and structures take shape. We shall refer to each unique combination as a *curricular mode* or *curricular system*. Sometimes an entire school program

---

[3] See, for definitions of non-graded structures, John I. Goodlad and Robert A. Anderson, *The Nongraded Elementary School* (New York: Harcourt, Brace and World, 1965).

utilizes only one system. Sometimes schools use several systems, or a multiple-systems approach. This language is relatively new, however. The school around the corner probably doesn't think of itself as representing one or more alternative curricular modes.

It is possible to develop a school program by creating curriculum systems and welding them into an effective totality. Whereas many past attempts to reform education have been attempts to develop and spread single ways of teaching and particular curricular plans or structures, we assume that the educational process aims at several very different kinds of objectives that require alternative curricular systems that are used in combination with each other.

Hence, the name *Alternative Models of Elementary Education* refers to the development of alternative curricular modalities or systems *and to alternative plans for weaving them into effective school programs.*

It is worth noting at this point that we should try to avoid the error of looking at education exclusively as something that teachers do to or for groups of children. It is possible to develop curricular modes in which individual children teach themselves. It is also possible to use democratically-organized groups of children who teach themselves. Technological aids to human behavior are beginning to open up fascinating and powerful new educational means. For example, automated data storage and retrieval systems will shortly make available to every local school scholarly knowledge on almost every subject. Computer-assisted games simulate reality and teach children complex processes that previously could only be described to them. Educational reform that limits itself to the concept of a "stand-up" teacher working with a group of children will find only a few of the possible systems for getting people to learn.

It should be noted also that the existing curriculum "Areas" (reading, arithmetic, social studies, science, art, music, physical education, and so on) represent only a few of the possibilities for selecting and organizing subject matter. In our emerging world we should be prepared to reselect and regroup things to teach.[4]

---

[4] See, for example, the proposals made by Philip Phenix, *Realms of Meaning* (New York: McGraw-Hill, 1964).

Furthermore, we must be prepared to develop ways of educating that may not be housed in places called schools. Usually in this book, we will continue to refer to schools and to elementary school curriculums, but many of the kinds of schooling and many of the curriculum modes we will discuss could be housed in many school environments or mediated through communication technology into homes or other places. Moreover, when we think "school," our mental image should not be a scene of rows of desks faced by a talking teacher. We should envision laboratories, libraries, theaters, seminar rooms, cartridge-loading motion picture projectors children can use, television tape libraries, and many other alternatives to the "classroom."

A last caution is that we have become conditioned to limited forms of educational environments — usually we think in terms of verbal learning in school as it is brought about by verbal, expository teaching. Most of us have much to learn if we are to be able to think adequately about the educative effects of social climates, social organizations, and things that at first sound as abstruse as "communication styles" and "dissonance situations." We are only beginning to appreciate the possible dimensions of the environment that can serve us by affecting children. Although recent developments are expanding our knowledge of teaching and learning, our sense of possible instructional forms for educating children, and our ability to make technology serve children's need to learn and to control their environment, each new discovery sharpens our awareness of what we do not know. *Anyone who would create a school needs first to accept the fact that only a small fraction of the decisions we have to make can be based on "hard" knowledge.*

The forces that affect decisions

Although we should try to make our decisions as deliberate and reasoned as possible, we have to recognize that many forces operate to determine the functions of the school — some of them arising from events that at first seem far-removed from education.

Social forces sometimes make the school an instrument of social policy. For example, the neighborhood elementary school has been used in some neighborhoods to maintain racial segregation (by drawing boundaries which send children of only one race to the school), whereas in other communities boundaries have been drawn to deliberately promote racial integration.

Traditions also affect the shape of the schools. For example, in the United States, elementary school teaching is still seen largely as women's work and much of the staff of elementary schools is made up of young women who teach for only a few years before they marry. The elementary school is greatly affected by the fact that so much of its staff is composed of inexperienced personnel and because many of the experienced teachers are females whose careers are secondary to the responsibilities engendered by marriage and childbearing. In the center of our cities, the shortage of career teachers is accentuated. As many as one-third of the teachers in some large school districts do not hold permanent licenses for teaching.

The sensitive position of education in the society also has its effect. For instance, many parents and other citizens react very quickly to events in the school. To reduce negative reactions, many teachers try to avoid controversial issues that might bring unpleasant response. When these teachers avoid political and social issues and other topics, their classrooms may become bland, safe places, where free-ranging inquiry is unknown.

In fact, there are so many forces acting on the school that unless the responsible authorities develop thoroughgoing and vigorous plans and carry them out with resolution, it is very likely that circumstances will operate to give the school a program that may not be at all what was hoped for.[5]

This problem is compounded by the fact that there are so many easy-to-implement, ready-made patterns for educational programs. It is almost automatic for school officials to group children by age, to have six grades, to buy basal readers and textbooks for spelling, social studies, and science. A brand new school can be opened and,

---

[5] For a thorough analysis of the forces that operate to shape educational policy, see Roald F. Campbell, Luverne L. Cunningham, and Roderick F. McPhee, *The Organization and Control of American Schools* (Columbus, Ohio: C. E. Merrill, 1965).

within a week, it can take on the character of the school down the road.

Furthermore, it is extremely hard work to develop a unique educational program — and one may find that deviation from the typical school program is not always regarded with approval. Sometimes an attempt to create a school tailored to the needs of a particular community and student body only arouses fear in the local community that the children will be harmed by not receiving the same school program given in other communities! Many fine attempts to improve schools have foundered because the community has had a negative view of "experimentation" in education.

Consequently, current school programs, influenced by the impact of social forces, tempted by tradition and contemporary practice, and watched by a nervous public, seek many fewer possible missions with a much smaller range of means than are possible. Therefore, as we consider each of the elements of educational programs, we shall look at many functions, means and structures that occur rarely but which have much promise. We also will include some possibilities that I firmly disagree with, but which occur with some frequency or have strong advocates. Consciously considering a wide range of solutions to the problems of developing an educational program permits the exploration and comparison of a great variety of views about the alternatives for creating schools.

The successive sections of the book begin with the identification of the forces that shape schools, with particular emphasis on the social patterns and human characteristics that resist innovation in educational forms. Next, we consider the development of educational purposes on the "missions" of the school. We then journey through the selection of means. Finally, we deal with the development of organizational structures and the consideration of alternative models of integrated educational components.

If this book makes a contribution, it will not be because it identifies a direction for elementary education, but because it helps identify the tasks involved in the creation of elementary education and the options that are available to those who would redirect their educational efforts. No matter how clear the alternatives are, however, and no matter how much one wants to improve education, sooner or later he must learn that changing education involves an attempt to change a ponderously large, bureaucratic institution, the American Public School. And, like all huge, bureaucratic complexes, it is permeated with forces that stabilize it by developing routines that resist change. In the following two chapters we will concentrate on the nature of the school bureaucracy and ways of changing it. For unless we cope with the stabilizing forces of the school, all our alternative models will turn out to be impossible dreams.

The press of events:
motives for decision

*Successful innovations of new practices in schools have to satisfy
not only the criterion of education plausibility or soundness;
they must also catch the mood of the public. For example,
teaching machines are currently (educational) failures because
they do not teach the "higher mental processes" such as
critical thinking — but the public is willing to buy them. At the
same time, "self-directed study," which can be valuable for
the child's education, has been driven underground by the
national drive toward standardization, automation, and
routine-teaching procedures applicable to everyone.**

2

Schools do not exist in a social vacuum. They are live,
"flesh-and-blood" organs of their societies. As such, they are
extremely complicated. One does not simple dream up models for schools and then go out and put them into action.
Even private schools are by no means free from their societies, as can easily be seen from their monotonous conformity
to one or two educational patterns.

Moreover, schools are often staffed by people who have
forceful needs and ideas of their own. One cannot create a
model for a school that the staff cannot or will not implement. Nor can one, in building an educational model, ignore the fact that the school itself has to be a stable institution, non-chaotic, orderly, and satisfying to its members.
Over the years, in fact, the school has developed a myriad of
bureaucratic routines that operate to preserve the *status
quo.*

Furthermore, the possibilities for schooling in any given
era are limited and extended by what is known about education at the time. Today, fresh educational ideas and new
technologies are both expanding our options at a rapid

---

* From Herbert A. Thelen, *Classroom Grouping for Teachability* (New
York: Wiley, 1967), p. 3.

rate. Before the computer, we could not have computer-assisted instruction. Now we can. Before trained subject-matter specialists for the elementary school were available, we could not employ them. Now there is beginning to be a supply of them. An un-dreamed-of variety of educational forms is taking shape. In one day recently, I watched a motion picture a group of children had made (and heard them explain it to me), observed a child learning economics through a computer-controlled game, and listened to a half dozen children discussing their original play and using a television tape recorder to prepare its production.

In this chapter we will consider several of the types of forces and conditions which affect the decisions that can be made to create and implement an educational model. In some senses, this chapter is partial — it represents only a fragment of what *could* be said about the forces and conditions that affect educational decisions. To provide a complete discussion of that topic would take several volumes. However, anything that will be said later about the development of models and their implementation will depend greatly on an understanding of the forces, rational and irrational, that press on any arena where decisions about education are made.

Out of all the possibilities, three basic sources of forces and possibilities will be considered in this chapter. First, we will treat the needs that are generated within the school itself — the institutional needs that create pressure to make certain kinds of decisions. Second, we will treat the needs and forces within communities as they operate to shape the school. Third, we will treat the limitations and possibilities of educational technology — the knowledge of education and structures and devices that make possible certain kinds of educational procedures and prohibit or limit others. Then we will discuss some of the types of organizations that can be created to legitimize and mediate the needs of the institution and community so that the forces that resent change do dominate, and planners can bring to the creation of the school the best in the state of the educational art.

The needs of the institution

Social institutions are organized to accomplish something — to perform some function. Within any institution we expect to find many actions that serve the agreed-on function of the organization. And so we do. We also find that there are many actions that have originated because they enhance the institution itself or make life within the institution more comfortable. Even though we rail against it, we create many routine arrangements that make our life predictable and comfortable. In so doing, we frequently create obstacles to innovation.

Some of the recent studies of mental hospitals are instructive in this regard. We are all agreed that the ostensible social function of the mental hospital is the care of the sick and, if we look inside a mental hospital, we will find that many of the things that are done there are indeed for the purpose of treatment. However, a careful look at the behavior of the hospital staff reveals that some of the things they do would be prescribed by no physician — things done to make the institution a more comfortable or a safer place for its own sake. For example, many therapists feel that the mentally ill should participate in problem-solving situations to the extent that they are able, in order to help them prepare themselves gradually for life outside the institution. However, many nurses and technicians try to keep the patients from facing complex or disturbing situations, because patients are more likely to become upset in problem-situations than in simple tranquil situations. Keeping things simple makes for a more peaceful institutional life, but one that runs counter to many of the beliefs about therapy and the things that should be done to enable the patient to become well.[1] In other words, by keeping the patient calm, the institution may be making it less likely that he will get well.

Recognizing this, therapists are giving attention to the creation

---

[1] John and Elaine Cumming, *Ego and Milieu* (New York: Atherton, 1962).

of therapeutic milieu in which all the personnel of the hospital are trained to resist the tendency to satisfy their institutional needs and to behave, wherever possible, in the interest of creating therapeutic environment.

In most human institutions we find the same kind of phenomenon. In the small Connecticut town where I live, the recreation center has become a well-developed institution. Recently, regulations concerning the use of tennis courts have been changed to require players to schedule their use of the courts in advance. This is not in reponse to a problem-situation regarding the function of the center (the courts are virtually empty during the week) but to satisfy the need for order of one of the directors of the center.

The school is no exception to the development of institutional need-satisfying behavior. A careful look at any school will quickly convince the observer that some of the actions of teachers and principals are clearly for educational purposes, whereas some are in response to institutional needs, while other actions serve both functions. Some of the behavior patterns that surround the physical maintenance of the school building will illustrate the general point. The personnel who clean the school frequently find that it is easier to clean the school if the chairs and tables are left in rows at the end of the working day. Frequently they will attempt to put pressure on the teachers to leave the chairs and tables in orderly rows, rather than grouped for various purposes. In many schools, the principal acquiesces and requires the teachers to leave the chairs in rows, resulting in extra work for the teacher who prefers another arrangement and favoring those teachers who prefer to seat their classes in rows to instruct them all at the same time.

In many large city schools one can observe a phenomenon known as "toilet recess." Toilet recess is a convention in large schools which have too few toilet facilities for convenience and where principals and faculty prefer not to have unsupervised children in the halls. Because the physical needs of the children do not permit them to wait through the half-day before using the toilet, such schools institute a scheduled "recess" in which each class takes its turn lining up for the toilets. The practice is unnatural and is offensive to the uninitiated observer, but it is common in most large city school districts and many small ones.

The library is another place where the effects of institutional needs can be observed easily. In order to ensure that each child in a school has some contact with the library on a regular basis, many schools schedule each class group for a "period" or more each week or two in the library. In a twenty- or thirty-room school, this practice means that the library has a class of children in it during nearly every hour that the school is in session. No sooner does one class leave than another takes its place. The librarian who simply lets the children browse on their own frequently has difficulty preparing the library for the class that follows. Many librarians have solved that problem by requiring silence in the library and by permitting only a few children to browse at a time, when they are to select only one or two books, sign them out, and then spend the remainder of the period reading them in silence. This grim business still takes place in a great many schools — and no doubt will continue until more and better library facilities (not to mention librarians) are provided.

The library problem, by the way, is compounded by another institutional need caused by the workload of classroom teachers. They should, of course, be with the children in the library when circumstances are as described above, so they can help the children with book selection. However, in many schools, library time, lunchtime, and time for visits by "special" teachers of physical education and the arts constitute the only time that the teacher is free from the direct supervision of children — hence the only time for reading, marking papers, preparing presentations, and the like.

There are literally thousands of behaviors, such as those described above, that arrive from the needs of institutional life rather than from educational intent. There has been entirely too little scholarship on this subject of the institutional character of the school, but we can discern several general categories of institutional need that arise and have to be dealt with in nearly every educational setting. Hence, we will briefly treat four general categories of institutional need:

Need for an orderly institution,
Need for feelings of competence,
Need to feel supported and accepted in the community, and
Needs generated by the workaday world of the teacher.

The need for social order within the institution

Schools are expected to be relatively orderly places. Wild tales are told by many people about the supposedly chaotic schools that existed in the United States during the "Progressive" Era. These stories are told to reinforce the belief that the school should be a calm, purposeful place.

The fact is that the elementary school has the task of creating a going, orderly society from a large group of young children, with only a few adults present. Initially, the children arrive very young — many of them with little experience in large groups and very little notion of how to behave autonomously yet responsively. Because so few adults are responsible for the behavior of so many children, the adults will often construct many activities with an eye to their effect on the control of the children. The "workbook" has become a time-honored instrument within the school, because it imposes controlled activity on the children. Textbooks have questions and exercises at the end of the chapter, not only because they provide for "review" of the material in the chapter, but because they can be assigned to keep the children busy and, consequently, under control.

Jonathan Kozol[2] describes one horror story after another in which the villains of the piece are the teachers and administrators in the Boston slums who impose bureaucratic regimens on the children instead of teaching them. What Kozol does not appear to understand is that the remedies must be institutional as well as in terms of personnel. He seems to feel that the problem is due to the specific people who teach and administer in the Boston schools and that changing them would improve the situation. Unfortunately,

---

[2] Jonathan Kozol, *Death at an Early Age* (Boston: Houghton Mifflin, 1967).

what he describes is typical (ordinary, even) in big cities. The institution is what is defective. A different way of schooling would change the teachers and administration and also would encourage different personnel to seek employment in the city schools.

Recitation teaching methods also provide easy control. The teacher asks questions, and the pupils respond. So long as this continues, the teacher has an easy time keeping the reins in his hand.[3]

Grading systems can also be shaped to provide control. Report cards often have places where teachers can legitimately comment to the parents on the behavior of the children. Grades — and later success in school — are used in some cases as threats to bring the misbehaving pupil into line. "If you don't learn this, you won't do well in high school," is a familiar admonition in the elementary school.

Another source of institutional need arises from the enormous individual differences of the children. These differences, large at birth, increase steadily through the years. Trying to teach all these diverse children in an orderly way imposes a severe strain on the teacher. To make the teaching tasks more manageable, the teachers of each grade impose pressure on the teachers of each preceding grade to teach *all* the children certain information and skills that can be, then, "counted on." The eternal hope is that if all children reach these minimal standards, then instruction can be standardized for all children, reducing the stress occasioned by the attempt to meet individual differences. In other words, the teachers are the source of much of the pressure to have clear levels or grades within the school and to make the preparation of the children for the next level a central task of each preceding level. Frequently, this pressure turns a "non-graded" school into a school that simply has more grades or levels than before — more "achievement-steps" for the children to climb. The strain of meeting individual differences often gives rise to arguments against the development of new and better educational programs. One hears school personnel say, "But

---

[3] See Louis Smith and William Geoffrey, *The Complexities of the Urban Classroom* (New York: Wiley, 1968) for a fascinating study of the institutional pressures on the teacher.

if we develop this new program, what will happen if some of the children transfer to another school? They won't have had the usual program (the old stuff) and it will go hard with them." In effect, this kind of argument represents approval of the failure of many schools to respond to pupils on their own terms. Translated, it means, "Never change the schools, because it will involve changing our routines." A corollary translation is "Standardize the students, so they will fit in better."

Over the years, the teaching staff has formed a professional sub-culture that has been heavily influenced by the need to develop an orderly child society. In the teachers' rooms of many schools, teachers who have difficulty controlling the children are held up to ridicule. Novice teachers are pressured by their "cooperating teachers" to learn how to "handle" the children smoothly. Principals are subject to this culture and they frequently take great pains to see that there is order in the lunchroom, the halls, the buses, and so on.

The ways that personnel are used in the school adds to this, of course. Until recently, teachers worked alone. Each teacher was assigned a specific number of children to teach and organize somehow into a coherent and orderly group. As a consequence, teachers who could not easily lead children were at a severe disadvantage. A bright and able young teacher simply could not survive in the school unless he also could manage the social aspects of teaching without undue difficulty. Furthermore, neither teacher training institutions nor public schools have developed any systematic ways of teaching teachers how to develop smoothly-functioning democratic groups of children — although they have exhorted the teacher to do so.

It does not have to be like this, of course. It is possible for school faculties, working together, to develop societies of schoolchildren who have the ability to organize themselves, to work together, and whose norms encourage intellectual pursuit. Teams of teachers, working together, could develop strategies for developing such school societies that would make questions of "discipline" and "control" seem almost absurd. Unquestionably the school does have the need for a reasonably orderly society. The real question is whether that society will be created with utmost care for its educational efficacy or whether it will grow haphazardly, with a need for control dominating the need to educate.[4]

The kinds of school that Jonathan Kozol describes are really educational accidents. The needs of the institutional personnel have been generated by a poorly-planned institution (the ghetto school as we often know it), and the result is horrendous. However, we are able to design very different institutions, and they would have very different needs *and* effects on children. The present structure encourages repressive behavior and discourages attempts to develop the unique capabilities of children. The kind of education envisioned by John Holt[5], for example, simply does not fit into the usual school structure; although it must be added that extraordinary teachers can and do pull it off.

The need to feel competent

The professional functionary within the school — the teacher — also has needs that are generated by his view of his professional position. One of his salient needs is to feel competent in his job.

This was revealed very clearly between 1958 and 1965 when the "New Mathematics" programs were introduced into the elementary schools. The mathematics programs were given much publicity and were promoted by college teachers of mathematics and education and supervisors within the public school systems themselves. Many teachers were convinced of the importance of improving mathematics education. Yet, many otherwise dedicated teachers voiced the hope that they would "retire before the new math really comes in." What they were really saying was that they did not feel competent to teach the kind of mathematics they believed was being ushered

---

[4] For a thorough discussion of the interpersonal dimensions of teaching, see: Bruce R. Joyce and Berj Harootunian, *The Structure of Teaching* (Chicago: Science Research Associates, 1967), Chapter Four.

[5] John Holt, *How Children Fail,* (New York: Pitman, 1964).

into the curriculum. The attempt to improve mathematics educa-tion quickly became the attempt to improve the mathematics edu-cation of the teacher, and just as rapidly it evolved into an attempt to bolster the egos of teachers who had felt themselves competent, but who soon felt threatened.

The role of the teacher exposes him to the judgment of many others, and a surprising percentage of people, including children, actually feel capable of judging the competence of the teachers they observe. Many teachers, quite naturally, feel strong desires to be approved and liked and respected by their students. They become extremely sensitive to the opinions of those who observe them teaching. We should not be surprised to find that this pressure com-bines with their already strong desires to feel competent, resulting in a powerful need to be active where they feel adequate and to shun those areas where they do not feel so confident.

The result is a powerful force for conservatism within the school. Every innovation — every change, even slight on the surface — requires the members of an institution to adjust by learning new behaviors. To some extent, all adjustments that require learning involve some risk of a feeling of incompetence. In teaching, the risk can be considerable, particularly because the average school pro-vides no place where the teacher can develop new competence in private. A teacher who wishes to perfect a new teaching strategy has to work out his training with his own students. He tries the new behavior on them and sees how it works, that is, how students re-spond. Since it is new to him, the chances are that it will be less effec-tive with *them* than most of the other things he does. Hence, unless the new behavior is unusually easy to learn, he is likely to receive distress signals from the students, and he well may respond by avoiding the new behavior altogether in the future.

Arno Bellack's recent research on the classroom has indicated the extent to which teacher-learner interaction develops into rou-tine patterns that appear to be very stable, difficult to change, and remarkably similar from classroom to classroom.[6]

---

[6] Arno Bellack and others, *The Language of the Classroom* (New York: Teachers College Press, 1967).

For an illustration of this process, we might consider how teachers have reacted recently to the suggestion that they employ game-type simulations in their teaching of social studies. Recently I participated in a workshop in which some selected and highly-motivated teachers were taught how to use simulation games for the social studies. One of the games was the "Legislative Game" which is a simulation — very realistic — of legislative processes at the national level. The game was demonstrated for the teachers, and they were given the kits used with the games. The curriculum director for the school district was present at the workshop, and he urged the teachers to try out that game or one of the others that were presented. After one week, no one had tried the games, so one of the workshop leaders and the curriculum director offered to participate as co-teachers if the teachers wished, the strategy being to spread any embarrassment that might develop in the situation. Still, no takers appeared, although several of the teachers had taken the game with them, and they appeared interested when it was demonstrated and discussed. Toward the end of the third week, however, two of the most capable teachers confided to me that they were actually using the game with small groups of children, practicing to develop their capability to use the device, but that they did not yet feel ready to expose themselves to the view of the other teachers in the workshop. Subsequent private questioning revealed that many of the teachers were engaged in their own private investigation, safe from the judgment of others.

It would not be prudent to universalize this homely example, but it is one concrete evidence of the need to feel competent at work in the school. Innovations of any kind — any teaching behavior of any kind that requires new patterns of activity — will be slow to come about in the school unless great care is taken to see that they are accompanied by devices that assist the teachers to become competent in them — and to feel that they appear competent in the new roles. After-school "in-service" courses will scarcely fill this need.

The student also needs to feel competent. He will resist teaching techniques, learner roles, and demands that stretch his confidence in his ability. Arno Bellack has documented with great care the gamelike character of many of the interchanges between teachers and students when they are in the school setting. The most common pattern that emerged from Bellack's studies was that the teacher tended to play the role of questioner, with the student responding and the teacher adding to the response or signifying satisfaction or dissatisfaction with what the student had said.[7] This cycle (teacher asks, pupil responds, teacher reacts) along with another, shorter cycle (teacher asks, pupil responds) made up over half of the amount of discourse that Bellack and his collaborators examined.

It is interesting to observe what happens when a teacher tries to break this pattern and, for example, attempts to induce the students to carry on a discussion among themselves. In many cases the students will resist the change. Why? At this point we can only speculate. But it seems fairly sure that one of the prime causes will be that the student, playing the easy "language game" of ask-respond-react, has a role in which he feels master of his situation. He knows what is coming and he can judge the kinds of demands that will be made on him. However, when the teacher tries to change the "rules" of the classroom game, the student is required to negotiate new roles — to learn new responses to different kinds of questions. In the case of participation in a discussion, he has to be prepared to evaluate the ideas of others and to submit to their evaluation of his contribution. Until he becomes accustomed to the new types of responses that he must make, he is likely to doubt his competence and, when he does so, we are likely to find him resisting the new procedures. This negative reaction will not be true of all students, or to the same degree. But it will be perceptible in many. Many educators whose methods do not fit into the easy pattern of the recitation "game" have reported this problem.[8]

Another example of student resistance to change occurred a few years ago at the University of Chicago Laboratory School, when

---

[7] Arno Bellack and others, *The Language of the Classroom* (New York: Teachers College Press, 1967).

[8] In the literature of "non-directed" teachers there are some wonderfully vivid examples. See Carl Rogers, *Client-Centered Therapy: Its Current Practice* (Boston: Houghton Mifflin, 1951); Nathaniel Cantor, *The Dynamics of Learning* (Buffalo, New York: Henry Stewart, 1956); A. S. Neill, *Summerhill* (New York: Holt, Rinehart and Winston, 1960).

quite capable students in the ninth grade were given the option of receiving English instruction under one of three conditions. The student could attend class in the normal manner. Or he could proceed with individual study, obtaining appointments with instructors when he felt the need for their guidance. Or he could follow an intermediate course, with relatively unstructured but regularly-scheduled seminars. One of the most interesting bits of information to come out of the experiment was the tremendous difficulty the school had getting children to take the second two options. Relatively gifted students — with a history of academic success behind them and attending school in a privileged environment which abounded with individual support and the capacity to help out strenuously if things did not work out well — preferred the safer, more structured course. At first it appeared that they did not want the freedom they had hitherto been clamoring for. More realistically, they probably feared for their competence. They were sure of their capacity to meet the demands posed by the familiar situation. They were unsure and tentative about their ability to meet the requirements of self-study.[9]

There is no need to belabor the point or to develop a list of all possible examples.[10] The forces emanating from the need for competence are conservative in nature and can be overcome only by taking pains to build competence in affected parties, by helping to build the feelings of competence (which, surprisingly, do not necessarily follow from the attainment of the new skills), by helping the members of the organization develop means of making their own accurate judgments about competence, and by providing an environment where they can develop new capacity without submitting half-developed skills to the scrutiny of the public. The need for competence also affects the kinds of innovation that will not take hold easily in the school. In general, the most durable innovations

---

[9] See Willard J. Congreve, "Independent Learning," *North Central Association Quarterly*, XL, Fall 1965, p. 233, for a thorough description of the experiment and the kinds of reactions that came from the faculty as well as from the students.

[10] A guide to other studies can be found in: Bruce R. Joyce and Berj Harootunian, *The Structure of Teaching* (Chicago: Science Research Associates, 1967), Chapter Four.

will be those which most readily help people feel competent. For example, the introduction of subject specialists in place of generalists is taking hold partly because it narrows the range of academic competencies needed by a teacher, making it easier for the teacher to feel (and to be) adequate.

Needs emanating from physical wants and conditions

The school is not exempt from the human biological needs. In addition, it cares for very young people who are also partly under the care of the home and the community. The school is a large-sized feeding station. It is also a recreation center. It takes care to exercise the young and to teach games that will fill the children's leisure. The school is a major community-health station, dispensing vaccines, providing dental care, serving as a base of operations for the public health nurse and the social worker. For the poor, the school may be a source of clothing and warmth. It is also the agency where the community keeps its watchful eye on the home, and through which the community is likely to intervene if there is neglect or if there are signs of unusual difficulty.

All of this adds up to a huge operation. And, in tending to the physical needs of its pupil personnel, the school generates needs of its own. For one thing, it keeps records, and these records, in turn, need to be tended. Filling in the records is an example; the teacher spends time interviewing children to obtain personal data about the home and the child himself. For another, the records engender conformity. A parent who wants to exempt his child from dental or medical care in the school will have to satisfy authorities on that count and may encounter disapproval.

The school schedule is one obvious place to see the effects of physical needs on the activities of the schools. Frequently, in setting up a schedule for the school, the principal will begin with the cafeteria schedule, then the physical education schedule. Then he will add the special teachers who are shared with other schools and thus are restricted in the time they can give his operation. After tending those needs, the principal will turn to the schedule demands of the remainder of the educational program. And, inescapably, what comes first gets certain kinds of priority. Feeding surely gets scheduled, whereas dramatics may have to be wedged in.

Over the years, therefore, the physical wants of the students have become institutionalized, and any modification in the rest of the institution has to take into account the institutional demands thus generated. As a simple illustration of this, let us examine the case of an experimental school developed a few years ago in the Midwest. The architect included coin-operated cafeteria facilities in the school, for two reasons. First, it saved the space normally used for cafeteria, allowing that space to be used for other purposes. Second, and interrelated, the coin-operated facility enabled each student to feed himself according to his own internal schedule — and more important, probably, to schedule his feeding around his educational needs, rather than vice versa.

Unfortunately, the state department of public health had created regulations concerning the feeding of people in schools that specifically forbade the use of prepackaged foods or vending machines. The rules, which had been made for what were good reasons many years before, were applied to the new school. Ultimately, the school was forced to adopt a modification of the conventional feeding arrangement. Hence, the educational program was forced to bend to the needs for feeding.

The abhorrent "toilet recess," referred to earlier, is a case of a practice that interrupts the educational schedule, regiments the pupils, and invades their privacy horribly. It has come about because of failure, on the part of school architects and budgeteers, to attend satisfactorily to a need that might have been foreseen, and *is* anticipated in many school designs.

We shall stop here the chronicle of needs that can be generated within the educational institution by the physical needs of man; but, as in the case of all the sources of institutional need, we will be dealing with this one throughout our discussion of educational models. Perhaps more than any other category of need, the physical ones are often neglected in plans for school reform, just because they are so obvious and so inescapable. The needs are unavoidable, but there are many possible institutional ways of meeting them, and we have to concern ourselves with the creation of alternative institutional forms if we are to learn how to create new educational alternatives.

Need for community support

The school is inextricably interwoven with its community, but the relation is symbiotic — each sustains the other. If the school *is* simply the community, then what is learned will never transcend folklore. If, on the other hand, what happens in the school is too foreign to the community, then the education will be rejected and the institution will be brought into line.

No one teaches for more than a few minutes before he realizes that what his students learn will be transmitted to their parents, by hearsay at least, and that their parents will soon form an opinion about that teacher and the substance of his teaching. The response can be excitement — the teacher may strive to teach not only his students but *through* his students. He may draw parents into activities and enlist their help, thus both widening his audience and his support. Or, the response may be caution — the teacher may become guarded and defensive, avoiding controversy and the possibility of offense, and seeking to lessen the involvement of parents.

Then, to carry on many activities, the school needs the community for actual physical help. Parents chaperone excursions, sew costumes for plays, contribute magazines and other materials, share their travel experiences. One of the reasons that it is so hard to teach in the inner city is that parent-school contact is limited and perfunctory in many cases and the school does not have the physical support of the parents. The teaching staff has to go it alone, provide nearly all of the energy for the enterprise. Furthermore, the teaching staff frequently, in inner-city areas, feels uncomfortable in the community and the community often feels uncomfortable with school personnel. The resulting alienation is often accompanied by the feeling that the community does not support the efforts of the school, and in some cases this has been true.

In the last few years the communities surrounding inner-city schools have been demanding a greater voice in the operation of their schools, and, while the efforts to bring this about will no doubt result in temporary strife and dislocations, the long run should see a more solid relationship between the school and the community, with the school staff feeling an increase of community support and liaison.[11]

For many years teachers did not feel they had the support of the community when they taught about controversial issues. As a result, in social studies, teachers developed what Hunt and Metcalf have called "closed areas," areas avoided by teachers. These included:

(1) ECONOMICS. While "open" to professional economists and many laymen, this field is so affected by taboos, confusion, and emotion that schools tend to avoid it as a subject for rational study.

(2) RACE AND MINORITY-GROUP RELATIONS. In recent years this field has become more open to reflective inquiry in schools, but in some places, fears, tensions, and confusions continue to make it a closed area.

(3) SOCIAL CLASS. Here is a "truly closed area" in the writers' judgment, "neatly ignored as a result of the widespread belief, 'There are no social classes in America.'"

(4) SEX, COURTSHIP, MARRIAGE. This area is more open to inquiry than it was a few years ago, but critical analysis of contradictions and problems is not usually encouraged.

(5) RELIGION AND MORALITY. Morality is somewhat more open to reflective inquiry than are religious beliefs, but both tend to form a closed area as far as schools are concerned.

(6) NATIONALISM AND PATRIOTISM. This area is one in which it

---

[11] See Muriel Crosby, *An Adventure in Human Relations* (Chicago: Follett, 1965). for an interesting and well-told story of a city's effort to develop a more complete partnership between school and community and, simultaneously, to revitalize the education of the inner-city children.

is difficult to question traditional beliefs, even if they are inconsistent with real behavior or the requirements of national survival.[12]

From this list we can see that the very heart of the social studies curriculum was imperiled by excluding those areas from discussion. Yet there were very few communities in which there was overt objection to the study of these topics — in many cases the teachers simply believed that they would not be supported if controversial issues were included.

In recent years the climate has shifted, and many schools are conscious of support for the teaching of what were formerly considered controversial issues. Civic groups such as B'nai B'rith and Americans for Democratic Action (ADA) actively encourage teaching about civil rights and liberties and, in this, they are actively joined by groups directly representing the interests of the Black community, poor people, and others whose philosophy includes the advocacy of a more open society. Yet other civic groups, such as the Foreign Policy Association, are promoting and supporting efforts to open the study of our foreign relations and the political and economic system generally.

In some communities, then, the formerly "closed" areas are opening in the schools. In other communities, support is not forthcoming and the social studies curriculum tends to confine itself to the "safe" areas.

The academic reform movement of the last few years[13] has illuminiated the ways that the school reacts to its feelings of support from its area. In some communities, the school felt that it had to adopt the "New Mathematics" and science programs as soon as they were available, because the community demanded it. In other communities, the faculties felt that the patrons were quite suspicious of the "strange" content being taught to their children. Dur-

---

[12] Maurice P. Hunt and Lawrence E. Metcalf, *High School Social Studies: Problems in Reflective Thinking and Social Understanding* (New York: Harper, 1955).

[13] See John I. Goodlad, *School Curriculum Reform* (New York: The Fund for the Advancement of Education, 1967).

ing the late 1950's, I found myself pressed into service as an apologist for the schools in both kinds of situations. In some cases I was explaining to parents how much teacher retraining was necessary to inaugurate new programs, thus apologizing for the slowness of the school to adopt new mathematics programs; in other cases I was explaining that there was nothing to be feared from the new programs, thus apologizing for the quickness with which those schools had reacted. In both roles, however, what struck me was not the suspicion of the parents, but the nervousness of the school staff about the reactions of the parents. *In many respects, the Need for a Feeling of Support exists independent of the actual amounts of support that are given.*

The dynamics of this process are not well understood and are in need of much systematic study. Throughout this book I will refer to this aspect of the need structure of the school, but most references will be speculative or based on my personal observations.

Needs generated by the workaday world of the teacher

Let us turn now to a third set of needs: those which come from the life of the teacher and his working conditions. The dynamics of the forces generated by virtue of the world and responsibilities of the teacher are quite different from those developed from the phsyical wants or community relations. Robert Schaefer has given an excellent description of the institutionalized role of the teacher.[14]

In the case of the average school, these effects severely limit the kinds of education that can be carried on.

In the first place, the days of the teacher, in most schools, are such that he is almost never free from the responsibilitiy of managing children. For thirty or more hours a week he must see that the needs and educational wants of his charges are being satisfied. He teaches a quantity of hours each week for which it is impossible to prepare properly. He is exhorted to respond to individual differences but he

---

[14] Robert J. Schaefer, *The School as a Center of Inquiry* (New York: Harper and Row, 1967).

is not given the time nor the technological support to make that possible. He has little time for scholarship. Summarily, his workload is crushing, unless he behaves like a technician. The result is a powerful drive to routinize teaching. He turns to the textbook, the workbook, the mass assignment. We can see this in each of the curriculum areas. The English teacher, while believing in the teaching of creative writing, tends instead to teach grammar, because that is easier to routinize! The science teacher, believing in theory-building, tends to teach laboratory procedures instead, because they are manageable. In the same vein, the social studies teacher turns from social theory to places and dates. Not all teachers do this, of course, nor all the time, but the tendency is marked.

Schaefer also points out that the teacher works under conditions that inhibit scholarship. The process of education is ill-understood and it cries for research. Yet the school often is asked to behave as if the answers to the mysteries of learning had already been found. It is not set up as a research community — a place of scholarship in which children, the society, the scholarly disciplines, and the processes of teaching and learning are being studied. Schaefer suggests that the need structure of the school could be radically changed if the school were established as such a center, because teachers would not then have to behave as if more were known about learning than is now the case; and, equally important, they would be enabled — even mandated — to live the life of scholars of their professional work.[15]

A third point that Schaefer makes is that the teacher is frequently compelled to work under unilateral patterns of leadership. The principal frequently regards his relationships with the teachers as a line relationship and he treats them as subordinates, rather than as colleagues. This has several noticeable effects. The teacher frequently is not given responsibility that he would need if he were to act as a professional. Second, it discourages independent thinkers from entering teaching — only those who are willing to submit to authoritarian control are likely to enter and stay. Third, it

---

[15] *Ibid.*

depresses the atmosphere of cooperative inquiry that would have to be established if the school were to operate as a center of inquiry.

In summary, the behavior of the teacher is partly a response to his workaday world. His responsibilities, the way he is treated, the kind of thinking that is expected of him, affect his behavior. With his colleagues, he establishes a kind of professional society that in its turn reflects the workaday world of all. *In the case of teachers, this professional society rarely demands scholarship, philosophical thinking or experimental behavior. Nor, under present conditions, would it be expected to contain those values. But change the workaday world of the teacher, and the need structure will change as well. The teachers' world can be one that promotes an entirely different set of norms.*

The interlocking need structure of the school

We have discussed several of the sources of behavior that emanate from the demands of life within the school as an institution. Obviously the kinds of educational institutions we are all familiar with represent only a small part of the spectrum of possible educational forms. Yet within each school there are likely to be generated needs from at least the five sources identified here. First, in every school, there will be need for some kind of social order. Social order can, of course, be achieved in such a way as to encourage professional autonomy and creativity. Second, teachers, students, and administration will need to feel competent at what they are doing. Those who do not will tend to withdraw from the situation or to become disruptive. In any school that wishes to have flexibility, provision will have to be made for people to learn new roles in protected situations, where the consequences of initial awkwardness are minimized and the individual has the opportunity to make his own stylistic adaptations to the new situations. If some provisions for experimentation are not developed, the need for competence will operate as a conservative force within the institution.

Third, the physical needs of the individuals have to be satisfied.

While there are many ways for accommodating them, they are critical and will make themselves felt. Fourth, the school knows that it is part of a society, and it needs to know that it has the support of the society. Especially, teachers and administrators are attuned to the wishes of the patrons and the official representatives of the public. What is important is to develop school–community relations that are cooperative and oriented toward the creation of vigorous educational programs, and to avoid relations that are unilateral and political.

Last, the workaday world of the teacher operates to produce institutional behavior that greatly affects what can be done, educationally, within the school.

The components of this complex of sources do not operate independently, of course. The need for social order affects the workaday world of the teacher (as when teachers are required to serve as hall and lunchroom monitors and playground supervisors.) Both in turn are related to the physical needs of the people in the school. The teacher's need to feel competent is related to the student's feelings of competence, and it is much easier for both to feel capable when they believe that the community is solidly behind what the school is doing.

As teachers are inducted into the teaching profession they are taught how to fit into the need structure of the most common forms that schools take today. They tend to adopt the teaching method and institutional roles that fit comfortably into this complex of needs. If we wish to create a new or unique educational model, we will have to create a new institutional need structure, or we are likely to find that the new types of education we developed look very much like the ones we were trying to depart from.

Forces and needs emanating from the community

Both public and private schools operate within a social milieu that greatly affects them. In the case of the public school, of course, it is clear that the very legal authority for the conduct of the school has its roots within the formal political and economic structure of the community, and the society maintains the public school in order to serve itself and its citizens. Private schools are also chartered by the state and they are generally required to operate within the general rules that are laid down for public schools. (A. S. Neill has included in his description of the Summerhill plan of education a really fine account of the process by which the English educational authorities permitted his really deviant school to operate, and yet submitted it to inspections that attempted to judge it on its own terms as well as on the usual terms applied to English schools.)[16]

In this section, however, we will not be so much concerned with the legal authorities as with the more informal but equally powerful forces that operate within the community to shape the school. Later in this chapter, in the section entitled "The Responsible Parties," we will deal directly with the roles and functions of boards of education and other educational authorities as they work with the informal sources of influence to develop operating units that can shape the schools rationally. At this point, we are more concerned with the kinds of influence that are generated out of the community structure whether or not they are expressed through the legal structure. For, like the school, the community organization, through its own momentum, tends to produce needs for certain kinds of educational practices. As in the case of the institutional needs of the school, the needs of the community can be considered in terms of sources emanating from the nature of the society.

Need to socialize the young

In order to perpetuate itself, the society socializes its children into the normative structure that pervades it. It teaches its children how to behave, what to believe, and it passes on to those children the technology of the society. This is true even in terms of the enormous urban-technological societies developing today, although it is also true that these societies permit variations in behavior that are much

---

[16] See A. S. Neill, *Summerhill* (New York: Holt, Rinehart and Winston, 1960).

greater than those in primitive societies — and the possible variations that might be permitted are still greater. The type of enculturation of the young that permits cultural growth and variation is
much more complex, however, than the type of enculturation that
simply perpetuates the existing social order. And, it is no less
urgent — the socialization of the young in order to perpetuate,
enhance, and accomplish flexibility in the society is a matter of the
greatest urgency.

It is partly for this reason that the schools were established. When
the society was simple and the cultural technology was meager, the
socialization of the young could easily be accomplished in the
home. Now, however, it requires an enormous bureaucracy and personnel trained to do all sorts of things that would be difficult to
carry out in the home. The complex symbolic technology of our culture — the language-mathematics domain — is essential for full
participation in the culture and it has become one of the major
functions of the school. Awareness of cultural norms and the posses-
sion of the subtle social skills that enable one to navigate in the
society are equally important, and they are also domains of the
function of the school.

Progression up the educational ladder has become of major
importance in determining the extent of cultural participation and
material success available to any individual, and this trend continues. Hence, the socialization for material enhancement has become
inextricably woven into the educational fabric of the Western
World.

To the extent that children from the inner city or the rural slums
are "culturally deprived," the school may take on the job of compensating for this lack. Hence, in recent years the term "compensatory education" has been used to describe the purpose of specific
programs developed for this purpose.[17] The compensation which is
referred to is for the loss in enculturation that occurs in some
inner-city and rural homes.

---

[17] As used in Benjamin S. Bloom, Allison Davis, and Robert Hess, *Compensatory
Education for Cultural Deprivation* (New York: Holt, Rinehart and Winston,
1965).

The enculturation functions of the school are so obvious and so taken for granted that the community need for the function can easily be overlooked when we are assessing the forces that shape the school. Yet, in the view of many citizens, any deviation from the enculturation role would have severe consequences. Some citizens actually fear any school activity that even implicitly challenges the status quo. For example, the hue and cry in the 1950's over the teaching of communism in the schools was motivated by the fear of some citizens that if children were taught about communism they would surely be seduced by it.

In a similar vein some schools have recently undertaken to regulate the haircuts their boys may have and the lengths of the skirts the girls may wear. When they engage in this kind of regulation, the schools are stating loudly by their actions that they fully accept the enculturation role and see their function as the induction of the young into the folkways of the previous generation.

The really critical question about the enculturation role of the schools was hinted at earlier. That is, will the school simply induct the student into the values and technology of the culture, or will it try to help the student attain and utilize the culture, but as a means of building a better one and as a matrix in which he can live an individually meaningful and distrinct existence?

Pressures will come from the community for both of these possible enculturation roles.

The need to understand the school

The community that supports the school sometimes begins to feel that it has raised an alien in its midst. One of the reactions to the "New Mathematics" and the "New Science" has been some parental apprehension that the school will teach the children some things that are beyond the parents themselves. Experimental schools, unless they are very careful, can meet suspicion and even censure by their community because of this kind of parental nervousness.

The community's need to comprehend its schools sometimes operates as quite a conservative force. A curious example of this has occurred recently in some of the big cities. Some of the parents in the inner cities have become convinced that one of the disadvantages that their children have suffered has been that they have not received the quality of education that is given to middle-class children. (This claim unquestionably has at least some basis in fact.) The attempt to provide compensatory education, as defined above, has been greeted in some inner-city neighborhoods with resistance. *These parents, believing that the disadvantage their children suffer is caused by differences in schooling, tend to reject an education that is differentiated deliberately, but for the purpose of "compensating" the original handicap that these children operate under.* In other words, these parents do not comprehend what compensatory education is all about, and they fear that it will close doors to their children rather than opening them — which is the intent of the procedure.

The need for the citizen to understand the education his child is given has resulted in some tragic events, as when the children of some parents have not been encouraged to reach for higher education, for fear that it would give them "airs;" or, put another way, it might alienate the children from their parents. It is a paradox that the very compensatory education that these parents desire for their children should result in suspicion and even antagonism.

Middle-class parents also have a need to understand their school. The previously-mentioned resistance to the mathematics and science programs was a middle-class phenomenon. *All* social strata react to education that they do not understand. If the history of architecture is taught in an elementary school classroom, for example, some parents will wonder why. If difficult philosophies, foreign ideas, controversial topics, are treated, the parent will tend to react.

A rather interesting sort of tension results from the fact that the school, being peopled largely by young people, belongs in large measure to a generation other than the one that is paying for it. Inevitably, the schools reflect some "younger" ideas and fashions. In democratic schools, the students have a legitimate participation in the regulation of affairs and in the selection of topics and ideas that will be explored. When this happens, some of the ferment of the school may be difficult for the previous generation to understand. If contemporary music is studied, especially contemporary popular music, there will be some reaction on this score. If the changing social scene or social problems involving young people are given much attention, some reverberation is likely.

The community's need to understand its school is natural and can be the source of much energy and support for the school. Some schools have attained great support for their programs simply by carrying on extensive public-relations efforts with their community, and have seen their efforts result in the development of powerful support, even pressure, to develop programs more innovative than were originally contemplated.

The need to protect and prepare

Not only does the community feel the need to socialize its young and to understand the agency to which it entrusts so much of its socialization, but it also feels protective toward the young and it feels responsibility to prepare them for the world they will have to cope with shortly. Anything that the community feels will remotely jeopardize the future of the young will be squelched in short order.

This process can be seen clearly in the reaction that many parents have to the progress their children make in the curriculum area of reading in the primary grades. Many parents make considerable effort, even in the first few months of school, to ascertain the speed with which their children are learning to read. If progress is not swift, the teacher is frequently questioned. He (usually she) is likely to be blamed if progress is not swift.

The teacher's frequent response to this is a retreat to orthodoxy. She may report, "All of the other children progressed well through the readiness program. Although John didn't do so well with the readiness exercises, we felt it best to start him on the primer rather than have him develop any feeling of being slower than the other children . . . ." Now, what parent could argue with *that*? Unfortunately, the defensive stance is not the most flexible of postures, and the cumulative effect can be inhibiting, indeed.

The enormous importance of higher education to the success of the child in later life has resulted in pressures on the schools to prepare all children for admission to college. Hence, the high school is exhorted to teach the orthodox college preparatory subjects, and the task of the junior high school and the elementary school can easily be seen as preparation for college. Even the tasks of the nursery school and the kindergarten, in this light, can appear to be the preparation of the student for the tasks of the primary school! (In truth, it is not at all unusual for nursery school and kindergarten teachers to judge their success by how well they have prepared the child for the first grade!) It is easy to see how this pressure can combine with the need for institutional order, described in the previous section, to create a school system where the major task of each grade is the preparation of the student for the grade or level that is to come. In fact, there is considerable parental pressure in some communities to have the requirements for each grade or level rather clearly spelled out so it is easy to assess progress and to assure the progression of the students from level to level. (It can be seen how this pressure can coincide with the teacher's need for order and structure to perpetuate the graded school.)

The needs that emanate from the community's efforts to socialize the young, the need to comprehend the school and to protect and prepare the children are all natural societal processes that spring from the general tasks of child-rearing. The next set of forces we will discuss, however, frequently results from a deliberate and rather fully self-conscious attempt to influence events.

The vested interest

Some parties within the community have an interest in affecting what is taught or how it is taught. In various ways they put pressure on the schools to teach the things that will further their cause or their fortunes.

One of the most common ways in which vested groups operate is to distribute free teaching aids or materials to the schools. Food and transportation companies are particularly ingenious at this pratice. Great posters have for years adorned classrooms, exhorting the students to have a "balanced diet," which, naturally, includes lots of _____. By this means, generations of children have been conditioned to believe that _____ (which really represents quite a lot of products) is really essential for a healthy, American life. Railroad and airplane travel have been sold from the apparently innocent bulletin boards of the schools in much the same way that food products have been advertised.

In addition to sending free materials (advertising) to schools, pressure groups have operated through direct legal means. Some religious groups have lobbied to obtain laws that require prayer and Bible reading in the schools, whereas other groups have lobbied just as assiduously for laws prohibiting any type of religious activity. Some patriotic groups have pressed for laws or board of education rulings that specify how much American History must be taught each year, others have lobbied for laws prohibiting the teaching of communism, while others have worked for the requirement that communism "be taught" and sometimes in a specified way!

The teaching of "evolution" in the schools — a great controversy which had its moment of high drama in the famous Scopes "Monkey Trial" during the 1920's — was the specific battlefield for groups representing different ideologies. Some religious groups felt that their religious tenets were definitely threatened by the theories of evolution, whereas those who believed strongly in the unrestricted freedom of scholarly inquiry wished to see all relevant and important scientific theories explored in the schools.

In many communities vested interest groups have succeeded in gerrymandering the lines of school attendance districts so that economic and racial segregation are maintained and promoted. Schools in many communities have their "Negro" school or the "school for the folks from the other side of the tracks" simply because schools were built and attendance areas defined to bring about that kind of segregation. Recently we have seen agitation to draw school attendance boundaries to promote the integration of economic and racially-different sections within the population.

The operation of pressure groups also occurs in some subtle and indirect ways. For example, the major source of teaching materials in the public schools of the United States has been the output of commercial publishing firms. In an effort to widen their market for textbooks as much as possible, they have been careful to exclude from those textbooks materials that might be offensive to any sector of the population. The major impact of this can be seen in social studies books, which have, until very recently, been confined to very "safe" material. Segregation, political issues, civil dangers, and the like have been avoided because there are some people who benefit from keeping discussion about those things to a minimum. Largely, then, the anticipation of what vested groups might say has served as a powerful editorial force operating upon the suppliers of educational materials. Recently there has been a cry to have a different kind of approach altogether, and now the same commercial firms are rushing to include in their books many of the same types of discussions that were so carefully avoided before — civil rights, communism, and so on.

The pressure of vested interest groups is a complex thing, and we should not dwell longer on it here. Like the other sources of pressures and needs that influence the school, it is most dangerous when it operates unnoticed and is most beneficial when it is made part of the open ferment that *can* attend the shaping of the school. Also like the other forces, it operates most powerfully when it combines with others.

The concatenation of forces within the community

In times of controversy, as when the educational program of a school is seriously challenged by the citizens of a community, the types of forces described above can operate together to have a controlling influence on the school. When this happens, the embattled staff of the school is likely, as indicated above, to retreat to orthodoxy, to teach the "safer" things, and, in summary, to be more average than the average.

Generally this works. A few years ago I had the opportunity to observe this in operation. An experimental school became challenged within a community for reasons that were not clear, but which I put down under the category, "Need to Comprehend the School". Despite an extensive public-relations effort, the school was apparently mystifying to the community. There was very little dissatisfaction with the way the "basic subjects" were being taught or the discipline of the school — in fact, nearly all the parents were impressed with the purposefulness of the students and the zest of the faculty. But the emphasis on independent study, the rich creative arts program, the amount of cooperative planning, and the general atmosphere of experimentation, probably more than anything else, gradually resulted in a feeling of suspicion which culminated in a number of citizens becoming candidates for the board of education on a platform that essentially was "make the _____ school like the other schools in the district."

The school staff reacted by doing more ordinary things in more ordinary ways and, as far as I know, the disturbance gradually died down.

Within the education profession, there are many apocalyptic tales of community pressure squashing school programs and faculties. While relatively few of these tales are based on fact (some most resoundingly *are* true!) they reflect the belief of many educators that community forces generally tolerate very little deviation from orthodox educational practice. As one superintendent put it, "My job is to see that our schools do what everybody else is doing, but a little better." While his view may be accurate, the consequence, of course, is to reduce greatly the potential diversity among schools in this nation and to dampen educational experimentation. Worse still, with such a climate, many experimental-minded young people, when choosing a career, tend to avoid education because they wish a profession where experimentation and the quest for knowledge will be more normal. One graduate student recently remarked to me, "I would really rather concentrate on education now. But I am going into experimental social psychology, because there I will be expected to innovate, whereas in education I shall have to do it against the resistance of many of my colleagues and the suspicion of the general public."

Community forces do not need to have that effect, of course, nor do they always. The *potential* obstacle to the development of alternative models for elementary education is substantial, however.

We turn now from a consideration of forces generated through social interaction to a consideration of the effect on education of the technological level of the times.

Technological possibilities and limitations

We are all prisoners of the level of our culture, and the decisions we can make are limited and extended by what the tools of our time enable us to do. In education as in other domains of endeavor, our developing technology continually changes our capability and exerts pressure to change.

We can distinguish two major areas of technological influence. The first is in the realm of ideas and the second is in the areas of technique. Although quite different in substance, these aspects of technology operate in much the same ways to influence educational practice.

Educational ideas

When a school board charges the superintendent of schools to see that a new school is brought into existence, the board usually envisions a certain kind of school — a school that is consonant with the concepts of education that the board members are familiar with. Until about 1955, the board of education expected the superintendent to estimate the new enrollment, divide that figure by the approximate number of children that current practice placed in a classroom, and use the quotient as the number of classrooms for the building. In some communities a library would also be expected, and in others a cafeteria and possibly an auditorium. It expected him to staff that school with teachers who were able to teach a wide variety of common school subjects and one or two teachers who would carry on "special" instruction in music, art, and physical education. Only a small library would be provided at first (only by 1960 did even half of the elementary schools in the United States have libraries *at all,* including many schools a hundred years old and more!), but textbooks would be provided in adequate numbers. One or two motion picture projectors would be ordered, a slide projector or two, an overhead projector, and two or three record players. Reflecting on these preparations, we can see the level of ideas and the educational tools that were envisioned by the board and by the superintendent. The children were to be divided into age groups to be taught by teachers using, largely, the textbook and such materials as the teacher made or induced the children to bring from home. The teacher would be expected to adjust instruction somewhat to accommodate the differences among the children — usually three "reading groups" and perhaps two in arithmetic was considered optimal at that time. "Whole class" teaching of science and social studies was considered acceptable. A small amount of laboratory equipment was supplied for science — the "kitchen physics" variety was the norm, if any experimentation was done at all.

While educational practice followed the above description, educational theory envisioned something quite different. It saw the teachers as the leaders of cooperative groups of children. These groups would, through solving problems of social importance, learn the scientific method, the great value issues shaping their times, and methods of cooperation and negotiation. In the process, the children would learn reading and the other practical arts.

In practice, the classroom was run by the textbook with very little cooperative inquiry or theoretical work. The practical arts, rather than being by-products of serious inquiry, became the basic subjects of the school. The great value issues of the time were rarely taught.

Since 1955, boards of education and superintendents have been made aware that a great many alternative kinds of education could be envisioned, and a great many possible technologies could be put together. Schools have been specially designed for team teaching and the use of academic specialists. The "egg crate" design of the past has become a slogan for out-of-date, unimaginative school architecture. Schools are being constructed with facilities for closed-circuit television instruction and even for videotape feedback to drama classes and other classes. Videotape and audio tape libraries are being added to some schools, and books are being placed on microfilm and other devices as well as in conventional binding. The "language laboratory" has been developed. Experimental laboratory sciences are being taught. Special packages of material have been prepared by advanced scholars, packages designed to induce children to debate the serious questions of philosophy and social movement that affect the changing time. Therapists are seriously suggesting that schools be conducted so as to advance healthy personality development — that the deliberate construction of a therapeutic milieu be a major part of the duties of the teacher. Computers enable an individualized instruction that was previously not really dreamed of in any situation in which each pupil did not have a personal tutor. At least one massive self-instructional system for teaching reading and basic arithmetic is being field-tested in schools.

While only a few of the schools in the nation markedly reflect the above changes, the important effect has been a resultant awareness, by those who must create schools, that there are a multitude of levels of ideas that can be used to construct educational plans or models. Theory and research about the development of the self, about intelligence and problem-solving ability, and about technologies for affecting these facets of development, among many others, are developing at a rapid rate. The consequence is that it is becoming clear that the technological capacity for creating an educational model and for carrying it out requires a level of philosophical and scientific sophistication and technical know-how vastly greater than was possessed by the pre-1955 board of education or superintendent, or, for that matter, can be possessed by them today. Only in the largest city and county school districts can there be within the entire school staff the competence to consider and engineer the more sophisticated alternatives. It is necessary, therefore, to consider ways that organizations for planning schools can be put together so that the desires of the legal authorities, the knowledge of the local situation, and the technological possibilities of the era can be brought together in the creation of the model that governs the creation of the school.

The responsible parties

We have considered the needs of the institution as they operate to shape the school, the natural societal forces that operate to affect the school program, and the fact that the technological possibilities of the time have put within our grasp a great many forms of education that require high levels of expertness for their realization. In this section we will consider the development of school-planning committees — "responsible parties" who can put together the education of a community.

Preventing mindlessness

The institutional needs and forces described earlier are natural. Some set of forces is generated simply by the fact of group life. It is malign when these forces simply operate mindlessly to shape the school. Then the need for social order can become pathological — order becomes sought for the sake of order.

A personal anecdote may illustrate this point. Early in my teaching career, I noticed, at the beginning of one school year, that the children in my class copied each piece of schoolwork onto fresh sheets of paper, in ink, before they let me see their work. By my standards, their work was incredibly neat. When I questioned the children about this, they informed me that they were previously required to redo each piece of work in that manner and, furthermore, if they made an error that required erasing, then they had to do the whole thing over again, rather than erase or "cross out" anything that they were to give me. I remonstrated with them, explaining that good, honest work was sufficient, and that I didn't want to have them spending their time copying work already completed. Throughout the year I worked on this, and gradually succeeded in weaning them from this habit. However, at the end of the year one of the children confessed to me that she always felt guilty whenever she gave me work with any erasure, however minor, and that she thought it was really better if she did the work over.

What had happened, of course, was that their teacher of the previous year had instituted the practice described above, and a multitude of other practices that kept the children very busy, very orderly, and which made neatness and prudence the watchword of the class. There was no experimental science, no discussion of the driving social issues of the time, no building of mathematical or social theory, no exploration of creative writing or literature — but there was order!

Not infrequently, we find entire schools that have given themselves to their need for order.

The mindless workings of community forces can be equally disastrous. Imagine an educational program that is just the product of pressure groups, jostling one another. Or a school so given over to the need for socialization that it is just a place where the tribal rituals of present-day America are carried out! For many years the school has inadvertently compounded the cultural disadvantage of the children of the poor. Even today we know very little about how to prevent the school from doing this. The needs of the institution actually conflict with the conditions necessary to bring about a vigorous compensatory education for those children. For years no forceful group within the community questioned the fact that controversial issues appeared in the curriculums of very few schools. For years, also, the *de facto* segregation of school attendance boundaries was a mindlessly accepted fact of American life.

On the other hand, the needs of the institution and the community are real. The teacher should not be prevented from expressing his needs, nor should any pressure group be simply squelched. The ferment of forces that arise from those sources are important motive forces. Were there no needs, there should be no action.

The task is to develop organizations for planning schools that can legitimize the consideration of institutional and community needs and forces and include with them consideration of the ideational and technical possibilities offered to those who would create a school today.

A committee of responsible parties

Who are these people who are responsible for the direction of the school? They are drawn from several sources:

(1) REPRESENTATIVES of the general public. This group is chosen to exercise some jurisdiction over provisions for education. For public schools in the United States, local boards of education are most common. However, state legislatures and boards of education, departments of public instruction and other agencies are frequently

constituted to exercise some direction over schools. Sometimes they choose to operate through general regulations or policies within which others may operate. In other cases (as especially local boards of education in small communities) they may become intimately involved with the shaping of the school. Even local boards may give great latitude to privately-financed schools, requiring only compliance with health regulations and building maintenance standards.

In any case, representatives of the general public should be involved in the creation of a new school. Even the most aloof trustees of a "private" school are representatives of the public and they are wise to include other representatives of the public in the committee that has charge of determining the direction of a school program. The community will react to any school, and the testing of community pressure and will is an important ingredient in the planning for any really bold educational plan that will have a good opportunity to succeed. Moreover, liaison with designated agencies is desirable throughout the planning stages.

(2) REPRESENTATIVES of the school administration. As early as possible in the development of a new school program — or in the regeneration of an existing one — some officials should be designated to exercise the necessary executive functions to see the planning through and to bring the school into existence. Whenever possible, the officials who are expected to work in the new school program should be included in this group. Throughout the planning process, these individuals should be expected to develop organizational and logistical procedures and to procure the expert assistance that the program planners will need. However, the representatives of the school administration do not need to conceive of themselves as the "directors" of the school in the full meaning of that term. The administrative organization will need to depend on the plan for the school which conceivably could call for an exceedingly nondirective form of leadership or even self-government by the students.

(3) INSTRUCTIONAL specialists ("teachers"). The planning group needs to include people who teach and who have the capacity to envision new and alternate educational forms. These people represent

the established knowledge about the educational process. The representatives of the public may have limited views of the possible functions and means of education (although in *some* communities they exceed the professional staff), whereas the leading teachers are students and even scholars of the educational process. As planning proceeds more and more toward the development of the means of the school, the instructional specialists will need to take more and more leadership for shaping the specific components of the school and bringing it into existence.

(4) TECHNOLOGICAL consultants. Because it is unlikely that any local situation will contain all the expert knowledge needed, the responsible parties should augment themselves with specialists in curriculum planning, educational technology, architecture, and school administration. The types of competency needed will become apparent as we describe the tasks involved in creating a model for a school.

(5) PATRONS of the school. Parents and children also need to be included among the responsible parties. Especially in the case of large school districts, where school boards and other representatives of the public are likely to be quite remote from the local situation, it becomes necessary to make special efforts to include patrons in the planning of a school. Children would not be involved in all aspects of planning but would react to ideas when the child's view seemed important. (In the actual operation of the school, children can play a prominent decision-making role, as we will see later; and in secondary schools, of course, the possibilities for their participation are considerable.)

The school committee

Imagine, then, a committee which is charged with the task of creating a school. It includes some representatives of the public, some school officials, some instructional specialists, some technological experts, and some parents and children.

The committee might be set up by the legally responsible parties. If a private school corporation is initiating the school, the corpora-

tion can set up the committee. Or, if a board of education is responsible, *it* can determine the membership or set in motion the
machinery for assembling it. Or, a school committee might be
assembled by people who hope to influence educational practice
although they have no legal authority themselves. For instance, a
firm of architects might decide to develop school models. If so, it
might assemble a representative body, including members of the
public for reality-testing purposes rather than because it is a political necessity.

Similarly, a group of technologists might decide to plan a school.
Again, they would include administrators and parents out of no
political motive but to test the viability of their model for potential
consumers.

This book is intended to be useful to all who would play the part
of Responsible Parties. It provides a system for analyzing the educational process at the institutional level (the school level), and a language for discussing the system. If it is successful it will be a practical guide for those who have the actual responsibility and initiative
to create a model for the school, and will also be visionary enough
for those who would reflect philosophically on the possibilities of
what man can do for himself through education.

In the next chapter we will look at the task of selecting goals to
guide the development of an educational model — the selection of
the mission for the school.

A sense of purpose:
the mission of the school

*The game is no longer to explore and conquer
your physical environment, nor to build empires
on the face of the earth, but to explore and
expand yourself, your institutions, and all of
human possibilities, to seek ever-receding
frontiers in the infinitely rich and varied
countryside of humanity.**

3

While a discussion of the goals of education logically needs to be placed here, and while the analysis of the tasks involved in the creation of the mission of the school is an important part of our conceptual scheme, it is with some misgivings that the treatment of educational objectives is given such prominence. These misgivings arise from two related sources. The first is that far too much of the public debate about education has consisted of sloganeering about the purposes of education with much too little attention to the development of means adquate to the proposed ends.

The debate about the inner-city schools is a good example. Every few months someone discovers afresh that we must do something about the schools for the culturally disadvantaged. The new arrival criticizes the cities for not doing a better job. He talks about rigid administration, poor teaching, inappropriate materials (*all* of his type make the original discovery that Dick and Jane do not live in the slums) and *de facto* segregation. Then does this plaintiff devote his life to research on compensatory education? He does not! Having discovered the problem, he leaves the solution to

---

* From George B. Leonard, "California: A New Game with New Rules."
Look, Volume 30, Number 13 (June 28, 1966), pp. 28–33.

others. Consequently, we still know almost nothing about the means of compensatory education. (Fortunately, the situation is improving, and we *are* finally seeing a perceptible amount of research into *that* problem.)

Our long history of empty debates about objectives has, then, made me wary.

The second source of my caution comes from my conviction, articulated throughout this chapter, that the ends of education are not really defined until the means for achieving them are identified. A desired end for which means have not been suggested is one which is, at least in our time, beyond our grasp.

Nonetheless, it is logical to discuss ends first, and we should. The more means we perceive, however, the wider our possibility of ends, and the more possible they are. Hence, this chapter and the one that follows should be read as a single unit. The separation of ends and means which is valid intellectually is unwise in a practical sense.

When the common school of the last century first opened its doors, its intended functions were obvious to all. It was to spread literacy across the land and, in so doing, to spread participation in the culture. And so it taught us to read and introduced us to the stories of the founding of our land. It helped some of us to love learning, and for the few fortunate enough to combine aptitude with means, it was the first step toward a higher education.

Because so many of us were needed in the fields and around the home, the school closed its doors at the beginning of summer and opened them at the ending of the harvest. It celebrated the days set aside to mark important national and religious events either by suspending classes or by ceremonies within the school building.

It was a Christian school, because anything else was unthinkable. There was Bible reading and praying and singing of hymns. There was strictness and obedience, because fracturing a rule was close to sinning, and toeing the mark was the way to Salvation.

The teachers were not specially trained. No special training was necessary for them to do what they were asked to do. And when special places were set aside to prepare young women to teach, they were training grounds in the original sense of *train* — the teacher was to administer the common education, not create a unique and personal world of discovery.

The child-study movement and the progressive revolution shook the fundamental, obvious, commonly-accepted purpose of the common school. The reformers, through their study of children, came to believe that the kind of school and home that seemed so obvious to us all was not necessarily the best kind of climate for mental and emotional health. They challenged our normal, automatic way of doing things. They came to believe, and taught us to understand, that punishing children did not help them to learn, and that competition was often destructive. They helped us to see how different were those children we were trying to educate in the same way.

The most challenging reformers had their eye not only on the child but on the society. The school, they suggested, does not need simply to transmit the culture to the young in the form that it exists *today* — instead, the school should teach the young to apply the methods of science to the improvement of democratic society. The school should teach the common faith of the mutual attempt to develop a more humane world.[1]

The resulting Progressive Movement never fully reformed the schools, although some of the progressive schools showed what a phenomenally rich and powerful education could be built, if one had the will.[2] However, it left a world much less certain of the functions of the elementary school, because it opened up the possibility of an infinitely rich spectrum of functions.

And so today, when we begin the task of creating an educational model, we are able to begin by attempting to define the mission of the school. We can ask a lot of interesting questions: What purposes will the school serve? Will it foster creativity or conformity? Will it produce social activists or placid acceptors of the status quo? Will it

---

[1] For a history of the Progressive Movement; see Lawrence Cremin, *The Transformation of the School* (New York: Knopf, 1961).

[2] The massive Eight Year Study is a rich source of information about these Schools. See Charles Dean Chamberlin and Enid Straw Chamberlin, *Did They Succeed in College?* (New York: Harper, 1942).

produce intellectuals of practical people? Will it help the little selves that come to it develop confidence and flexibility, or will it concentrate on other things and allow the growing self to shift for itself?

An essential task in the creation of an educational model is the selection of the mission of the school. The Responsible Parties have no more formidable challenge, for along with the multitude of possible directions the school can take, planners have to know that in selecting one direction they will have to neglect many other worthwhile directions. They also need to recognize that if the educational model for the school is not derived from a consciously-selected statement of mission — the school will, in the final analysis, develop purposes. The purposes may not be consciously formulated. They may only be implicit in the means that are selected. But they will be there. If they are not consciously derived, however, they may actually work against the interests of the individual and the society. In many schools the educational program is in some respects detrimental to the person and to the community.[3]

A strong mission is essential to a school that would be great. For a vigorous education to come about, the school has to stand for something — something that galvanizes the efforts of the staff and students, that unifies the program, that symbolizes the effort. Without a strong sense of mission, the school will probably be submerged by pressures to be "normal," "average," and, hence, relatively ineffectual.

Direct and latent functions

The task of selecting the mission of the school is complicated by the fact that the school not only accomplishes its directly-intended purposes, but it tends to develop latent functions that are by-products of the central effort. For an example of the development of a latent function, let us use the example of the "track" system as it operates in many European countries.

In many European countries an examination is given at the end

---

[3] Solon T. Kimball and James E. McClellan, Jr., *Education and the New America* (New York: Vintage, 1964).

of the elementary school years. On the basis of the results of this examination, the child's academic future is determined. The highest scorers are henceforth prepared for college, whereas lower scorers are prepared for trade or technical schools, or given a terminal general education. Once categorized, a student only rarely can switch from one of the lower "tracks" to the academic preparatory tracks. Whereas the direct purpose of the examination is to match students to appropriate courses, the indirect or latent effect is to influence very heavily the occupational possibilities for each individual, because these are tied very closely to academic training.

The ultimate effect is to perpetuate the existing class system, because the students from the upper and middle classes tend to survive this competitive system much better than those from the lower economic classes. A comment by the headmaster of one of the English public schools sums up the situation:

"I should agree with those who hold that moribund class distinctions are being given artificial respiration by our educational system."[4]

It is extremely important for those who define the mission of the school to develop an appreciation of the latent functions that are likely to develop, and, as the school ages, it is important that its mission be revised and its means be recast to ensure that it does not unwittingly undermine one purpose in the course of its attempt to achieve another.

The spectrum of missions: identifying the alternatives

The possible functions of elementary education are so numerous that the task of identifying them can be bewildering unless we impose a structure on it. This structure should enable us to generate the central, unifying objectives the school will strive for. It is those central objectives that focus the efforts of the school and, hence, form its mission.

---

[4] John Dancey, Headmaster of Marlborough, 1963, quoted in Anthony Sampson, *Anatomy of Britain Today* (New York: Harper and Row, 1965) p. 197.

The mission of the school can be defined in terms of the domains through which it (the school) enters into the life of the student. For education is an attempt to enter our life and change it. The product of education is always seen in terms of a developed capacity to respond to reality in new ways. The primary task in selecting the mission of the school is to identify the domains through which the school will enter the life of the learner in order to change his responses to living in the world.

To bring order to this task, we can divide these domains into three, with the caution that the categories overlap somewhat:

(1) We can attempt to improve the capacity of the learner through direct intervention in the personal domain (as through a direct attempt to improve his intelligence);

(2) We can attempt to enter the social domain, to change him at a point where he is in interaction with his fellow man (as when we attempt to teach him social or economic skills); or

(3) We can attempt to reach him through an academic domain, by teaching him academic skills and ways of dealing intellectually with complexity (as when we attempt to teach him mathematics).

Let us use these three categories, the personal, the social, and the academic, to build a system that will enable us to sort out some of the possible functions of the school, and to generate combinations of functions that can serve as the missions or the guiding objectives of school programs. We may begin by looking a little more closely at each of the points of entry.

The strategy of the scholar as a point of entry: the academic domain

We turn now to focuses that have their origins in the academic disciplines. These are characterized by the attempt to intervene in the life of the student by teaching him ideas of techniques that have been developed by scholars. Probably more schools use academic content as their point of entry than any other approach. Mathematics are taught with the belief that the ways of thinking of the mathematician and his way of calculating will be useful in the life of the learner. History is taught, or the ways of thinking of historians, with the hope that the sweep of history will help the growing student orient himself in the flow of humanity. Content from the sciences is taught — or less frequently, the systems of thinking employed by scientists are introduced, to help the child learn the technologies of his modern world.

Less frequently, aesthetics, ethics, and humanitarian philosophies are taught to the child. More often than those, we find foreign languages, literature, or the social sciences — although none of these is common in American public schools.

The accumulated knowledge of the human race is increasingly concentrated in the hands of professional scholars. Not only in the humanities, sciences, and social sciences is knowledge produced systematically and at an explosive rate, but many pursuits that were at first the result of the practical imagination of men (such as marine architecture and agriculture) have become the objects of systematic scholarship. The larger universities presently provide offices for people studying just about every conceivable human activity.

The elementary school is the first formal link between this scholarly activity and the child. It can function to make the scholarly world accessible to the child and to prepare him for a lifelong relationship to scholarly material.

In the view of many people, the elementary school should find its primary functions in the academic domain. Some of these people simply see academic learning as the route to all development in all domains — they tend to brand any other function as "anti-intellectual" and therefore bad.[5] Others, however, are increasingly concerned with the complexity of the modern world and the

---

[5] Richard Hofstadter appears to be reasonably characterized in this way. He simply does not seem to see any functions for the school other than academic ones. See Richard Hofstadter, *Anti-Intellectualism in America* (New York: Knopf, 1963).

need for every person who can, to be able to handle it concep-
tually. They see the organized scholarly disciplines as the only possible source of this knowledge.

Increasingly, we find the view that there is nothing incompatible
between the personal, social, and academic domains. Before
considering a reconciliation of the three domains of function,
however, we should discuss the alternative academic missions of the
school. Let us turn, therefore, to the question: "What can be the
missions of the school in the academic domain?"

A technical–symbolic mission

Far and away, the most common academic mission is to transmit
the technical and symbolic systems that we use to communicate.
That is to say, reading, writing and arithmetic receive the greatest
emphasis in today's elementary schools. Especially what are called
the nursery, kindergarten, and primary school years, spanning from
age three or four to about nine, are devoted almost exclusively to
language and number development. In the middle grades we find
map skills, study skills, information-location techniques, the
writing of summaries, and the like.

In recent years there has been a resurgence of interest in foreign
languages for elementary school children — not as literature and
rarely (in practice) to develop cross-cultural understanding, but
chiefly for oral and, sometimes, written proficiency. Usually this is
simply an extension of the popular symbolic-systems mission of the
school, although the matter is confused by the fact that achievement
of a foreign tongue confers certain kinds of prestige in America.

The fact that the technical-symbolic mission is so well-established
and is so likely to be agreed on as one of the missions of the school
encourages us to minimize a discussion of it here — to spare the
reader what he already knows. The minimal treatment, however,
should not obscure the enormous role of this function in today's
schools and, quite possibly, in those of some years to come. However, as we shall see in the next chapter, technological changes are
likely to change substantially the means that will be employed to
attain technical-symbolic goals.

A background of information: broad fields coverage

A less dominant, but equally common approach to elementary school children has been to try to present a broad overview of many fields. If one examines middle-grade science textbooks, for example, one finds small sections introducing an enormous quantity of topics. Or, in the social studies, the common practice is to hit the high spots of the political history of the United States or the Western world, and the general economic geography picture of the contemporary world. In mathematics, the tradition has been to cover the fundamental processes and related ideas.

The justification for the broad approach has been that the elementary child needs a store of background information from which he can delve deeply in later years. The school functions to provide him with the basic information and skills that he will use later on when his study becomes more deeply academic. Hence, by acquainting him with the broad outlines of governmental functioning, we prepare him for the serious study of political behavior in the high school. In a sense, therefore, the broad superficial approach is *preparation* for later academic study, and implies only a minor placing for the academic mission during the elementary school years.

Structural control: a serious introduction to academia

Since the publication of the influential book by Jerome Bruner[6] there has been much attention to treating a discipline so that its important organizing concepts are emphasized. The thesis is that within each scholarly discipline there is a network of ideas that shows the major relationships within the field. For example, the sociologist uses ideas like "norms," "values," "sanctions," "roles," to

---

[6] Jerome S. Bruner, *The Process of Education* (Cambridge, Massachusetts: Harvard University Press, 1961).

describe what has been learned about small groups. Hence, if one were to follow the structural principle, he would build a course on small groups around these ideas we have just mentioned.[7] In mathematics, one would teach the fundamental operations (addition, subtraction, multiplication, division) in such a way that the ideas or principles that control those operations were revealed and used to organize the material. In science, biology courses would be organized around ideas like "structure" and "function" that unify the content, whereas units on "machines" would be held together with ideas like "force," "mechanical advantage," and so on.

To develop content so that it provides structural control, one would examine the discipline to determine its network of organizing ideas and then use those ideas as guidelines to the selection of content. For example, the University of Georgia Anthropology Project is preparing a "map" of the anthropology field, and then building materials for courses from grades one to seven. They have identified "cultural universals" as the fundamental ideas that anthropologists use to organize their discipline, and in each grade the children are introduced to those ideas, using illustrative materials from many cultural groups. For example, when "religion" is introduced as a universal, the child is presented with information about the operation of religion in several cultures. "Family" and other ideas that hold anthropology together are treated in similar fashion.

Bruner's statement of the advantages of the structures principle has been taken seriously by many of the leaders of the academic reform movement, and we now have the development of curriculum materials in several areas that use the structural principle — (grammar and spelling courses using principles from linguistics, mathematics courses using mathematics principles, and so on. (Even reading programs are being developed using phonetics, linguistics, and semantics as the source of unifying ideas.) Bruner sees four advantages:

---

[7] For an application of the structures principle to the teaching of the social sciences, see Bruce R. Joyce, *Strategies for Elementary Social Science Education* (Chicago: Science Research Associates, 1965).

(1) The structural ideas provide a conceptual map of the field that aids memory. The learner, in a sense, has places to put information when he receives it.

(2) The student who learns the structural ideas has a sense of control over the area that is not yielded by factual coverage alone.

(3) Organizing concepts provide a basis for applying learning to practical situations. One has the ideas needed to manipulate the content so that it aids in solving problems.

(4) Organizing concepts are what the scholar uses. By teaching them to the young child, we enable that child to "think," using the tools that the advanced scholar employs.

These ideas are so attractive that they have dominated much of the academic reform movement of the last fifteen years.[8] They imply that a basic function of the elementary school years is to initiate the child into the types of conceptual systems that scholars use. There are several fundamental purposes that underlie this goal: Some scholars hope that the approach will have a generally elevating effect on the children by helping them feel the power of the organizing ideas of the disciplines, that it may even increase their intelligence. Others hope that the structural ideas will help provide the children with an intellectual map or system that will help them comprehend the world and solve problems. Still others hope that the contact will impel some of the more gifted students to seek scholarly careers.

To some extent, all of these possible objectives are legitimate and plausible, but they all suffer from some difficulties:

Those who foresee an elevating effect can argue that the contact with cognitively complex ideas may help the children to become more complex intellectually. But which disciplines should be used? Is the clear structure of the developed physical sciences better than the multiple structures of English and history?

Those who see the mission as the provision of an intellectual map, drawn from the disciplines, are arguing from strength,

---

[8] See Robert W. Heath (ed.), *The New Curricula* (New York: Harper, 1964) for an excellent overview of the curriculum projects utilizing the structural principle for selection of content.

because the disciplines are constructed with organization and analyze reality as their fundamental purposes. This approach, also, suffers from the problem of selection. However, it is often argued that exposure to *any* two or three disciplines is as good as exposure to any others — that the mission is to provide a map — that the systems from the disciplines provide problem-solving ability in the special area and, also, show what can be done in general.

Those who see the mission as the induction of the gifted into scholarship can argue that such salesmanship needs to begin early if it is to succeed against competing lures. Detractors of this approach feel that proselyting the young is not a legitimate function of the elementary school.

The important problem is getting the alternatives clear. Three sorts of missions that involve teaching the organizing ideas of the disciplines are available: to develop cognitive complexity; to provide cognitive maps; and to induce scholarly careers.

The questions about "which disciplines" are more properly left to the curriculum systems planners of the school, for they are really questions of means. For the Responsible Parties, the question is whether to give any emphasis in the mission of the school to the teaching of the structures of the disciplines because of some intended effect on the students.

Modes of inquiry: teaching the scholarly processes

A discipline can be conceived of as a community of discourse,[9] a place where a community of scholars studies, expands, and revises knowledge about that domain. On the growing edge of the disciplines, knowledge is being revised and reconceptualized at a rapid

---

[9] The term "community of discourse" is used here in a somewhat different sense than it has been used by Arthur R. King, Jr. and John A. Brownell, *The Curriculum and the Disciplines of Knowledge* (New York: Wiley, 1966). King and Brownell have devoted their entire book to the problem of the analysis of the disciplines. As expected, they use some similar terms but with slightly different meanings than will be found here.

rate. It is here that the real methods of the real scholars are being employed in the struggle to increase knowledge and understanding or to create something new. Many people feel that in the ways that the disciplines develop new creations (what we can term the "modes of inquiry" of the disciplines) we can find the most useful content for the child. For, first, as the child learns how knowledge is produced, he will learn what knowledge is — he will grasp the revisionary character of the constructs that man employs and invents in order to understand and manipulate the world. Second, it is argued that present information and concepts are rapidly going out of date. What we teach the child now may well be seen as "untrue" by the time he reaches maturity; but the ways the scholar works are more durable and they enable one to "keep up" better with what is going on. Third, if one is led into the experimental edge of an area, he will learn the most important fundamental ideas used in the discipline — the ones that are used to guide current inquiry — and he will be led into the discourse by which knowledge is held and revised. In a sense, he will be made a part of the community of scholars. Fourth, it is argued, the methods of scholarship are problem-solving methods of high utility. If one learns how to develop and revise and check out hypotheses, then one has a tool to apply to all of one's life problems. Hence, the most valuable part of the disciplines (viewed this way) in daily life is the part that deals with inquiry within the field.[10]

Several curriculum experimentation projects have employed this approach in the development of their materials. For example, the American Association for the Advancement of Science has developed procedures for introducing even primary-grade children to the processes by which the scientist collects and organizes data, builds ideas, and revises them. At the University of Illinois, elementary school science project has selected just one science, astronomy,

---

[10] Joseph J. Schwab and Paul Brandwein, *The Teaching of Science* (Cambridge, Massachusetts: Harvard University Press, 1962). Also, American Association for the Advancement of Science, *The New School Science: A Report to School Administrators on Regional Orientation Conferences in Science* (Washington, D. C.: American Association for the Advancement of Science, 1963).

and has developed an extensive set of units designed to teach students how the astronomer works The child is taught much geometry, for example, in order to apply it to investigations of the type that the astronomer performs.

Fox and Lippitt[11] of the University of Michigan have taken the same approach, but with respect to the social sciences. They have developed programs designed to achieve the objective of teaching the child the research methodology of "social science." He learns to make observations, and to organize them and build concepts. He learns how to make inferences and to distinguish inferring from the making of value judgments. He is even presented with "scientific reports" that are written from accounts of real experiments in social science.

So far, the application of the "modes of inquiry" principle to the elementary school has been tried very little. There have been a great many attempts to teach the organizing concepts of the disciplines more or less straight, but fewer attempts that have emphasized the processes of developing and revising knowledge.

However, the theory of the Progressive Movement greatly emphasized the child's learning of the scientific method through carrying on projects and solving problems that he, or he and his class group, were interested in. Throughout the writings of Dewey, Kilpatrick, Counts, and Bode, and, more recently, in the writings of Thelen and Miel, we find the assumption that the child learns the disciplines through practicing them. "Practicing them" means engaging in the activity the scholar uses when he attempts to solve problems. However, the assumptions of the Progressives were that the child would develop the problems. The teacher, knowing the discipline, would lead the child to develop control over scientific or scholarly processes and knowledge.

Many of the curriculum reformers operating currently seem to be unaware of this aspect of the Progressive movement and dismiss the

---

[11] Ronald Lippitt and Robert Fox (directors), *Social Studies in the Elementary School* (Ann Arbor: University of Michigan). Project supported by the United States Office of Education.

Progressive era as one devoted entirely to the individual and societal domains.[12] The reason for this is to be found partly in the political aspects of the Progressive reform movement, which so often
involved so forceful an attempt to make education more relevant to
the child and the needs of the society, that the academic issues often
were eclipsed.

Emphasize broad philosophical schools or problems

A possible but little used mission of the school would be to help
children approach the aesthetic, ethical, and broadly humanitarian
philosophies of the time. We see this approach recommended for
higher education, as in the writings of Robert Maynard Hutchins,
Harold Taylor, and others, but it has never caught on as a central
focus of the elementary school. Religious schools, of course, have
attempted to inculcate particular philosophical positions, but a
decentralized philosophical approach in public education is rare.
Some of the flavor is present in the Quaker schools of Philadelphia
and in a few of the old English schools, but we still know very little
about it as a possible approach to elementary education.

Possible academic emphases

From the foregoing, it should be clear that when one decides to
select content from any discipline (as, for example, history) the possible emphases are several. Let us recapitulate by listing a few of the
alternative possibilities.

---

[12] John Dewey, *Democracy and Education. An Introduction to the Philosophy of
Education* (New York: Macmillan, 1916); Herbert A. Thelen, *Education and
the Human Quest* (New York: Harper, 1961); Alice Miel and Peggy Brogan,
More Than Social Studies: A View of Social Learning in the Elementary School
(Englewood Cliffs, New Jersey: Prentice-Hall, 1957).

Figure one

Alternate functions within the academic domain

(1) Emphasize general symbolic proficiency. (Reading, writing, arithmetic, technical methods)
(2) Emphasize information from selected disciplines. (History, geography, literature, etc.)
(3) Emphasize major concepts from the disciplines.
    a. Treat broad, related fields together (social studies, language, arts, science).
    b. Treat a few disciplines separately (economics, physics, history, music).
(4) Emphasize modes of inquiry (ways of thinking) of the disciplines.
    a. Treat theory-building, scientific method in general.
    b. Treat knowledge-creation within a few, selected disciplines.
(5) Emphasize broad philosophical schools or problems. (Aesthetics, humanitarian issues, ethics.)

Again, these involve only a few of the possibilities. As we look at educational means in the next chapter, we explore a few more possibilities, but they really are endless, and no one has such clear advantages that we can resolve the problem of selection on *that* basis.

Let us now turn to a very different domain of influence on the student — the domain of his very person.

Focusing directly on personal capacity: the personal domain

The human organism has many potential capacities for responding to its environment. There is intelligence, including the ability to solve problems, to analyze and synthesize information, to build new ideas. There is creativity, or the capacity to take the environment and do new and interesting things with it. There is the organization of the inner self, the feeling of adequacy, or openness, of ability to grow and to face complexity. There is independence or autonomy — the capacity to respond fearlessly and on one's own terms. There are warmth and feelings of affiliation, that enable a comfortable and non-threatening response.

It is possible for the school to try to function to increase directly one or more of these capacities. The school may emphasize creativity, for example, and shape itself to do everything possible to teach students to make a creative, aesthetic response to life. Or the school may organize itself around the attempt to increase intelligence and rationality. It may seek means that have a high likelihood of improving the ability to think. It may focus on means of increasing the personality development of the individual.

A school that sees its mission in the development of personal capacity will emphasize the individual in everything it does. It will try to challenge him, to free him, to teach him how to teach himself. Such a school may pay some attention to social and academic demands, but it will concentrate on the personal capacity of the individual.

Various educational theorists have advocated interesting ways of approaching the task of improving the learner's general capacity to deal with the world. Let us look briefly at six of the types of functions that have been advocated within this personal domain. Figure Two provides a brief outline, with the names of leading theorists in parentheses.

Figure two

Alternate functions within the personal domain

(1) The developing organization of the self. (There are various views of this. See the works of Fromm, Rogers, Maslow, Snygg, and Combs, as listed in the text.)

(2) The development of productive thinking capacity. (Including creativity, flexibility, ability to produce alternatives. See J. Hunt, Torrance, Rokeach.)

(3) The development of a personal meaning. (Here, see Fromm, Phenix, Dewey, Lindser.)

(4) The development of Self-Teaching and problem-solving ability. (See Thelen, Brunes, Hullfish and Smith, D. Hunt.)

(5) The development of aesthetic capacity. (See Santayana, Ducasse, Dewey.)

(6) The development of motivation to achieve. (See Atkinson, Hansen, Bloom.)

(1) *The developing organization of the self.* In recent years a large number of educators and psychologists, many of them from the "phenomenalist" school of personal psychology, have believed that a central mission of education should be focused on the development of a strong self — on the creation of a person who feels adequate and who reaches out warmly and integratively to others. These theorists believe that the function of the school lies in helping the child find and develop a healthy self — one with great capacity for personal and social development.[13] Education should help him find direction rather than impose it on him. We will look rather closely at this position in the next chapter when we examine various approaches to the selection of educational means.

(2) *The development of productive thinking capacity.*[14] Creative problem-solving, the ability to produce alternatives, the capacity to integrate material into new forms — these could be the mission of the school. Theorists like Torrance, Taylor, and Thelen have seen creative thinking as the central purpose of the school. Psychologists like Hunt, Barcon, Rokeach, and Wertheimer have stud-

---

[13] See Erich Fromm, *The Same Society* (New York: Rinehart, 1955.); Erich Fromm. *Escape from Freedom* (New York: Farrar and Rinehart, 1941); Erich Fromm, *The Art of Loving* (New York: Harper, 1956).

[14] Calvin Taylor, (ed.), *Creativity: Progress and Potential* (New York: McGraw-Hill, 1964); Frank Barron, *Creativity and Psychological Health: Origins of Personal Vitality and Creative Freedom* (Princeton, New Jersey: Van Nostrand, 1963); E. Paul Torrance, *Gifted Children in the Classroom* (New York: Macmillan, 1965); Max Wertheimer, *Productive Thinking* (New York: Harper, 1945).

ied the characteristics of creativity and the kinds of environments that stimulate it.

(3) *The development of a personal meaning.* Other theorists have emphasized the capacity to respond to others — to seek the common cause and to avoid alienation through affiliation with mankind. Writers like Fromm, Phenix, and Lindser[15] have described the process by which man discovers himself and finds meaning in a social world. In so doing, they have defined another possible point of entry for the school.

(4) *The development of self-teaching and problem-solving ability.* Another avenue is to attempt to increase the student's capacity to solve problems independently and to plan and organize independent lines of inquiry. We find this emphasis in the writing of Dewey, Holt, Hullfish and Smith, and Miel, among others.[16]

The view of intelligence as problem-solving ability has been encouraged with the recent popularizations of Piaget's work[17] and the view of intelligence as malleable rather than fixed has increased the plausibility of direct focusing on intelligence as a mission of the school.

(5) *The development of aesthetic capacity.* Quite a different point of entry is to try to affect the aesthetic capacity of the student — to change his response to beauty in the world and to imbue him with the drive to enhance the beauty in his life and his physical

---

[15] Philip Phenix, *Education and the Common Good* (New York: Harper, 1961).

[16] John Dewey, *Democracy and Education: An Introduction to the Philosophy of Education* (New York: Macmillan, 1916); John Dewey, *How We Think* (Boston: Heath, 1910); John Dewey, *The Child and the Curriculum* and *The School and Society* (Chicago: University of Chicago Press, 1960, 1956); John Dewey, *Reconstruction in Philosophy* (New York: Henry Holt, 1920); Henry G. Hullfish and Philip G. Smith, *Reflective Thinking: The Method of Education* (New York: Dodd, Mead, 1961).

[17] J. McVey Hunt, *Intelligence and Experience* (New York: Ronald Press, 1963).

and social environments. In the works of Ducasse, Berttel, Eisner, Santayana, and again, Dewey, we can find this type of approach.

(6) *The development of motivation to achieve.* Another distinctive approach is to try to arouse the student's desire to improve himself — to master knowledge and skills. Described by the psychologists McClelland and Atkinson,[18] among others, we find the approach recommended by educators like Hansen and we can see it in the philosophy of many of the programs of compensatory education which frequently try to arouse the desire of the inner-city child to develop himself more fully.

Alternative focuses on personal capacity

We have identified six of the personal capacities of characteristics that can give focus to the school program and, in each case, some of the theorists or researchers who recommend or explore each particular capacity. All of the six probably sound like worthy ends to the reader. Any would serve nobly as the driving mission of a fairly vigorous school. Yet they are only a few of the possible focuses of a school program. And only one or two of them actually have been the focus of more than a handful of school programs.

Let us further compound the problem by looking at possible vantages from which we might attempt to focus on the interaction of the learner with his society.

Focusing directly on interaction with the society: the social domain

The school might seek to enter the learner's life in such a way as to affect directly his relations with his culture and his society.

---

[18] David C. McClelland, *The Achievement Motive* (New York: Appleton-Century-Crofts, 1953); John W. Atkinson, *Achievement Motivation* (New York: Wiley, 1966); Carl Hansen, *Amidon* (Englewood Cliffs, New Jersey: Prentice-Hall, 1962).

Enculturation

The school provides this effect, of course, when it seeks to enculturate him — to teach him the norms and values of the society and the meaning of his cultural heritage, which is the most common way schools try to affect social relations. There are several types of possible focus besides enculturation.

Internationalism and social activism

The school could try to commit the student to a life of service and social activism. I have known a school, for instance, where the children are involved in social work from the middle elementary years and where many of them take part in political activities and the doings of international organizations. These activities reflect the focus of that school on developing the social commitment of the students. In the work of Kenworthy, Preston, and Cahn we can see such a determination.[19]

Cooperative problem-solving

Another societal focus was recommended by Dewey, who saw the school committing the student to the cooperative problem-solving method. The school would be operated as a miniature democracy in which the young citizens would learn the arts of cooperative inquiry and how to apply the scientific method to the problems that interested them as individuals and which confronted them as social beings. While John Dewey was the most formal and thorough spokesman of this view, we find it, in quite different forms today, in

---

[19] Leonard S. Kenworthy, *Introducing Children to the World* (New York: Harper, 1955); Ralph C. Preston, *Improving the Teaching of World Affairs* (Englewood Cliffs, New Jersey: Prentice-Hall, 1956). The National Council for the Social Studies, *The Glen Falls Story* (Washington, D. C.: National Education Association, 1964) provides an interesting description of an entire community school's effort to carry out this objective.

the work of Thelen, Miel, Michaelis, and others.[20] Recently, we have seen this as an emphasis on social activism in some of the experimental schools of Washington, D.C. and other cities.

Economic competence

Another objective might be the development of economic independence. The school might emphasize the skills and knowledge that are essential for economic survival and development. This is a more common mission for technical junior and senior high schools than it is for elementary schools, but many people see reading and arithmetic as the central elementary school "subjects" because of their potential economic usefulness.

Nationalism

In the schools of many nations we have seen an attempt to dominate the social education of the child with a commitment to nationalistic ends. In William L. Shirer's *The Rise and Fall of the Third Reich* we have an excellent description of the program to induct the youth of Germany during the 1930's into the service of the state. Today we can see the emphasis, in less extreme forms, in many schools of many nations.[21]

Human relations

Another approach to social education is to attempt to improve human relations directly. Such a mission characterized the school improvement program of the Wilmington, Delaware public schools

---

[20] See Herbert A. Thelen, *Education and the Human Quest* (New York: Harper, 1961); Alice Miel and Peggy Brogan, *More than Social Studies: A View of Social Learning in the Elementary School* (Englewood Cliffs, New Jersey: Prentice-Hall, 1957); John U. Michaelis, *Social Studies for Children in a Democracy* (Englewood Cliffs, New Jersey: Prentice-Hall, 1963).

[21] William L. Shirer, *The Rise and Fall of the Third Reich* (New York: Simon and Schuster, 1960).

in the late 1950's and early 1960's under the direction of Muriel Crosby.[22] The philosophy of the Bank Street School[23] reflected this same emphasis, and we can see it in the work of Shaftel, Taba, and the Cooks, among others.

Many people feel today that one of the central missions of the urban school should be to combat the alienation of mass society and to help people find meaning and affiliation within the emerging "Brave New World". There is still no powerful theoretical statement on this question, but the work of Sykes and Durkheim are worth consulting.

The possible ways of approaching the student at the point of his interaction with his society are as numerous as those through which we could mount a direct attempt to develop his personal ability. And, of course, personal and social development can be seen together. The attempt, for example, to develop a creative response might be combined with a focus on thinking creatively with respect to the society. Similarly, the attempt to focus on personal problem-solving ability might be combined with a focus on cooperative problem-solving.

The approach to personality development outlined by psychologists Harvey, Hunt, and Schroder describes the intellectual capacity to deal with complexity simultaneously with the capacity to handle interpersonal relations integratively. Hence, their structure provides a way of looking at intellectual and interpersonal complexity together.[24]

---

[22] Muriel Crosby, *An Adventure in Human Relations* (Chicago: Follett, 1965); Fannie R. Shaftel and George Shaftel, *Role-Playing for Social Values: Decision-Making in the Social Studies* (Englewood Cliffs, New Jersey: Prentice-Hall, 1967); Hilda Taba, *Thinking in Elementary School Children* (San Francisco: San Francisco State College, 1964); Hilda Taba, *Intergroup Education in Public Schools* (Washington, D. C.: American Council on Education, 1952); Lloyd and Elaine Cook, *School Problems in Human Relations* (New York: McGraw-Hill, 1957); Lloyd and Elaine Cook, *Intergroup Education* (New York: McGraw-Hill, 1954).

[23] Lucy Sprague Mitchell, *Our Children and Our Schools* (New York: Simon and Schuster, 1950).

[24] O. J. Harvey, David E. Hunt and Harold N. Schroder, *Conceptual Systems and Personality Organization* (New York: Wiley, 1961).

Figure three

Entering the social domain: alternate functions

(1) Enculturation: socializing the child to his culture and transmitting his cultural heritage.
(2) Developing competence as an international citizen.
(3) Developing cooperative problem-solving capacity. (Democratic-scientific approach, political and social activism).
(4) Developing economic competence and social mobility.
(5) Promoting nationalistic fervor.
(6) Improving human relations: increasing affiliation and decreasing alienation.

Figure Three, above, outlines the six approaches to social intervention that we have been describing. Again, they represent only a very few of the possibilities, and the combinations of social and personal objectives scarcely begin to describe the alternative missions a school can seek. Let us now further complicate the problem by looking at ways we can use the scholarly disciplines as the sources of intervention strategies.

Three domains of function

Let us now look at the three domains of function as they are presented in Figure Four and see how we can use this structure to analyze the missions of existing schools and to generate alternative missions. Figure Four simply combines Figures One, Two, and Three, so that we can see the possible emphases in the three domains when they are considered together.

Shall a school emphasize internationalism? Or will it concentrate on the development of intelligence? Should it teach information or concentrate on the modes of inquiry of the disciplines? Shall it try to do all these things?

FIGURE FOUR   *The Missions of the School: Three Domains of Function*

POINT OF ENTRY		
Intervention through Academic Strategies	*Intervention through Personal Capacity*	*Intervention through Social Relations*
1. Symbolic-technical proficiency (reading, arithmetic, etc.)	1. Self-organization or concept	1. Enculturation
2. Information from selected disciplines (commonly history, geography and literature)	2. Productive thinking	2. Internationalism
3. Structure of knowledge (concepts from disciplines)	3. Personal meaning	3. Cooperative problem-solving and social activism
4. Modes of inquiry (how scholars think)	4. Self-teaching and problem-solving	4. Economic competence
5. Broad philosophical schools or problems (aesthetics, ethics, etc.)	5. Aesthetic capacity	5. Nationalism
	6. Motivation to achieve	6. Human relations: affiliation vs. alienation

Selecting the mission of the school

As indicated in the introduction to this book, the ordinary patterns of schooling seem to us so obvious and normal, that standing back from our task and developing strong, well-thought-out missions for each new school that is brought into existence is a task that has not come naturally to the Responsible Parties. Hence, across the land we have a scene of relatively small educational variety.

Creating a sense of mission for the school, however, is a complex and difficult task. It involves answering serious questions within each of the possible domains of function:

Which of the personal capacities of the individual will be focused on?

Of the possible ways of affecting societal orientation and relations, which will be chosen for the greatest emphasis?

What will be the emphasis within the academic domain?

For a fully rational approach to these questions, we respect the position of the educator, Ralph W. Tyler.[25] Tyler suggests that the selection of the objectives of the school should be made only after serious study of the student, the society, and the academic sources of content. The recent volumes of the Project on Instruction of the National Education Association have taken much the same position, recommending that the Responsible Parties engage in a continuous study of student, society, and subject matter and continually revise and refocus the objectives of the school.[26]

For the Responsible Parties to do this effectively, they must augment themselves with specialists on child development, societal analysis, and the academic disciplines. They need to provide themselves with expert advice on the various ways that these domains can be analyzed; and, as the school is developed, procedures for continuing and deepening the study of relevant factors should be built into its organization.

If this is not done, the school will tend to drift with the winds of the educational fads. As an example, let us look into the recent developments within the academic disciplines. For many years the science that was taught within the school was of the "kitchen-physics" variety, with children and teachers experimenting with materials and phenomena that were near at hand. Most of the experts in the teaching of elementary school science felt that the child, exploring his environment gradually, should be helped to employ the scientific method and to build theories and discover the concepts of the sciences inductively. In actuality, very few elementary school teachers felt competent to teach science, and the area languished, except in a small percentage of schools. In recent years,

---

[25] Ralph W. Tyler, *Basic Principles of Curriculum and Instruction* (Chicago: University of Chicago Press, 1950).

[26] National Education Association Project on the Instructional Program of the Public Schools, Ole Sand, Director, *Schools for the Sixties* (Washington, D. C.: National Education Association, 1963).

academic scholars have begun to recommend that the methods of the scientist — his modes of inquiry into phenomena — be made the center of the curriculum and that science instruction be rather formal and direct in the teaching of inductive and deductive procedures. Recognizing the lacks in teacher preparation in science, these scientists are attempting to build teaching materials that are very easy to administer by the untutored — in these circles the term "teacherproof materials" has become fashionable. Throughout the nation, schools are adopting these materials, *because it is the current doctrine to do so.* Now, the materials may have a beneficial effect on the children — that is not the question at issue here. But faddism is not a proper basis on which to make a serious curriculum change.

To avoid it, however, the Responsible Parties need to be quite sophisticated about the alternatives that are possible for them.

When developing the central mission of the school, the Responsible Parties will want to take into account the conditions of the local community and the characteristics of the children who are likely to make up the school population. The mission for a bohemian, intellectual community might be very different from that for a middle-class suburb, for example, and the task of the school for a foreign-speaking population in a rural area would likely be defined differently from that for a polyglot urban community. A school for the gifted might seek different ends than a school for the culturally disadvantaged, and so on.[27]

The mission of the school might be defined in terms of only one function, as in the case of Summerhill. Or, it might be quite eclectic and seek to include functions from all three domains.

In any event, the educational purpose of the school should be sharply-etched and strong. It should select from the thousands of desirable objectives the few that are to give focus and character to

---

[27] Bruce R. Joyce and Berj Harootunian, *The Structure of Teaching* (Chicago: Science Research Associates, 1967). Chapter Two gives a blow-by-blow description of a faculty attempting to develop an educational program that takes into account the conditions of the community and the characteristics of the children.

the school program. A realistic, well-defined selection of functions will enable the development of educational means that are coherent and strong and which will accomplish many other purposes as well, because of the momentum that will be generated. The example of the traditional English "Public" schools is instructive. Drawing as they did from the upper classes, they made character, honor, and self-reliance their watchwords. These schools came to stand for those objectives. A new student was quickly swept up in them and passed them on to younger students in his turn. Put pedantically, the schools had a clear function around which it was relatively easy to develop a coherent program. Not that those schools ignored academic learning or other types of functions. They were for many years the chief sources of students for the universities. But the fundamental social purpose provided the matrix against which academic learning went on.[28]

Operational objectives

Once the few major functions of the school have been selected within each domain, they need to be considered in relation to each other and prepared for use in the selection of educational means — the tactics that will be used to induce the students to learn. The Responsible Parties need to see that the faculty of the school translates the mission into working objectives that can guide the selection of educational means. *An educational objective, or set of objectives, is not useful until it is linked with the means for achieving it. We might even say that the operational definition of a statement of objectives is the statement of the procedures that will be followed with respect to it.*

A study by Ammons is instructive in this regard.[29] She studied the curriculum guides of a great number of school districts within a

---

[28] See Anthony Sampson, *Anatomy of Britain Today* (New York: Harper and Row, 1965) for a fascinating description of the function of the public schools in British society.

[29] Margaret Ammons, "The Objectives of Schools." *Elementary School Journal,* 62, pp. 47–63.

radius around Chicago and discovered that nearly all of them had very long statements of many objectives that were, in the first place, not stated in a form that could be followed as a guide for the selection of means, and, second, were not communicated to the teachers of the districts nor used by them for the development of programs. Those school districts had made statements of objectives that were not complete with linkage to the means for implementing them. Had an effort been made to develop means for them, it would have been discovered that they were inadequate and they would have been improved. Had means been developed for each of the objectives, then what the teachers were doing would have been related to the objectives. Let us turn our attention to some of the alternative characteristics that objectives can have — characteristics that affect their potential as guides for the shaping of the school.[30]

Priority

Objectives can be stated generally and include many things, or they can establish high priority for a few things. I have already stated my preference in this respect, but more needs to be said about the function of the school with respect to other institutions. It is clear that many agencies operate to educate children. (Home, church, government, and so on.) Equally, schools can do other things besides educate (dental care, hot lunch programs, recreation, and so on). The function of the school needs to be ascertained in such a way that the relations between school and other agencies is made as clear as possible, and so that relations among these agencies are specified. For example, the home functions to push the child toward the political preferences of the adults. The school can function to help the child analyze political affairs. What is the function of the child in helping the child to analyze why people

---

[30] National Education Association Project on Instruction, Ole Sand, Director, produced several volumes that describe in great detail the selection of educational objectives. See Project on the Instructional Program of the Public Schools, Ole Sand, Director. *Planning and Organizing for Teaching* and *Deciding What to Teach* (Washington, D. C.: National Education Association, 1963).

vote as their parents do, or what are the pros and cons of the positions advocated by the various political parties? Can medical care be organized through other agencies as well as it can through the school? If not, then what should be the relation of the medical care program to the science and health curriculums? These and other questions need careful attention. They add up to the establishment of the major functions of the school — and hence to those things which will be given priority in the school.

Imperativeness

Objectives can be stated in a "achieve them if you can" manner, or in a "these are must!" fashion. The social objectives of the English Public Schools were fairly imperative. If you did not develop what was then called "character," you were in for a hard time. There was much imperativeness in the objectives of the school. An extreme example of an objective with little imperativeness is taken from the curriculum guide of an elementary school I know. It goes, "Readiness to participate in the democratic process varies widely among individuals and should be developed accordingly." That objective simply does not sound as though it will sadden anyone if a child should not become "ready".

Those selecting the functions of the school need to consider how imperative objectives should be. If the democratic process seems to them of excruciating importance, then they want every child to develop all the democratic capacity that he can. They may want the objective to have, much force. On the other hand, they may want to leave much to the judgment of the teachers and the characteristics of the child.

Specificity

Statements of educational function serve in different ways depending on their generality or specificity. For example, the Oakleaf School in Pittsburgh is being developed by a team of experts in self-instruction. They are selecting specific sets of objectives that can guide a carefully-designed sequential program in which each child goes from one learning task to another until the larger objectives have been achieved. They have been *very* specific, therefore, in developing the objectives for the Oakleaf School, as the objectives are to be applied directly to the selection of the learner's program.[31]

On the other extreme, one can develop objectives that are to be used by teachers simply as guidelines for selecting objectives for specific learners. In this case, the objectives are kept deliberately general and have little imperativeness. An objective such as "knowledge of world history," on the other hand, is so general as to be meaningless. It could not even be used as a guideline. In general, specificity is necessary when the whole program is to be laid out in detail by the planners. Generality is useful when the statement of function is simply to guide the development of the specific educational programs by teachers working with specific children.

Gradedness

Gradedness is another quality that can be present in objectives to a greater or lesser degree. By gradedness is meant the ordering of objectives and assignment of them to different age levels or other levels of children. For example, one can assign certain functions or objectives to the nursery school, some to the kindergarten, some to the first grade, and so on. Or, one can develop a statement of which of the objectives comes first, second, and so on, and then let students of any age work up to them. Or, one can simply have overall objectives and leave out gradedness altogether.

Gradedness has been a conspicuous characteristic of the objectives in American Elementary schools. Teacher, parents, and children alike speak of the "second grade work" and so on. Many view

---

[31] Bruce R. Joyce and Berj Harootunian, *The Structure of Teaching* (Chicago: Science Research Associates, 1967) for a thorough description of the Individually-Prescribed Instruction Program at Oakleaf and other schools.

this as the creation of "lock-steps" that hold back the gifted and frustrate and slow[32] but obviously the majority opinion favors gradedness.

Gradedness is useful if one wishes to delineate certain functions for certain age levels of children. It can even be useful if one wishes simply to develop a ladder of objectives up which the child may climb, scholastically speaking, until he reaches the top. It is less useful if one wishes to see much of the content of education come from the inquiry of the individual child or group of children. In fact, of course, gradedness inhibits the selection of content by children and teacher, by specifying it for them. The Responsible Parties should be chary of specifying gradedness, leaving any specification of sequential objectives to those who must plan the curricular systems.

Behaviorality

The major effort to improve educational objectives has involved trying to get them stated in a way that specifies the student behaviors that are to be developed or changed in order to achieve the function of the school.[33] The reasoning goes that education by its very nature is intended to change or develop behavior and that any educational objective, to be meaningful, has to identify the kind of behavior that the learner should manifest once the objective has been achieved. Not to state educational objectives behaviorally, then, is to avoid functions that involve changing children. Hence the objective stated by another school district that I know ("To take a child where we find him and take him as far as he can go") is no

---

[32] John I. Goodlad and Robert A. Anderson, *The Nongraded Elementary School* (New York: Harcourt, Brace and World, 1965).

[33] Ralph W. Tyler. *Basic Principles of Curriculum and Instruction* (Chicago: University of Chicago Press, 1950); Robert F. Mager, *Preparing Objectives for Programed Instruction* (Palo Alto, California: Fearon, 1962); W. James Popham and John D. McNeil, "The Influence of Taped Instructional Programs on Certain Cognitive and Affective Behavior of Teachers" (Paper presented to the Annual Meeting of the American Educational Research Association, Chicago, February 1965).

objective at all, for it doesn't tell us how we can identify the target of our educational efforts. "To take the learner where?" we may ask. And, "What will he be able to do when he has learned?" "How can we tell when he has learned?" Another example of a non-behavioral objective cropped up in a brand new book on the social studies. The author lists, under the heading of "Skills to Be Developed," the following:

"Have the children trace the major episodes in the development of the states rights theory, offering a cause and effect relationship to explain the major revisions of the theory in its course of development." This author has confused an educational activity, or means, with an educational end, or, in this case, a "skill to be developed." What he has given us cannot serve to give direction to the activity.

Hence, it is usually recommended that educational purposes be stated rather precisely in terms of the kinds of student behaviors that are to be encouraged. For example, "ability to think creatively," while rather general, can be defined by citing situations in which creative thinking could be manifested, as when writing stories, solving problems, developing concepts. "Skill in reading maps," can also be defined. We know what it is, what a student should be able to do when that objective is achieved. Popham and McNeil have done some interesting research which indicates that teachers who set behavioral objectives get more educational output from their students than do teachers whose objectives are rather less behavioral.[34] There is little research that can be cited on the schoolwide basis, but one reason for this, as Ammons and others have discovered, is that the educational purposes of schools are rarely stated in adequately behavioral terms.

The Taxonomy of Educational Objectives[35] provides for the school faculty a comprehensive grade to the delineation of objectives in what are called the Cognitive and the Affective Domains. The taxonomy is helpful in intensifying various kinds of objectives and, especially, in placing them in behavioral form.

---

[34] *Ibid.*

[35] Benjamin Bloom and others. *Taxonomy of Educational Objectives, Handbook I: Cognitive Domain* (New York: David McKay, 1956).

The statement of function

The selection of the functions of a school can be identified in the following steps:

(1) Each of the domains of possible function is examined and purposes are set within each domain.
(2) The objectives for the three domains are compared and combined, eliminating inconsistencies and determining where each domain can serve the other.
(3) The objectives are grouped together so that systems of means can be organized to achieve each cluster of objectives.
(4) Decisions are made about priority, imperativeness, specificity, and gradedness.
(5) The objectives are placed in behavioral form — each objective including a statement that enables us to identify the student behavior.

Once these tasks have been accomplished, the function of the school has been identified. It is then possible to make the objectives operational by selecting the means that will be likely to achieve the objectives. If we are unable to identify the means for any given objective, we will have to discard it. Also, we may find that the objectives are too general, or too specific, or that we need to consider the amount of gradedness we have provided for, and so on. The process of the selection of means, if it is well done, will provide us with much information about the feasibility and adequacy of the objectives.

The selection of the mission of the school, its domains of function, is a philosophical and analytical task. The selection of means is more technical. Whereas the Responsible Parties will want to be immersed in the creation of the mission of the school, they will want to oversee the development of its means, but much of the actual creation of means will have to be done by specialists. In the old days the school board member knew as much about teaching as did the teacher. Today he will listen while others talk about feedback, computer-assisted instruction, dissonance situations, creating social norms, and the like and, he may wonder, "Is this new jargon for the old stuff?" Let us proceed and see for ourselves.

A sample mission, with working objectives

To illustrate, let us visit with the Responsible Parties for an imaginary new elementary school and examine the process they journeyed through to develop the mission and working objectives for the school. Let us assume that the school is located in a small city school district with a representative range of problems and possibilities. Let us place this city within the hinterland of a much larger city about one hundred miles away.

The Responsible Parties in our example consist of one member of the board of education, three citizens from the neighborhood where the school will be located (two elected by a neighborhood council and the third recommended by a local businessman's group), the curriculum director and director of elementary education from the school district, three teachers and the principal of the school-to-be, and a technologist from the state department of education. The principal and one of the teachers will function as the executive secretaries of the Responsible Parties. They and the other teachers will be responsible for liaison between the Responsible Parties and the school as it develops. The teachers will also later serve as coordinators of the curricular systems of the school and will take chief responsibility for staff training. A committee of students will be available for discussions.

The first task of the Responsible Parties is to identify a mission for the school. To accomplish this they will augment themselves with technical consultants from time to time. The principal and the teachers, working with the curriculum director, will then develop working objectives for the school. The Responsible Parties will present the statement of mission and the working objectives to the board of education and the district curriculum council for their approval and information.

Then the Responsible Parties will assume a more supervisory and advisory role. The teacher-members, principal, curriculum director and director of elementary education, with the addition of other staff for the new school, will develop the plans for the means of the school: the social, technological and curricular systems of the school, and also a plan for the organizational structure of the school. This group will constitute the curricular council for the school and will be responsible for the actual school operation. The council will report periodically to the Responsible Parties.

That is in the future, however. The task at hand is the development of the purposes for this new school.

The community

The council begins with a report from the curriculum director's office which describes the neighborhood, including housing conditions, incomes, types of community organization and facilities, interest of parents in school affairs and estimates of future support and desire to share in the educational enterprise.

The report indicates that the area is a new development of lower-priced homes. Almost all families have adequate incomes to meet their fixed expenses and some luxuries. Fewer than five per cent of the working males are laborers and fewer than five per cent are professional men. In twenty per cent of the households both parents work. The homes are exceptionally stable — fewer than ten per cent of the households have a history of divorce or separation. All customary shopping facilities are available within the tract, and a large recreation complex has been constructed by the builder and turned over to a community organization which operates it. Most of the residents previously lived in the inner part of the city and have moved to this semi-suburban area in search of better housing and better schools, recreation and neighbors for their children. Parents tend to be active in local affairs but show very little interest in city, state, or national affairs. The tract is racially mixed, but the races are in different sections, and there is much tension over the future racial composition of the development. The parents tend to be young, with young children. Adolescents attend a high school which is one of four in the city.

The report occupies several sessions and results in a request to the curriculum director that his staff poll a sample of the citizens to ascertain their desire for participation in educational affairs, their view of the problems facing the community, and their feeling about the direction the school should take.

The children

The next report comes from the elementary education office and concerns the children, who presently are being transported to older schools in the district, pending the completion of the neighborhood school. The report covers many aspects of the children.

Intelligence tests indicate a wide range of ability, with the mean IQ about 100. Achievement test scores in the traditional subject areas reflect the national distribution with a range and mode which are typical for this type of community. The racial groups are approximately equivalent in terms of tests of intelligence and achievement.

Racial and ethnic attitudes are not clearly defined in the younger children, but by age nine a racial cleavage appears and steadily widens.

Typically the children travel in the nearby region with their parents, but one-third of the ten-year-olds have been to the nearby large city only once or twice.

Even the older children show little acquaintance with local, national, or international social and political affairs. Fewer than ten per cent read widely in or out of school.

Adolescents in the community generally continue through high school, but fewer than ten per cent of the college age group attend college. (The national average for a similar community is about twenty-five per cent.) As children get older, their engagement with school seems to diminish. Many of the adolescents who are interviewed seem to feel that much of their school life is meaningless. Even some of the highest-achieving students (but not all) say that although they try to get high grades, they do so for later benefit rather than because the work interests them greatly.

Neither parents nor students have many suggestions for the improvement of the school program, however, although parents want a "good strong" program — and students, especially older ones, want more interesting studies and more share in determining their lives in school.

The report on the children is lengthy. Many technical sections are deferred for later use by the school staff.

Subject matter

With help from members of the state department of education supervisory staff, the Responsible Parties then hear reports on recent developments in academic subject fields. Approaches to academic disciplines such as those sketched earlier in this chapter are explored. Various types of objectives in reading and language teaching are identified and explored. The purposes of foreign language teaching in elementary schools are explored.

Technology and educational theory

Although educational technology refers to means, rather than ends, reports are presented on recent developments in educational technology for the very good reason indicated in the preceding chapter — because technology makes new ends possible to achieve. The development of the purposes of the school requires, then, a general idea of what we can reasonably hope to bring about by educational means.

Thus, the Responsible Parties hear from experts who recommend that education begin early — as early as age three, in order to bring about a more rapid and, eventually, a greater development of intelligence.[36]

Other experts suggest that advancing developments in self-teaching devices make possible a greater personalization of instruc-

---

[36] For a development of this position, see Carl Bereiter and Siegfried Engelmann, *Teaching Disadvantaged Children in the Preschool* (Englewood Cliffs, New Jersey: Prentice-Hall, 1966).

tion — that a school can be organized so that students can have more individual choice about what they will study and proceed at their own pace, moreso than previously.[37] They also advise that the availability of several types of new data storage and retrieval facilities enable the inquiry of groups to be more far-ranging. New instructional systems facilitate a direct teaching of the modes of inquiry of the disciplines — a teaching task which has been limited by the availability of teachers prepared to do that job. Various other developments are explored in some detail.[38]

The building

What has the physical plant to do with the mission of the school? It bears the same relationship as do developments in means, because buildings are more suited to the accomplishment of some ends than others.

For example, school buildings affect the kind of social system the school can develop.

Some buildings permit easy movement of individuals and groups from area to area, making independent and group inquiry relatively easy, thus facilitating the means appropriate to certain ends. Also, the building affects the options the child and teacher will have in the learning situation. For instance, some provide for the inclusion of random-access systems of videotapes, audio tapes, films, and books, so that, from individual carrels, students can retrieve information in many forms.

A third effect of the school building is to determine potential use of the school as a community center. A building can be planned to make many types of community usage possible and desirable. Also, the educational program may extend to community-wide activities (parents and children together may explore dramatics, music, and many other things).

---

[37] For a general review, see Bruce R. Joyce, "Staff Utilization," *Review of Educational Research, XXXVII*, No. 3 (June 1967), pp. 94–107.

[38] We will discuss this kind of technology more fully in Chapter Three.

Fourth, the school is an aesthetic entity. It creates beauty or dullness, encourages by its example, or discourages by its forbidding mien.[39]

The Responsible Parties study these ideas, and many more. Architects present and defend their plans. An architectural consultant successfully defends the position that the ultimate plan of the school should not be created until the means of education are roughly defined, so that the building will facilitate them fully. (It will be adaptable, as well, if really well-designed, of course.)

Debate

Gradually, the various Responsible Parties begin to form opinions about the possible purposes the school should serve. Different members are stimulated by different information or ideas. Some members are impressed by a local psychologist who argues that the school's central mission should be to help individuals to find themselves and meaning in their personal lives. He believes that the current urbanization, materialism, and standardization in the society are compounding to alienate man from man and that a major responsibility of the school is to help each individual develop on his own terms and learn to find warmth and understanding in *the modern world*.[40] Other members are struck by the racial situation in the local community. They see the community situation as America in microcosm — something to be capitalized on. If the students can learn to build a democracy in this situation, they can learn about the trails of building democracy everywhere.[41]

Other members feel that intellectual development should be paramount and that the nursery and kindergarten years should be

---

[39] See Fund for the Advancement of Education, *Profiles of Significant Schools* (New York: The Ford Foundation, 1967) for a description of some very interesting school buildings.

[40] This will be recognized as the kind of argument made in Edgar B. Friedenberg, *Coming of Age in America: Conformity and Acquiescence* (New York: Random House, 1965).

[41] Here we see the basic idea in John Dewey, *Democracy and Education: An Introduction to the Philosophy of Education* (New York: Macmillan, 1916).

given to the development of general intellect, the primary years divided between the technological–symbolic domains and the ways of inquiry of scholars, gradually giving way to an emphasis on the application of the disciplines to the study of history and contemporary society.

One evening an artist argues persuasively for the dedication of the school to aesthetic pursuits. The world, he suggests, is in greatest need of beauty, beauty in human relations, in cities, in the way life is lived.

Another evening several parents argue the position that the primary purpose of the school is to provide a firm foundation in the basic skills and knowledge on which the high school and college can build.[42]

During the debate, many other views are aired. Gradually consensus begins to be reached on the following ideas:

First, the distinctive mission of the school in its early years should combine the social and academic domains. The social emphasis should be on human relations and a commitment to improving them through cooperative action. The closely related academic emphasis should be through learning the analytic tools that scholars use to analyze and understand human relations. The Responsible Parties have become convinced that the social activism and racial problems of the local community should be focused on and that the lack of knowledge and interest in national and international affairs should be remedied. They have also become convinced that academic strategies provide the best avenue to the study of social problems and the development of social skills.

The statement of mission, then, includes the following paragraph:

> This school will stand for the social and intellectual development of the children of this community. Its students will explore themselves and their community, learning to employ the social sciences in the analysis of community dynamics and their own human relation-

---

[42] For thorough development of this view, see the book by the former Washington, D. C. Superintendent of Schools, Carl Hansen, *Amidon* (Englewood Cliffs, New Jersey: Prentice-Hall, 1962).

ships. The school will represent commitment to the building of a richer social world and to the free and vigorous exploration of alternative paths to a better society. Democratic skills and values will be learned, but not by rote. They will be examined and reaffirmed in a form appropriate to the times and to these young people.

The second mission of the school emerges from the concern of the responsible parties that the children develop the intellectual skills for their future self-education and that they grow comfortable with the scientific ideas affecting the shape of their future world. Thus, another paragraph in the statement of mission reads:

> In accordance with personal need and capacity, each child will be enabled to develop the reading, mathematical, and study skills necessary to modern life. With his peers he will study the scientific thinking and technological developments that will give power to the future citizen if they are controlled by him.

The third central mission of the school is devoted to helping the individual to develop on his own terms:

> In this school each student will be given the opportunity to explore himself and things of importance to him. The atmosphere of the school will encourage vigorous personal exploration and tolerance of the unique development of others.

These three missions seem like a great deal for a school to focus on, but the members are unable to agree on the deletion of any one, and the teachers and curriculum specialists believe that a program can be developed that will do a reasonable job in all three areas. Accordingly, they set about the development of working objectives that can be used for the planning of the means the school will attempt to employ. All the working objectives are developed in behavioral terms — they meet Tyler's specification that an educational objective state the behavior expected and the content or area the behavior will apply to.[43] None of them is specific — all are in general terms. The degrees of gradedness and imperativeness are indicated in parentheses after the statement of each objective.

---

[43] Ralph W. Tyler, *Basic Principles of Curriculum and Instruction* (Chicago: University of Chicago Press, 1950).

From the first mission of the school, the following objectives are developed (the behaviors are italicized):

(1) *Commitment* to social participation and the enhancement of the society. (Gradedness: For younger children, social participation will be emphasized. The complexity and realism of social issues will increase with age. For the older children, national and international issues will receive equal attention with local involvement. Imperativeness: High at all levels.)

(2) *Skill* in cooperative social action. (Gradedness: None. Heavy emphasis at all levels. Imperativeness: High.)

(3) *Skill in analyzing* human relationships. *Skill in using* the modes of inquiry of the social sciences to *analyze* society and culture. (Gradedness: Low emphasis with young children, increasing with age. Imperativeness: Also increasing.)

(4) *To empathize* with other people and *appreciate* alternate frames of reference. *Skill* in *analyzing* alternate positions. (Gradedness: None. Degree of intellectuality: increasing. Imperativeness: Very high.)

From the second mission of the school, the following objectives are constructed:

(5) *Reading. Skill* in techniques of reading. *Appreciation* of literature. *Skill* in library research to solve problems. *Habit* of wide personal reading. (Gradedness: Emphasis on general language development before age five, then individualized by readiness with heavy emphasis until independence is achieved. Thereafter no instruction unless specific need arises. Imperativeness: High, but individual pacing critical.)

(6) *Mathematics. Skill* in the fundamental operations. *Knowledge* of basic mathematical theory of real numbers, sets, rational numbers. *Skill* in representing and solving problems, mathematics. *Knowledge* of rudiments of computer technology. (Gradedness: Very little emphasis before about age eight. Then, by readiness, individualized instruction in skills. Explorations of theory in upper grades, depending on progress. Imperativeness: High, but pacing important.)

(7) *Science and technology. Knowledge* of the modes of inquiry used by scientists. *Knowledge* of cybernetic technology and its application to human problems. *Skill* in building and testing hypotheses in areas of interest. (Gradedness: Equal emphasis in all levels. Increasing abstractness of theories explored and complexity of techniques. Imperativeness: Moderately high.)

The third mission gives rise to the following objectives:

(8) *Commitment* to exploring himself and his world and developing his own capacities. (Gradedness: None. Critical emphasis in early years. Imperativeness: Very high.)

(9) *Skill* in initiating and carrying out self-education. (Gradedness: None. Imperativeness: Very high.)

These nine objectives become the working guidelines of the school. They are used to give focus to the development of the school environment — the means of education to be employed. To see how the objectives function, we will revisit them throughout our discussion of educational means and structures in the next two chapters.

The reader will note that the arts, music, and physical education, among other common areas of attention, are not directly dealt with in working objectives of the school. Nor are dramatics or the dance, among other vital areas not customarily included in elementary schools. The commitment to self-education in the third mission of the school, however, includes the possibility of creating optional and self-instructional programs in those areas or including them in the effort to involve students in personal development. They may also receive heavy emphasis as part of the exploration of the community and society, depending on the means that are chosen.

This illustrates, however, the hard choice that faces us in the selection of a guiding mission. There are more valuable possibilities than we can possibly achieve. By implication, what we leave out affects development as surely as what we leave in.

The means of education, 1:
the social system of the school

*At the level of the small group, society has always been able
to cohere. We infer, therefore, that if civilization is to stand,
it must maintain, in the relation between the groups that
make up society and the central direction of society, some of
the features of the small group itself. If we do not solve this
problem, the effort to achieve our most high-minded purposes
may lead us not to Utopia but to Byzantium.**

4

The world that presses us also presses on our children. Sometimes it arouses them. Sometimes it maddens them. At still
other times it pushes against them so hard that it shapes
them. At all points in their lives the enormous weight of the
culture lies over and around them — a veritable sea of
values, skills, ideas, and "normal" behaviors.

It is in the environment that the means of education lie.
The pragmatists have taught us that the critical process in
education is the point of interaction between learner and the
social and physical world that surrounds him.[1] They have
given us the knowledge that, once we know the mission of
our school, our task becomes the arrangement of the environment in such a way as to bring about the changes in the
learner that are embodied in the mission. The most difficult
intellectual task for the Responsible Parties is to help the
faculty create a milieu that will achieve the working objectives of the school. We live in a means-oriented culture. We
treasure our social patterns. The task of persuading people

---

* From George C. Homans, *The Human Group* (New York: Harcourt,
Brace and World, 1950), p. 468.

[1] William Heard Kilpatrick, *The Philosophy of Education* (New
York: Macmillan, 1951).

to seek new educational ends is relatively easy compared with getting them to try new means or to relinquish old ones.

Furthermore, to learn to think effectively about educational means, we have to learn to analyze the educational dimensions of the world that surrounds the learner. And thinking in term of "environments" is still awkward for many people. To begin with, we find that different aspects or dimensions of the environment operate in different ways.

In this chapter we will discuss three environmental dimensions that have substantial impact on the student. These dimensions constitute the means of the school — they are the available tools that can be used to help the student develop.

First, there is the social system of the school. Although it is rarely planned for in the schools of today, the social system within the school probably has the greatest impact on the learner.

Second, there is the technological system of the school — the artifacts and communication apparatus that enable the learner to have access to information and ideas, to conduct experiments, and to receive feedback about his behavior.

Third, there is the curricular system of the school, or the system for initiating and monitoring learning, for presenting ideas and problems to the learner and tracking his progress.

Thinking of the means of education as three separate but interacting dimensions of the environment may seem somewhat strange to a layman reading this book, for he has probably been conditioned to the idea that the means of education are the textbook the student reads and the lectures and demonstrations given by the teacher. At most, he may have envisioned a group of learners led by a skillful teacher who is able to help them "discover for themselves" by studying things that "really matter to them personally."

However, the means of education are more complex and more subtle than that. And they have meaning only when they are firmly hitched to the objectives of the school, just as objectives are not meaningful until means have been found for achieving them.

However, let us first look at the means of education — the creation of social systems, technological systems and curricular systems. Then let us take up the question of the creation of means-ends systems or curricular modes, and look at some school programs and specific curriculum areas. Finally, let us look at the creation of multiple-systems approaches to schooling.

Social systems as educational means

Within every human group there soon develops a social system; that is, the patterns of interaction become less random and more patterned, so that coherent sets of values, norms, roles develop that order the group and make relationships within it predictable and relatively stable. Also, the system develops mechanisms that link to other social systems surrounding it — what Homans refers to as the "external system" relationships.[2] The social system affects the members of the group greatly. It prescribes what behaviors are approved and which ones will be disapproved. It imbues the members with its values. It specifies how decisions will be made and status accorded. It delineates the kinds of relationships people will have — whether they will be cooperative or unilateral, austere or loving, honest or dishonest.

The social system within an institution does not absolutely control the social behavior within the institution, but it has a powerful effect on it, and, in the case of most people, sets limits on what they may do and may omit doing.

In his fascinating essays on mental institutions, Erving Goffman has opened for discussion the kinds of control exerted within social institutions.[3]

There is a deplorable dearth of research on the social system of the elementary school, but a number of items of research have opened the way to understanding some of the factors that operate within school societies.[4]

---

[2] George C. Homans, *The Human Group* (New York: Harcourt, Brace and World, 1950),

[3] Erving Goffman, *Asylums* (Garden City, New York: Doubleday Anchor Books, 1961).

[4] See Bruce R. Joyce and Berj Harootunian, *The Structure of Teaching* (Chicago: Science Research Associates, 1967). Chapter Four describes much of the research that has been done on social relations within the school and interprets the finding for teachers.

The student society

Coleman's research has confirmed what any observer should expect: the students in a school form values and norms that severely affect the behavior of their fellow students. Where students approve intellectual activity, for example, their peers tend to achieve more academic learning. This is true for the most able students as well as for others.[5] Although Coleman's research was done in high schools, it is no doubt true that, in elementary schools as well, the interaction of the students results in the development of values and expected behaviors that can work with or against the educational function of the school as conceived by those responsible for the direction of the school.

Institutionalized leadership

A good many years ago, Waller observed that within schools there tended to develop impersonal, institutional patterns of leadership rather than personal leadership patterns. Put another way, teachers tended to use impersonal devices rather than depend on their leadership skills and personality. Waller has observed that teachers tended to say "We must learn this because the principal (or curriculum guide) says so," thus invoking the authority of the institution. Such leadership, Waller observed, was adequate for lecture methods of instruction, but not good for democratic-process methods or for counseling the students.[6] In other words, the leadership patterns of the school social system are related to the educational possibilities. The creation of non-institutional leadership patterns would be a requisite to the employment of many kinds of educational methods.

---

[5] James S. Coleman, *The Adolescent Society* (Glencoe, Illinois: The Free Press, 1963).

[6] Willard Waller, *The Sociology of Teaching* (New York: Wiley, 1965). Originally published in 1932.

Social contagion

Many of the social behaviors manifested by teachers may be imitated by, and hence may influence, the students. This may occur even among classes of young children. Almost thirty years ago, Anderson and Brewer[7] demonstrated that in kindergarten classrooms where teachers were "dominative" toward the children, the children tended to be "dominative" toward each other on the playground. Where teachers were more "integrative" and respecting of the children, the children were more "integrative" toward each other. What happens, then, is that the children become infected with the social behavior of the teacher, and their system of behavior toward each other tends to take on the character of the teacher's behavior toward them.

Patterns of interaction and teaching strategies

Bellack and his associates have investigated the discourse of the classroom when lessons are being carried on. They have discovered that there are rather stable patterns of interaction that result in certain teacher and student roles which would be hard to change. For example, the teacher tends to ask many questions. Students are accustomed to this, and they are prepared to respond. Teachers, in turn, react by approving or disapproving what the students have said. This pattern is well suited to recitation styles of teaching. What would happen if the teacher were to put the question-asking burden on the students, and induce them to develop and test hypotheses, for example? More than likely the students would resist the change in their roles. The patterns that Bellack has found are comfortable ones — the student knows what to do, how to cope

---

[7] Harold H. Anderson and Helen M. Brewer, "Studies of Teachers' Classroom Personalities," *Applied Psychology Monographs*, No. 6, 1945.

with the classroom situation, and he is very likely to undermine attempts to teach him inductively.[8]

Any school that wishes to employ self-instruction, cooperative inquiry, or any other means that is not a moral part of the educational system as it now goes on can expect that the changes of instructional strategy will have to be accompanied by corresponding changes in the social system of the school. If the social system is not made to cooperate — be a part of — the educational strategy, then all other aspects of educational method will probably have little effect on the student.

Social pressure as an educational method

A number of interesting studies (conducted especially at the college level) have shown that the social climate of schools is contagious. An idea or value that is part of the normative structure of the school is likely to be transmitted to the students.[9] This is important for two reasons. First, because the norms of the school *will* be transmitted to the students whether it is planned for or not, and may work for or against the educational program by chance. Second, the educational program can take advantage of the fact that there *will* be a social system. A school that wishes to encourage self-instruction, for example, can try to develop high values that will support independent scholarly behavior.

The school and its social milieu

The environment around the school is another factor that is bound to have its effect, whether it is planned for or not. One kind of influence, of course, derives from the fact that the families in

---

[8] The interpretations are mine, not Bellack's. See Arno Bellack, and others, *The Language of the Classroom* (New York: Teachers College Press, Columbia University, 1967).

[9] Philip Jacob, *Changing Values in College* (New York: Harper, 1956) provides an interesting summary and interpretation of the investigations done at that level. Theodore Newcomb, *Personality and Social Change* (New York, Harper, 1947) is a challenging case study of the process at Bennington College during the 1930's.

some neighborhoods teach their children things that make the children more susceptible to formal education than do the families in other neighborhoods. Academic achievement is a close correlate of the economic and educational level in the home. In a sense, one might say that the educational climate of some homes is in tune with the educational climate of some schools. In other cases, it is out of tune. The school can either try to adapt itself, or it can try to change the community. In either case, the influence is constant and serious.

Another social influence is that the society transmits its taboos and mandates to the school, virtually intact. We have discussed earlier the fact that social studies teachers have found that many topics are virtually impossible to discuss with their students without a negative reaction from the parents. Our very political and economic systems have been difficult to discuss critically, for example. Communism has been hard to approach. Until recently, sex education has been a sensitive area. There are other sensitive topics.[10] Again, the school can adapt, or it can try to change the community, but for a school program to ignore its social milieu is to undermine itself.

A third general social influence comes from the kinds of life experience that the community provides. In some communities one meets only slum dwellers. In others, only middle-class suburbanites. In others, one is exposed to a polyglot urban community. In each case, the opportunities for social learning vary considerably. The author has taught in communities where the children were widely-traveled and in a community where few of the children had been more than twenty miles from home — to give some idea of the range that is possible.

A therapeutic milieu

A fascinating book by John and Elaine Cumming[11] describes the dimensions of the social environment that affect the mental health

---

[10] See Maurice P. Hunt and Lawrence E. Metcalf, *High School Social Studies: Problems in Reflective Thinking and Social Understanding* (New York: Harper, 1955).

[11] John and Elaine Cumming, *Ego and Milieu* (New York: Atherton, 1962).

of people. Some environments encourage extreme dependence while others encourage autonomy. Some press us to conformity, others free us. Some are punitive and make us feel guilty. Others are supportive and reassure us. Some climates tear at self-confidence and others induce us to explore new things.

Rosenthal and his associates[12] have recently reported research that suggests that the expectations the teacher has for the child greatly influence the development of the child. They suggest that when the teacher communicates high expectations to the child, he responds with greater growth. It is hard to imagine more dramatic evidence about the potency of the social system.

The social climate has to be a part of any system of educational means that would affect the child's feelings, self-image, creativity and ability to think boldly. If people are to make democratic decisions, it will be because the environment supports debate, open-mindedness and the struggle for compromise. Where they teach themselves, it will be because they have confidence in their decisions and in the supportiveness of the environment. The therapeutic — and the damaging — aspects of the milieu serve to remind us again that the social system has to be an integral part of the educational program.

Educational aspects
of the social system

We will concentrate on several aspects of the social system that can be incorporated into the educational program. These are:

The Normative Structure of the School,

The Student Roles that are Developed, and

The Teacher Roles.

We could include others. However, under these headings it is possible to consider most of the aspects of the social system that

---

[12] Robert Rosenthal and L. Jacobson, *Pygmalion in the Classroom* (New York: Holt, Rinehart and Winston, 1968).

have been studied well enough, at this writing, to enable us to describe the various ways they can be used to affect learning.

The normative structure of the school

The norms of the school are made up of the values that are espoused by the educational community (the children and the school staff), the norms or expected behaviors that are encouraged in that community, and the informal sanctions or rewards and punishments that are employed. Each of these can take on several shapes. Values, for instance, can be materialistic. In such a community the value of education that would be stressed is its material value — the child would be imbued with the idea that he should study in order to achieve vocational success later. When this argument is used by teachers, they are promoting that value. It is often thought that, in communities where education is not prized by the homes, the teachers should stress the vocational value of education in order to increase the salience of education in the minds of the children.

Another possibility is to promote the value of academic achievement. In that case the student would be exposed to a community of people who prize academic learning greatly. Some critics of the schools[13] feel that the school faculties fail to manifest and infect their students with high intellectual values, but that the school generally reflects the prevailing atmosphere of the wider society. Whether these critics are correct or not, there is no doubt that a school program could include provision for developing strong academic values in its society. The school could also charge itself with "creative-thinking" values, if it wished to promote innovative thinking among the students. Bruner has argued persuasively that the school that promotes intuitive thinking will have to value intuitive thinking in clear and prominent ways. The students will need to see teachers thinking creatively, encouraging the making and testing of hypotheses, and so on. If the school values the "right

[13] For example, see Richard Hofstadter, *Anti-Intellectualism in America* (New York: Knopf, 1963).

answer" too much, then students may be reluctant to venture the intuitive answers that are essential to creative enterprise.[14]

What we are saying, of course, is that in order to bring about any kind of behavior, the school has to value it. To achieve any of the kinds of educational function that we described in Chapter One, the school's normative structure has to radiate its valuing of that kind of behavior. If students are to learn to "practice the disciplines" it will be because that behavior is valued. If they are to enhance the self-concepts of the learner, it will be because those learners know they are valued and because they have come to value each other.

The principle of direction, for the "values" aspect of the social system, then, is fairly simple:

The possible directions of values in the school society are as numerous as are the possibilities for educational function. If the value structure of the school is to serve the functions that have been selected for the school, then the values implied in the functions have to dominate the social system of the school.

Hence, if creative academic thinking is to be the function of the school, then the normative structure should support it. If democratic processes are to be encouraged, then the normative structure has to encourage democratic cooperation. If mastery of basic material is to be the central function of the school, then the norms should encourage behavior that leads to that goal. If self-teaching is to be a function, then the school should encourage self-teaching independence, self-criticism and evaluation, and the like.

Mechanisms for developing the normative structure

It is one thing to decide what the norms should support. It is quite another thing to create the norms in the actual society of the school. It is especially difficult because the school society is made up of children and adults who traditionally do not share a peer culture. Usually the school depends on the parents and the community rela-

---

[14] Jerome S. Bruner, *The Process of Education* (Cambridge, Massachusetts: Harvard University Press, 1961).

tionships to transmit to the children the norms that are needed by the school community. When the home and community do not inculcate those values and norms (as in the case of the culturally-disadvantaged), then the school ordinarily is powerless to affect the children — or at least it does not engage very many of them. Where school teachers and parents do not effectively reinforce each other, the school culture frequently becomes a tug-of-war between children and teachers.

However, it is clearly possible for many things to be done to develop a normative structure that will facilitate the function of the school. While we cannot deal with all the possibilities, we can outline a few of the more obvious methods that can be used.

Rewards and punishments

Through grades, reports to parents, prizes, honors, smiles, words of encouragement, tolerance, the faculty rewards and punishes the behaviors of the students. These sanctions have two effects — they let the students know which kinds of behaviors the faculty approves of and disapproves of, and they have a depressing or encouraging effect on those student behaviors. If the faculty gives prizes for creative thinking, writing, acting, composing, and pays little attention to academic achievement of the conventional sort, then we can expect that the students' attention will be, to some extent, drawn toward the creative and away from achievement. If independence, self-teaching, and personal inquiry are rewarded, we can expect much the same kind of effect.

In the average elementary school of today, of course, behaviors other than achievement of the basic skills in reading, writing and arithmetic are rarely rewarded to any extent — consequently, every child knows that those are the expectations of the faculty, and he usually governs himself accordingly.[15]

---

[15] A set of research studies by the author and his colleagues has established empirically that the rewards and punishments given by young teachers are focused almost entirely on achievement of knowledge and skills. See Clark Brown, "The Relationship of Initial Teaching Styles and Selected Variables in Student Teaching" (Unpublished doctoral dissertation, Teachers College, Columbia University, 1967).

Example

The adults in the school are quite visible, and, students may identify with their teachers by imitating them. So the faculty can manifest, through example, the behaviors that they want to encourage in
their students. A faculty that reads widely and discusses the arts and
contemporary political affairs constantly is likely to have a student
body that does the same. Faculties that venture hypotheses and
offer them for the checking, faculties that share their own creative
efforts with their students as well as demanding creativity from the
children will find that their example produces results. Not with
every child or all of the time, of course, but the effect can be substantial.

Bandura and Walters[16] have provided a theoretical rationale for
this position and Anderson and Brewer[17] have reported a study
which indicates clearly the extent which the model of the teacher
influences the younger children.

Symbolism and ceremony

An elementary school that is carpeted, book-lined, that includes
an attractive theater and areas for music and art, that is hung with
paintings, is a building that "stands" for academic learning. If it
includes opportunities for the younger children to present plays
and concerts, opportunities for the older ones to debate contemporary issues publicly, then it becomes, in its visible action, a symbol
of creative academic inquiry. If it is a supportive, helpful place,
where student helps student and where the library is open and
inviting, then it develops "character" as a place of learning. The
more pronounced the symbolic value of the school is developed, the
greater is likely to be its salience as an influence on the children.

---

[16] Albert Bandura and Richard H. Walters, *Social Learning and Personality
Development* (New York: Holt, Rinehart and Winston, 1963).

[17] Harold H. Anderson and Helen M. Brewer, "Studies of Teachers' Classroom
Personalities," *Applied Psychology Monographs,* No. 6, 1945.

Informal contacts between teacher and pupil

If the school can be a place of much informal, personal contact between students and faculty, then the values and norms of the adults have a much larger chance of being absorbed by the children. Generally, there are two devices for accomplishing this. In the first place, the school can be operated generally on an informal basis, with easy leisurely contacts characterizing all activities. In the second place, opportunities can be created for students and faculty to have contact at times and in areas which are divorced from the usual business of the school. For example, if hobby clubs, trips to plays and ball games and community improvement activities are not part of the "curriculum," they can become part of the "extra-curriculum" that facilitates the desired personal contact.

Gradualness in normative change

A distinctive characteristic of the normative aspects of the social system is that they tend to be highly stable and, barring catastrophe, change but slowly. The use of rewarding, example, symbolism, and the development of informal contacts with students will have their effect on an existing system, but slowly. However, one of the characteristics of a school population is that it changes at regular intervals, so that the concerted efforts of all the adults in the environment can have a marked effect on the children. The four-year-olds enter school not knowing what it is. It can instantly become a place of supportive inquiry or a punishing, competitive grind. The children zoom away from some schools as soon as they are freed and the teachers are glad to see them go. In other schools they linger, and the faculty lingers too. In some schools the student who asks questions is sticking his neck out. In others, students' questions are an invitation to an academic journey. The processes that bring about these different climates are subtle, slow-working, and as crucial as any means of education we can presently imagine.

Nearly all present-day elementary schools are vulnerable to the criticism that their normative structure has simply come into being by the natural workings of the relationships between the teachers and the children. Frequently the resultant climate works against the other means of education, rather than reinforcing them.

Developing student roles

Another aspect of the social system that develops (whether it is planned for or not) is the role-expectation of the students. By way of introduction to this subject the reader might think back to a seminar he has participated in where the instructor alternately lectured and led discussions. A half-asleep student, woolgathering behind his attentive expression, senses a change in the instructor's voice. He rouses himself, brings his attention back to the subject, and concentrates very hard on the last remarks of the instructor. Why? Because he has sensed that the instructor is reaching one of those points where the lecture will cease and the students will bear responsibility for the discussion. Put another way, we may say that the students' roles are about to change.

Our little anecdote illustrates two things at once. First, students fulfill certain roles within the school social system, and these roles can be extremely varied. Second, students learn their roles in a variety of ways. Indirect factors, such as the manner in which instruction is given, shape the roles that the students learn. When Bellack found that there were certain definite patterns to the use of language in the classroom, he drew attention to the fact that the interchanges between students and teacher have a certain gamelike quality and each of the "players" soon learns his roles. For example, if the teacher is a "quizmaster," that is, if he spends much instructional time asking students questions that cause them to recite information they have memorized, the students will soon learn to play roles as "reciters." They will memorize and then wait to be questioned about the material. In such a situation, were a teacher to begin to ask them searching questions, the students would be quite awkward playing the role of discussers or inquirers. The teacher would probably find that the students would resist the change in role, because once they have learned a role and accommodated to it, they have learned to cope adequately with the demands made on them. New demands make their place in the social system of the school uncertain — until they have learned new roles, students are unable to predict how they will fare in the new environment. Consequently, they resist the change.

The normal student role in the schools of today is a fairly passive one. The student is expected to work hard to master information and skills that have been selected for him. He is to do assignments with mastery of the material in mind and, when it is called for, he is to produce "creative" writing samples or "original" ideas. He is to be cooperative in accomplishing the set work, and attentive, if not enthusiastic, about this work. *The student is taught these roles directly by the teachers. The teachers organize the work of the school so that it spells out the responsibilities the students are to take.*

Equally, it is possible to teach the student alternative roles. However, it must be remembered that the roles have to be taught. A school that hopes to shape the roles the students will play will find that it must prepare the students for those roles. For example, if students are to be responsible for developing their own learning projects, they have to be taught how to do this. If they are to evaluate their own progress, they have to learn how to do so. If they are to cooperate with other students to develop cooperative projects, then they have to learn how to do that. If they are to be wide-ranging inquirers, they have to learn how to use resources, how to plan excursions, how to interview, to debate, to state and test hypotheses.

While the age of the students and their capabilities influence to some extent the roles they can play, it is an amazing thing to see kindergarteners who have learned to share in the planning of their day, conduct experiments cooperatively (such as growing snap beans under several conditions to test hypotheses they have developed), make up creative stories and dances, take their own attendance, and, most of all, teach newcomers to their groups how to do these things.

The beauty of the social system is that it is self-perpetuating. Once we get it going, it maintains itself, or tries to, and needs less energy from outside it.

However, it is taxing to teach elementary school students to fulfill desirable roles. Such teaching needs to be planned carefully and possibly requires the services of specialists. For example, some faculty members can construct units of study which are aimed deliberately at the teaching of roles and can specialize in teaching social roles: they can coach other teachers in this area, demonstrate techniques, and actually move from class to class, helping to set up the social system. With their help, the entire faculty might plan units to initiate the school year in such a way that they teach the student roles that will be needed throughout the rest of the program.

It is important that the entire school staff, including the non-teaching faculty, be aware of the kinds of roles that the students are learning to fulfill. For example, if teachers organize students to seek information independently, then the library and other instructional resources have to be prepared to facilitate that kind of inquiry. (An inquiry-centered school, in fact, probably requires many more staff members in the instructional resources centers and fewer in the conventional classroom roles.) The school climate does not have to be completely uniform but neither should it tear the student apart by demanding contradictory roles.

Developing teacher roles

As in the case of the learner, the possible roles that can be fulfilled by teachers are numerous indeed. It is possible to create a school in which several kinds of roles, useful for different purposes, are fulfilled by different groups of teachers. Or, it is possible for teachers to move from role to role, depending on the need. We can briefly examine some of the major ones.

Cooperative group leader

In this role the teacher helps students to organize themselves, to analyze themselves as an inquiring group, to become more efficient as learners who set their own goals for learning, and to develop procedures for achieving those goals.

Organizer of others

This role requires that the teacher identify and institute procedures for organizing groups to work toward predetermined goals. The role is especially useful where there are extremes of misbehavior or disorganization.

Conveyer of information

This person must be a skillful lecturer, developer of teaching materials, and organizer.

Therapist

This highly specialized role is the civilized man's answer to a "disciplinarian." Unlike the disciplinarian, however, he is not a punisher so much as a student of social behavior. He engages in the development of programs to help students who do not fit into the school society.

Self-instruction specialist

This role requires the teacher to diagnose learning problems and prescribe self-instructional materials. He helps the student orient himself to the materials and work his way through them.

Instructional resources specialist

In this role a teacher creates and organizes instructional resources and teaches students how to use them.

Counselor

More a personal inquiry specialist, he helps students analyze their learning needs and prepare to do something about them.

Subject matter specialist

In this role a teacher is primarily a student of an academic discipline. He serves as a resource to students and other teachers with respect to the study of the discipline.

Even the most superficial analysis of these roles will quickly reveal why the author is no supporter of the so-called "self-contained" classroom, in which a single teacher tries to handle all these roles with respect to a group of twenty or twenty-five students. The job is simply too demanding.

In another publication[18] I have described the roles which have to be performed by a teacher who heads a large team of teachers and is supported by contemporary technical support systems (See Chapter Five for descriptions of support systems). Some excerpts from a day in the life of this teacher may help to clarify the multiple roles a master teacher will be filling in the near future.[19]

A day with a teacher

October 22, Some Year in the Future

8:00 A.M.: Harvey Thompson convenes a meeting of his direct-instruction staff to discuss two aspects of the educational program.

The first agenda item is a new project that involves the computer support center. Technicians at the center have developed a model store, and Thompson's team and the computer center staff are working out ways students can use simulation to learn the economic principles that operate as a store purchases goods, sets prices, creates advertising programs, and organizes its personnel. The students are to learn the economic principles by making decisions in the game-type situation. As they make decisions about the price of a product, they will receive feedback on sales and will be able to adjust prices, advertising, and other factors to see if they can increase the sales of the

---

[18] Bruce R. Joyce, *Man, Media, and Machines* (Washington, D. C.: National Education Association Center for the Study of Instruction, 1967).

[19] The following account is taken from *Man, Media, and Machines*, p. 16 ff.

product.[20] The program has been used successfully with older children, but this is the first attempt to apply it to the seven-to-nine age bracket. A staff member of the evaluation center will observe the process and advise about the testing program. The social science specialist from the independent inquiry center also will be an observer and consultant; if the experiment works, the material may have use there.

Thompson and his staff select twenty children to take part in the initial project. If all goes well, the number of students who participate will be increased. Although his team has much help from computer personnel, Thompson wants to proceed slowly so the team can train themselves to use the simulation effectively and to follow up with instruction that does not take place in the center. He also wants to give George Bryant, who has a social science background, a chance to explore whether he wants to continue to prepare to be a specialist in computer application.

9:00 A.M.: Harvey Thompson leads ten children in discussion of a science project on static electricity. Tommy Allen observes, because he will be following up on what Harvey does during the rest of the week. Thompson handles two project groups regularly — this advanced one and a group of difficult children he hopes to reach through their interest in science.

10:00 A.M.: Harvey and George are in the computer support center watching their students operate the simulated store. The experience is so positive that the decision is made to continue with that group of children on a regular basis and to begin the simulation with another group. Harvey arranges to brief the computer staff fully on the social studies program — the matrix of the game simulation. Harvey and George begin to discuss ways of establishing relationships between the store game and the rest of the program. It is George's task to see that there is follow-up when the children get back under the wing of the direct-instruction team.

Harvey also arranges for two members of the computer support staff to bring the simulated store directly into the team suite after the trial period is over. He feels that the trial should be held in the center

---

[20] Readers will recognize that this is no mythical game but one of the several computer-based economics games presently being experimented with by Dr. Richard Wing and his associates at the Board of Cooperative Educational Services for Northern Westchester County, Yorktown Heights, New York.

area, where he and the computer support staff can review and revise the materials. But when it becomes a regular part of the social studies program, the simulation should be moved to the team suite.

10:50 A.M.: Harvey watches the end of the discussions of the current events film, conducted by Florence, Marge, Joan, and Maureen. Joan has tape-recorded her session so Harvey or Marge can help her analyze and improve her teaching. It is weekly routine for each member to record or videotape a lesson and review it with another team member. The team also routinely makes videotape recordings of large group presentations or demonstrations for more flexible use with smaller groups of students.

11:00 A.M.: Harvey spends the next hour preparing a set of creative writing activities which will be used with most of the children in the instructional group. There has been too little spontaneous creative writing from the children, so they will try some "stimulator" activities. The two hundred children will be grouped into teams for writing poems, stories, plays, radio dramas, and a newspaper. The instructional team will act as consultants. The work of each student will be used to stimulate others.

This mythical teacher works as team leader, lecturer, seminar leader, organizer of support systems, counselor, and trainer of teachers, all in less than half of one day. Her life is arduous, certainly, and demands great interpersonal as well as technical capacity. But only such personal leaders will cause the development of modern educational devices to serve the creative growth of children rather than the creation of an Orwellian world of mechanical horror.

The interlocking social system: an example of facilitation and autonomy

Developing a social system is not a piecemeal business. Developing abrasive, driving teacher roles and conforming, acquiescent student roles would not do at all, for example. The students could not respond to the ferment generated by the teachers. The teacher and student roles need to fit together with the normative structure to create the exciting mix that makes the social system an effective educator.

To see the interlocking nature of the components of the social system let us look very briefly at the nature of a teaching strategy which is actually developed from a model of society.

The most common example we have of the derivation of teaching strategy from a model of society is the translations that have been made of conceptions of democratic process into teaching method. Dewey's *Democracy and Education*[21] postulated that, in fact, the entire school should be organized as a miniature democracy in which students would participate in the development of the social system, and would, through this participation, gradually learn how to apply the scientific method to the perfection of human society, and would thus be prepared for citizenship in a democracy. This work has been extended into a conception of the social studies which has been well formulated by John U. Michaelis[22], who made central to the method of teaching the creation of a democratic group which would define and attack problems of social significance.

Let us look closely at the method that Herbert Thelen used to translate a democratic process model into a teaching strategy. Thelen begins with a set of postulates. He feels the need for a social image of man, "a man who builds with other men the rules and agreements that constitute social reality."[23] He sees the necessity for each individual to contribute "to the establishment and modification of the rules . . . to determine both its prohibitions and freedoms for action."[24] He states that the rules of conduct in all fields are interpreted within a larger body of ideas, ideals, resources, and plans, and so on, that constitute the culture of a society.

> In groups and societies a cyclical process exists: individuals, interdependently seeking to meet their needs, must establish a social order

---

[21] John Dewey, *Democracy and Education: An Introduction to the Philosophy of Education* (New York: Macmillan, 1916).

[22] John U. Michaelis, *Social Studies for Children in a Democracy* (Englewood Cliffs, New Jersey: Prentice-Hall, 1963).

[23] Herbert A. Thelen, *Education and the Human Quest* (New York: Harper, 1961), p. 80.

[24] *Ibid.*

(and in the process they develop groups and societies). The social order determines in varying degrees what ideas, values and actions are possible, valid, and 'appropriate.' Working within these rules, and stimulated by the need for rules, the culture develops. The individual studies his reaction to the rules, and reinterprets them to discover their meaning for the way of life he seeks. Through this quest, he changes his own way of life, and this, in turn influences the way of life of others; but as the way of life changes, the rules must be revised, and new controls and agreements have to be hammered out and incorporated in the social order.[25]

Thelen feels that education has failed to capitalize on this model largely because it has failed to realize that knowledge is a part of the continuous business of negotiating and renegotiating the social order. Some people have made the error of attempting to teach knowledge without teaching the process of negotiation by which it is manufactured and revised. However, he proposes:

> The educational model based on these working suppositions is Group Investigation. Given a group of students and a teacher in a classroom, some sort of social order, classroom culture, and 'climate' is bound to develop. It may develop around the basic value of comfort, of politeness and middle class morals and manners, or of keeping the teacher happy and secure. In these all too frequent cases the gaining of knowledge collapses to the learning of information, the meaning of information is respectively to stimulate bull sessions, develop conformity, or provide the teacher with materials to show off with.
>
> We propose instead that the teacher's task is to participate in the activities of developing the social order in the classroom for the purpose of orienting it to inquiry, and that the 'house rules' to be developed are the methods and attitudes of the knowledge disciplines to be taught. The teacher influences the emerging social order toward inquiry when he 'brings out' and capitalizes on difference in the way students act and interpret the role of investigator — which is also the role of members in the classroom group. Under these conditions, the gaining of knowledge could serve initially only to validate the student's portrayal of the investigator role; but as the way of life of inquiring which by then will be inseparable (but not identical) with

---

[25] Herbert A. Thelen, *Education and the Human Quest* (New York: Harper, 1961), p. 80.

meeting personal needs in the group — will have a powerful appeal in itself. And of course, knowledge learnt in its essential, even if microcosmic, social context will be utilizable in the larger arena as well.[26]

Thelen goes on to postulate the particular elements of a teaching strategy:

> The first requirement for group investigation is a teachable group: one which can develop a sense of common cause, one whose members can stimulate each other, and one whose members are psychologically compatible and complementary. The students are assigned a consultant (teacher) who confronts them with a stimulus situation to which they can react and discover basic conflicts among their attitudes, ideas, and modes of perception. On the basis of this information, they identify the problem to be investigated, analyze the roles required to solve it, organize themselves to take these roles, act, report and evaluate the results. These steps are illuminated by reading, possibly by some short range personal investigation, and by consultation with experts. The group is concerned with its own effectiveness, with its discussion of its own process as related to the goals of the investigation.[27]

The kind of climate Thelen advocates is developed in a school environment by the ways the normative structure, the teacher roles, and the learner roles come together. If the learner is taught that his role is that of initiator, seeker, explorer; if the learner learns that his role is to support and assist others; if the teacher roles are those of helper, advisor, cheerleader; if the norms encourage independence and self judgment, exploration and vigor; then the climate is likely to be enabling. If any of these ingredients are missing, then facilitation is greatly reduced. If a group of fellow-students is derisive, if a few faculty members are punitive, if norms vacillate between independence and conformity, then the climate becomes nervous and behavior becomes more circumspect, intellectually speaking, and no climate of inquiry comes into being.

---

[26] *Ibid.*, p. 81.
[27] *Ibid.*, p. 82.

Creating the social system of the school

Creating the social climate of the school is phenomenally easy and maddeningly difficult, simultaneously. On the one hand it is an obvious business. One simply selects the kind of learner roles, teacher roles, and normative sturcture that will facilitate the mission of the school, and then he is ready. But is he? Teachers have to learn new roles and how to teach new roles to the students. The norms may not be the kind of things that the teachers have been encouraging all along, and learning to reward new student behaviors, for example, may be quite difficult. Comparatively few teachers are familiar with the processes of creating a new social situation, and the school culture has proved highly resistant to change in many cases.[28]

Therefore, the entire faculty has to understand and agree on the kind of social system that is to be developed and they should believe in the creation of that kind of society. This does not mean, of course, that they have to create a society in which all roles are rigidly prescribed. The most free and spontaneous environments are the result of the careful creation of roles and norms that encourage and permit freedom of activity. But agreement and understanding are crucial. Then also, the faculty needs to have available to them experts in the development of social milieus — persons who can help create the new roles and who can help train the faculty to develop them and carry them out.

In the preceding chapter we examined school missions that were developed by mythical Responsible Parties. Those missions resulted in several working objectives that required a special social system within the school. For example:

One objective implied that students would study human relations, something that can be done only in an open climate where the norms support individuality and regard for others. To develop such a climate, teachers will have to learn to handle democratic

---

[28] For example, see the illustrations in Matthew Miles (ed.), *Innovation in Education* (New York: Teachers College Press, Columbia University, 1963).

groups and to teach the children to fulfill roles as participants in a searching, cooperative society.

Another objective was to commit learner self-development. Such an objective is probably best achieved by planning a social system which encourages self-development both by approving it and by making it easy to do.

Learning skills through independent study also demands a special social climate where self direction is important and in which cooperation rather than competition is the watchword. Other objectives are less dependent on social means. However, we will see later (pp. 195 ff.) that even those objectives that are not directly achieved through the workings of the social system of the school are indirectly supported by the social environment.

Also, while the social system is powerful by itself, it is important to recognize the interdependence of the social technological and curricular systems of the school. None of these makes sense without the others. Hence, before we consider further the development of social systems, let us discuss the nature of the technological and curricular systems and, when we return to the development of the social system, it shall be in terms of what we will call curricular modes, or integrated social, technological and curricular systems.

The means of education, 2:
the technical support systems
of the school

*Our own utopian renaissance receives its impetus from a desire to
extend the mastery of man over nature. Its greatest vigor stems
from a dissatisfaction with the limitations of man's existing
control over his physical environment. Its greatest threat consists
precisely in its potential as a means for extending the control of
man over man.**

5

The technological support system
of the school

It may seem odd, at first, to put the technical support systems
of the school on the same plane with the social system and
the curricular system. Surely books, teaching machines,
computer simulations, motion picture machines and the like
are not equal to the interaction of the people in the school or
the system for deciding what things should be learned and
how. On closer inspection, however, it should become apparent that the purpose of technology is to provide options for
the human beings in any environment. The number of
options, good options, that exist within an environment
greatly limit or extend the kinds of things that people can do
in that milieu. Educational technology, or the development
of tools for learning and systems for employing them, are of
enormous importance for what they enable people to do
within the environment of the school. Hence, we speak of
technological support systems, or the systems of tools that
provide options for learning. It should be recognized,

* From Robert Boguslaw, *The New Utopians: A Study of System Design
and Social Change* (Englewood Cliffs, N.J.: Prentice-Hall, 1965), p. 204.

however, that technology does not refer only to mechanical devices. Books are an example of a non-mechanical support. Musical instruments are another. The skill of a teacher can serve as one.

Within the present limits of educational technology, there are four types of functioning technological systems that can support the learner and the teacher in their school environment:

Data Storage and Retrieval Systems,

Instructional Systems,

Information Processing Systems, and

Materials Creation and Consultation Systems.

In the development of a school it is possible to create these four types of systems in many forms and in many stages of adequacy. It is interesting to contrast the options that they can bring about in contrast to those in a school environment that contains only textbooks and a small library of resource books.

Data storage and retrieval systems

The learner and the teacher both need access to information. Whenever they inquire together, whenever the learner develops his independent line of study, whenever the teacher prepares to lead a class, the need arises. The possibilities today are seemingly endless and fascinating as well.

(1) BOOK LIBRARIES. The oldest and still one of the most exciting data systems is the library of books. And, there have never been so many children's books on so many subjects. An adequate library for an elementary school of five hundred pupils is estimated to be in the neighborhood of _____ volumes, with a substantial allowance for book loss, which is deemed to be an essential part of high library usage today.

In the elementary school library we are still lacking many titles on important topics. Literature, foreign countries, social problems and issues, art and architecture are among the areas where there are still far too few titles to permit the library to function adequately. It is to be hoped, of course, that, as more schools establish more out-standing libraries, there will come a greater supply of informational books and fiction of more kinds from the publishers.

The first-class library is organized and staffed so that storage and retrieval of informational titles and of fiction and poetry is rapid and easy, and available to all the students and staff of the school for many hours each week.

(2) VIDEOTAPE and audio tape libraries. Music, poetry reading, plays, lectures, and many other forms are now being recorded and can become part of the storage and retrieval system of the school. An enormous variety of topics can be included. The more advanced systems provide for the creation, by the school staff, of material to be added to the system.

(3) MOTION PICTURES, still picutres, and film strips. These media have been well-developed for some time, and a great supply of titles is now available. There is shortage of many of the same topics that are short in books, but foreign nations are now being represented in more and more ways. A relatively new development is the "concept film," a short film dealing with a limited topic. At the Agnes Russell School in Teachers College, Columbia University, Louis Forsdale and his associates have taught children to make their own library of homemade concept films.

(4) DATA STORAGE and retrieval systems on limited topics. A very new development is the creation of random-access data storage and retrieval systems on specific topics. The author and his wife have created, with a research team, a pair of data storage and retrieval systems, one about a New Mexico pueblo and the other about a New England town. Each system includes several thousand written passages, color slides, tape recordings, and other material on the topics that are involved, These "informational" modules range over several hundred categories that include nearly all known aspects of the two cultures. Children are able to use these systems to withdraw information relative to their inquiries about these two cultures. They can compare housing, child-rearing, religions, agriculture, political life, and the social class systems, among other aspects.[1]

---

[1] See Bruce R. Joyce, "Social Sciencing," *The Instructor, LXXVIII,* No. 2, (October 1968), pp. 85–92.

The purpose is to make available to the children an enormous fund of data relative to areas they may study — to provide a huge, open-ended fund of knowledge that is not, however, structured for them, but which they can retrieve and structure for themselves.

Children as young as six years old are able to withdraw and use information from these systems, which promises that they will have utility over the range of elementary school ages and, of course, utility for older students. We will look more closely at these potential uses when we examine specific curricular modes (see pp. 195 ff.).

Whereas data storage and retrieval systems are open-ended resources for the inquiry of the students and teachers of the school, let us examine how instructional systems serve quite different purposes in rather different ways.

Instructional systems

It is possible to create systems of books, machines and instructions that enable students, working singly or together, to teach themselves. Whenever a specific behavioral objective has been identified, one can consider the possiblity of developing a self-instructional system to induce the learner to achieve that objective.

(1) TEXTBOOKS are frequently crude instructional systems. They can be used by students to teach themselves mathematics, for example, and geography, and many other topics. They are crude because, on the whole, they require substantial teacher help and they are not as tightly organized as it is possible to make an instructional system.

(2) LANGUAGE LABORATORIES and their tapes are a familiar example of an instructional system that has a role for the teacher built into it. A complete language laboratory provides a guided course into the language. The student is presented with topics, listens to tapes of others speaking the language, is able to practice and to receive "feedback" by listening to his voice and comparing it with that of the taped native speaker. The system also includes tests and means of scoring the tests so that the student can gauge his own progress. Such a system, in short, provides the entire course, and minimal help is needed from the teacher or attendant who may be in the classroom with the student.

(3) PROGRAMMED INSTRUCTION sequences are becoming more common. They consist of step-by-step exercises in which the student is guided to the gradual achievement of limited objectives by as errorless a procedure as possible. Sets of programmed sequences can lead to quite complicated topics. There are entire courses in linguistics, mathematics, statistics, and psychology available in programmed textbooks.

The Research and Development Center of the University of Pittsburgh, with the Baldwin–Whitehall School District of suburban Pittsburgh, has developed programmed sequences for teaching much of the reading, arithmetic, and science to be included in the program of elementary schools.[2]

(4) TELEVISION COURSES are also available. Some are sets of lectures and demonstrations — really simply televised classroom courses. Others use the medium to make available illustrations that ordinarily could not be used in the classroom, as when a class in oceanography shows films of large specimens and scenes from the deep.

(5) SELF-INSTRUCTIONAL PACKAGES date from the 1920's when the schools of Winnetka, Illinois developed units by which students could teach themselves. In the Winnetka system — known as the Winnetka Plan — the student contracted to do units and then studied on his own to fulfill his contracts.

(6) SIMULATIONS — the cybernetic stance. One of the newest and most exciting developments in technology for education is the development of means of simulating real-life processes in the forms of progressive games that the student can "play" to learn about those processes. For example, at the Board of Cooperative Educational Services of Northern Westchester County, New York (BOCES), children are playing three computer-based games that teach them economic principles. One game enables them to simulate the role of the owner of a toy store. They stock the store, manipulate prices, select advertising campaigns, observe their sales, and make profits, or go bankrupt. Another game simulates a rapidly-

---

[2] See Bruce R. Joyce and Berj Harootunian, *The Structure of Teaching* (Chicago: Science Research Associates, 1967), pp. 81–84, for a description of those programs.

developing nation. They play the roles of economic planners of that nation, and observe the effects of their decisions. In the third game, they play the roles of the kings of ancient Sumeria, and they make such decisions for their kingdom as selecting the amounts of grain to be stored, used, and planted, and receiving continual feedback on the effects of their decisions.[3]

Karl and Margaret Foltz Smith[4] have done an excellent job of describing the use of cybernetic principles of learning to develop instructional sequences that involve simulation and other devices. Essentially the procedure involves an analysis of the process that the student will be introduced to, and then the construction of a situation (game) that can be controlled to vary the factors he encounters or the degree of complexity of the problems he faces. For instance, the Legislative Game, developed by James Coleman and his associates at Johns Hopkins University, enables the committee system to be included or excluded so the student can see how it affects the total legislative process.

The technique of simulation is greatly enhanced by the use of computers, for they enable much more complex processes to be used. Today the training of airplane pilots and astronauts is done largely in extremely complex simulations that enable them to encounter and solve the problems they will meet later, but within the "protected" environment of the game.

(7) MULTI-MEDIA SYSTEMS. Entire courses are now being packaged for groups and for individuals — courses that include laboratory experiments, programmed texts, films, and other materials. Some of these instructional systems need some help from the teacher. Others are designed to be self-administering or are for administration by teachers who may have minimal training in the areas that the course covers. Courses in science, mathematics, social psychology, anthropology, reading, and English grammar are now available for the elementary school. Much of the energy of the cur-

---

[3] These games are being experimented with under the directions of Richard Wing, Board of Cooperative Educational Services, Yorktown, New York.

[4] Karl U. and Margaret Foltz Smith, *Cybernetic Principles of Learning and Educational Design* (New York: Holt, Rinehart and Winston, 1966).

rent academic reform movement has gone into the development of instructional systems.[5]

Most school districts have depended on the large, well-funded "national" curricular projects for their multi-media systems. Some large cities, notably Denver, Colorado, have organized curriculum development staffs that have been able to produce complex multi-media systems.

The use of integrated instructional systems is extremely difficult to conceive fully without considering our third use of technological support — for information processing.

Information processing

The need for information processing is acute and, whether it is provided or not, it has a lot to do with the things that can be accomplished within the school environment. An anecdote from my early teaching experience will introduce the problem area, because it is surely a very typical one.

On my first day of teaching, I prepared a rather elaborate set of tests and problem-situations to help me get to know the students. I had a complex arithmetic test, a spelling test, a test of reading achievement, an inventory of experiences (places visited recently and the like), an inventory of interests and concerns (things they would like to learn, for example), a geography test, and a history test. In order not to delay the children's education, I administered these devices over a period of about a week while we began to work and plan together.

The first night of my teaching, therefore, I took home with me thirty-five examples of creative writing that my students had produced, and thirty-five arithmetic papers that included forty examples each, plus some problems to solve. Before we proceed further,

---

[5] See Robert W. Heath (ed.), *The New Curricula* (New York: Harper, 1964), for a guide to many of these systems and the thinking that has motivated them. Also, John I. Goodlad, *School Curriculum Reform* (New York: The Fund for the Advancement of Education, 1967) describes many of these curricular systems and their rationalizations.

just imagine what I had done to myself: I had over fourteen hundred arithmetic examples or problems! What are the possible permutations and combinations of interests, skills, errors, concepts known or incorrect, that could be extracted from that mass of data? Further, on looking through the stuff during that week, I found that all my charges were enormously different from each other. Some had huge vocabularies and perfect grammar. Some had small vocabularies and perfect grammar. Some had huge vocabularies, perfect grammar, and wrote dull stories that were copies of ones they had read. Need we go on? Some could add, but not subtract. Some could add, and subtract, and perform every other operation, but could not solve problems. I could not even read some of the handwriting.

I was flattened by the mass of data. Worse, in my commitment to working with each child on his own terms, I realized that even if I were able to prepare curriculums tailored to the needs of those children, I would have still more brutal time ahead, trying to track their progress and recast my diagnoses. To finish the sad story, I realized that if I really let the children share in planning their activities, I would be in the dark most of the time about what they were doing and whether they were learning anything from the activities. Fortunately, looking back, I chose that dark course. (I deferred the other tests and problems and never did get around to giving them to the children.)

My experience, of course, is absolutely typical. And, from that experience, we can extract several of the most pressing possibilities for data processing in the school.

Begin with:

Diagnosis and prescription

Imagine the options the teacher and the children would have if they were backed up by a diagnostic tests and assessment instruments of other kinds, report the results and recommended prescriptions, and keep track of changes in the situation. Suppose that that service included original test construction as well as the use of existing devices.

Add:

Tracking progress and providing feedback

Suppose that that service were continuous — that the charting of progress and activities were available and could be made available to the children and the teachers.

Add:

Individualized instructional systems

Suppose, further, that diagnosis, prescription, and tracking progress were joined to self-instructional materials that enabled students to teach themselves at their own rates and with their own individual curriculums.

Add:

Integrated instructional systems

To complete the picture, suppose the processes were linked to the integrated multi-media systems so intimate knowledge were available on each child and the system could be continually adjusted to him.

These four functions are just a beginning of the uses of data processing systems, of course. The alternatives that can now be engineered, given the present state of the art, will be numerous, indeed.

Technology as responsive or controlling

Clearly, the point has been reached where it is possible to provide the student and the teacher with a formidable array of technological supports. Clearly, also, it is possible to develop, outside of the setting of the school, technological systems that use many devices and which are intended to "carry" the instructional program. Now there is much controversy over this type of use of technology. Many people believe that, in certain curriculum areas such as science, there will not be an adequate supply of trained teachers for several decades, and the solution is to build integrated instructional systems that will do the job. Others feel that the only real learning comes about through the encounter between the child and a teacher who can sense his life concerns and interests and can build experiences around them.

We will return to this lively, healthy issue shortly. First, however, let us look at the nature and prospects for curricular support systems.

A proposal for a national support system[6]

We are all limited, in every kind of endeavor, by the information we have and the tools that are at hand. In the field of education there are needs for both information and tools at three levels of operation. One of these levels can be called the curricular or institutional level. At that level school faculties or district curricular divisions or committees develop overall educational plans and designs for courses. At this level there is a serious need for *information* about alternative ways of organizing curricula and the ability to identify *tools* for implementing various curricular conceptions. A second level is the instructional level, in which teachers design and carry out plans for specific groups of children or for individuals. At that level there is need for *information* about different patterns of instruction within curricular areas or courses and *tools* of instruction for making the patterns work. The third level is the learning level and is the point at which the student sets goals and teaches himself. At that level there is a need for *information* about self-instructional materials and a need for *tools* that can be procured easily and readily.

Why all three levels? Why not just aim directly at the youngster and build systems to facilitate his inquiry? Simply because his inquiry takes place within a framework of implicit or explicit decisions made at the other levels. Self-instruction has very different

---

[6] This proposal was developed by Elizabeth C. Wilson, George Usdansky, Edmund Hoffmaster, and Charles Proctor, of the Montgomery County, Maryland Public Schools, Louise Tyler of U.C.L.A., Martin Haberman of the Central Atlantic Regional Educational Laboratory, and the author, who served as amanuensis.

possibilities and meanings within various programmatic frameworks. For instance, if a social studies curriculum emphasizing the methods of social science and lays stress on contemporary urban problems, it will help teachers organize instruction and assemble materials that fit those approaches. In turn it will be likely that tools for teaching himself how to apply social science methods to urban problems will be provided to the learner and, also, that he will have the opportunity to use them. In other words, both the type and content of self-instructional materials are heavily dependent on curricular and instructional decisions. The student is not alone in the school. He is surrounded by other people and processes who mold his learnings.

Let us turn now to what might be the content of data banks at these three levels and then examine procedures for creating them.

A curriculum bank

Today there exist many alternatives for developing and implementing curricular plans, and the possible paths are multiplying at a good rate. There is a tendency for schools to choose from many fewer options than are now available, and it is difficult for local school personnel to identify clear alternatives and their implications. It is also difficult for them to make judgments about the practicality of some of the alternatives. Take, for example, the situation in science alone. Presently we can discern approaches that separate the disciplines, and others that treat them together. Some emphasize the methods of science while others emphasize basic knowledge. Some move from student-initiated inquiry, whereas others structure the learning situation. All of the above approaches are supported, to some extent, by available learning materials. Some other approaches are not backed up by materials unless the teacher creates them himself.

It is extremely important that school faculties, curriculum directors, and people in charge of the procurement of instructional materials know what curricular alternatives have been developed, how they can operate, and how well they are supported by materials. It is equally important for them to know what kinds of conceptions of curriculum have been thought of but which have not yet been backed up by the preparation of materials through which children can explore independently.

It is possible to develop a curriculum bank which identifies the alternative conceptions of curriculum and instruction that are presently available in all of the curriculum areas from the nursery school through the community college level. The bank can identify the major segments of materials that are available to support each of those conceptions of curriculum and to compare and contrast them in such a way that a teacher, curriculum director, principal, superintendent, or member of a board of education can have instant access to those alternative conceptions, providing the possibility of choice among the conceptions that he wishes to implement. If such a bank were made available, we feel the Kettering Foundation would have made a major attack on the glassy homogeneity of the American school.

An instructional bank

A second area in which support systems are badly needed is the area of instructional decision-making. The problem is analogous to the curriculum problem. Teachers need to know how to conceptualize particular units or segments of instruction *within* various curriculum frameworks and what kinds of materials and approaches are available to implement their plans. For example, teachers of world history in the senior high school might be provided with sophisticated resource units around topics derived from various conceptions of the organization of the world history course.* Each resource unit might provide objectives, descriptions of relevant learning activities, lists of materials that are available to enable those activities to go on, and the sources from which those materials can be procured most easily. As curriculum projects multiply, the diversity among commercial publishers grows, and activity by local school districts increases, we are seeing the creation of

---

* There are, in fact, about a half-dozen different organizational patterns which are currently used in world history courses.

wider and wider ranges of approaches and instructional materials. If this is to benefit instruction, the teacher must have at his fingertips a data bank which can identify for him the flow of materials that he can use and that his children can use to teach themselves.

A data bank for children

Thus far we have suggested two types of data bank. Both of these are necessary to the actual utilization of a data bank of materials designed for use by children. In the course of developing a data bank to assist curricular and instructional decision-making, a conceptual framework will emerge which permits the development of a data bank of materials for children. Three data banks, then, are needed. One would serve as a support system for making curricular decisions at the institutional level. A second would function as support system for the making of instructional decisions by teachers. The third bank would provide materials for use by children. *The materials for the children should not be all of the same kind.* The materials for children need to flow from different views of self-instruction as those conceptions fit different curricular and instructional purposes.

At least three kinds of individualized learning materials are required within the school setting, kinds which are different from each other in content, in type of learning activity, and in type of objective. One kind of material is tight, highly sequenced, and directed toward specifically-conceived behavioral objectives. The learner teaches himself through these materials but he is guided very closely by them. A frequent form is the programmed instruction sequence. The prototype curriculum built of many units of this kind of material is the IPI or Individually Prescribed Instructional curriculum which is being developed at the Research and Development Center at the University of Pittsburgh. The development of this kind of self-instructional material requires a curriculum framework in which sets of behavioral objectives are generated and organized sequentially and in which special units of material are prepared for each objective. These instructional materials also tend to be logical, formal, and have been most frequently applied to the "basic skills areas" such as computation and word attack skills in the area of reading. However, they have potential for application to many other curriculum areas. They actually exist in such diverse areas as computer-programming and poetry-writing.

Another type of material for self-teaching is designed to be molded by the encounter of the learner with the material. Here the learner participates highly in the shaping of the learning activity. A good example of this is a book of folk songs for the guitar. No one would seriously expect the young guitarist to follow literally what is written down in the instructions. The material is to stimulate, to suggest, to point out possiblities, to enthuse. But in the course of administering the material to himself the learner will reshape the objectives, re-create the directions, accept some suggestions and reject others, and move off himself. Similarly, a file of letters from soldiers to their families during the Civil War with a few suggestions of ways of looking at them, provides the particular learner who is ready to work with that material with something he could mold and shape in his mind. It may stimulate him to poetry; it may bring tears; it may even cause him to become a historian, but in any case *he* shapes the direction. We need many kinds of material to support the idiosyncratic learning activity of the individual student.

A third kind of self-instructional material is a support system for groups of children who are studying together. For example, data storage and retrieval systems on world cultures that can be entered randomly, provide a resource that individuals and groups of children can use in which they structure much of the inquiry. Similarly, there are units which can be used by children to teach themselves the modes of inquiry of the disciplines. For example, the Lippitt and Fox materials consist of self-instructional units for the fourth, fifth, and sixth grade in social psychology. These units teach the children how to use attitude inventories, to make sociograms, in short, to analyze the social structure of face-to-face groups.

Game-type simulations are another example of self-instructional materials that support group activity.

Today it is possible to build materials that are suited to various types of learning styles. For instance, some children no doubt will profit from motion pictures who would not profit from what seems like the same material embodied in a book. The converse is true. Similarly, motion pictures can say things that books cannot and, again, the reverse is true. Alternative learning styles can be accommodated in a curriculum bank by the sophisticated use of what are coming to be called "multimedia materials."

A unified bank

Imagine, then, a central curriculum and instruction bank which makes available to the school alternative ways of organizing curriculum and instruction and provides inventories of materials to support these conceptions of instruction. Imagine also that that curriculum bank provides resource units within topics which identify objectives and learning activities, as well as inventories of specific materials and where they are located. Suppose that in addition the bank provided materials that can be put into the hands of children — self-instructional materials, directed at certain objectives and differentiated by curriculum modes, media, and style. With such a service, any school would be in a position to select a particular curricular pattern, to back it up with appropriate resource materials, and to support these with the kinds of materials that suit the purposes of the school and the preferred conception of self-instruction. At its fullest level of development, such a bank would enable a school to conceive of its curriculum, give guidance to the teachers who are responsible for the education of particular children, and to provide both highly sequenced and open-ended self-instructional materials usable by individuals or groups.

The means of education, 3:
the curricular systems of the school

*The curriculum is only superficially 'what a man ought to know';
it is more fundamentally how to become a man-in-the-world.**

6

Through the social system, the school affects its students by
being the kind of place it is.[1] Through its technological
system it affects its students by giving them options.
Through the curricular system it affects the student by
attempting to initiate learning — by exposing him to experiences designed to induce him to attain skills and knowledge, or to change what he feels or values. A curricular
system is a plan for exposing students to context, for teaching strategies, and for analyzing what happens as a result of
the exposure.

What kind of organization will the school program have
in terms of subjects or curriculum areas? What principles
will guide the selection of content the student will be
exposed to and the problems that will be constructed for
him to encounter? What kind of sequence will be developed
to organize the progression of events in the curriculum
areas? What major ideas, principles, or values will be
repeated throughout the program and through the years,
giving continuity to the program? What teaching strategies

---

* From Paul Goodman, *Growing up Absurd* (New York: Random House,
1956), p. 83.

[1] This fortunate phrase is from Lawrence Downey, *The Secondary Phase
of Education* (Waltham, Massachusetts: Blaisdell, 1966).

will be used? Will the students be encouraged to study alone, will they be organized into inquiring groups, will they be presented with organized instructional sequences controlled by computers? What systems of evaluation will be developed? The answers to this complex of questions result in a system for initiating and monitoring learning within the school setting. The system suggests what teachers and children should do in order to carry on a coherent program of learning.

Tightness and emergence

A curricular system can be quite specific and tightly spelled out. It can specify the roles of students and teachers, the content to be taught, and the materials and strategies to be used. It can tell when and how things are to be done from year to year. As an alternative, it can be constructed as a guideline — a plan that helps keep the program coherent, but in which most of the actual decision-making is done by the teachers with the children. The curricular system can be extremely loose, in fact, and can encourage groups of children to create the content and develop attacks on it with minimal leadership from the teachers, who serve as advisors and counselors. A plan in which context and strategies emerge and are flexible is no less a plan, however, than one that specifically defines what everyone will do and when.

Selecting curriculum areas

To develop the whole school program in one large piece is an overwhelming task. To make it manageable, curriculum areas or focuses are frequently selected and curricular systems are built around each focus.

Any one of the central missions of the school can serve to focus a curriculum area. Hence, curricular systems can be built around "creative thinking," "commitment to humane values," or "the modes of thinking of the sciences," and so on. Or the working objectives of the school can be grouped together to form organizing centers. For example, if objectives dealing with the development of technical and symbolic skills, as in reading, were combined with objectives dealing with aesthetic sensitivity and a language, litera- ture curriculum areas might emerge.

Which disciplines?

Traditionally the elementary school has selected curriculum areas by grouping the academic disciplines in the generally tradi- tional way: humanities, social sciences, and sciences, with the addi- tion of the "basic skills area" including reading, writing, and com- putation. The humanities have been represented chiefly through history and some literature, although very few elementary schools have really well-developed literature programs. Sometimes foreign languages are included. During the last fifty years the social sciences usually have been a blend of geography, history, government, and community study, and the sciences have been generally treated together. The primary grades have devoted most of their instruc- tional time to the basic skills, including computational content from mathematics, which we can think of as the broadly useful aca- demic tools. These basic skills have so dominated the primary grades, in fact, that it is rare to find a school with a well-developed program that serves the academic domain in any other way.

In addition to the humanities, social sciences, sciences, and the basic skills, the elementary schools usually have included some attention to art and music and physical education, with strong emphasis on skills of performance. Crafts, singing, and the playing of games have dominated those areas in most schools.

If we open up the possibilities and consider afresh the many aca- demic disciplines, the areas of practical skills, and the personal and social domain, then the first compelling conclusion we must reach is that we must make a selection. Most of the possible, teachable con- tent must be left out. The school is going to have to function by compressing academic and other content, by letting a few things stand for many things, or by using some other system that enables an intelligent approach to a huge body of material. We will not dis- cuss one possible way of selecting *academic* content — that of teach- ing a few units or courses from *each* of the disciplines — because it clearly appears to be excessively unwieldy. Such a policy would result in thirty or forty curriculum areas, which is impractical and, fortunately, not at all necessary. What are some of the other ways of selecting content from the possible mass?

Synthesizing the disciplines

One possibility is to take several related disciplines and to weld them together into one curriculum area. There is a tradition of this in elementary education. The sciences, as we indicated earlier, are often treated together. (The aforementioned American Association for the Advancement of Science program uses this approach with the methods of science.) The language arts area was developed to permit reading, writing, spelling, grammar, and literature to be dealt with in a unified way, with common objectives. The social studies area was developed as a problem-solving approach to the social sciences, in which all would be treated together as they applied to problem areas.

Philip Phenix[2] has suggested that the disciplines be grouped for instruction in ways analogous to their methods or function for human life. For example, he suggests that one curriculum area, termed "empirics," might deal with both those social and natural sciences that use empirical methods. Another, called "symbolics," might deal with those domains such as English, foreign languages, semantics, and mathematics, which use symbols. A third might be aesthetics, another ethics, and so on. Phenix has provided a striking idea, because he suggests on a practical level that there may be imaginative ways of grouping subjects that will be more efficient than the one we are more accustomed to. For example, an "empirics" curriculum area might be able to teach all the modes of inquiry in terms of what they have in common, with illustrations from some of the areas. "Symbolics" could be built around understanding what a symbol system is. Focusing on the common elements in the disciplines could be exceedingly efficient and, through reiteration of a few important ideas, could lend itself to a powerful curriculum.

---

[2] Philip Phenix, *Realms of Meaning* (New York: McGraw-Hill, 1964).

Illustrating the disciplines

Many scholars feel that the discipline loses value when it is not treated on its own terms.[3] If one adopts that view, unless he wishes to include all the discrete disciplines in the curriculum, he may select a few to illustrate the rest. For example, we might teach one of the sciences in depth, so that the child learns its ideas or methods; or we might cover it thoroughly, on the assumption that the learning so developed will be analogous to what would be accomplished if all the represented areas were treated. If one learns how the physicist works, it might be argued, he will have little trouble later if he needs to study how the chemist works.

When we illustrate the disciplines, we assume they are related in some way, that they operate similarly. Hence, we might illustrate all the social sciences with one social science, all the sciences with one, all the humanities with one, all the performing arts with one, and so forth. Or, if we took the Phenix view, one discipline might represent aesthetics, another ethics, still another empirics or symbolics.

The socially useful

Another principle of selection is to permit the demands of the social domain to operate. This really is the principle that has given rise to the dominance of reading, the language arts, and computation in the curriculum. Even the social studies area was invented so that content from the social sciences would be the socially useful.

To operate on this principle, we must analyze the disciplines and demands of society simultaneously. It is interesting to note that many people who favor teaching the modes of inquiry of the disciplines do so because they see the modes as the most useful part of the disciplines in life situations. The same claim, as noted earlier, is

---

[3] For example, see Bernard Berelson (ed.), *The Social Studies and the Social Sciences* (New York: Harcourt, Brace, and World, 1963) in which scholars assume that the social sciences, taught "straight," are the best social education.

made for the organizing concepts of the disciplines. Those who favor a linguistic approach to the teaching of reading and language do so not only because it will reveal the structure of linguistics, but also because they believe that knowledge so controlled will be more useful — that the reading and other aspects of language use will be improved because of the linguistic content. We can apply the "socially-useful" principle in combination with the others above. For example, we can integrate the social sciences in the study of contemporary cultures, or we can utilize the structure of one, as anthropology or political science. We can build a great deal of content around contemporary social problems and then use the structure of one or several of the disciplines as the framework within which it is approached.

The personally meaningful

Another possibility is to permit personal needs of the individual to influence what will be taught. We can teach or permit a child to learn some aspects of science or social science because a student's interests lead him in that direction. This approach permits the personal domain to control the academic domain to a large extent. The student, it is argued, involves himself in pursuit of problems that interest him. As he pursues personally meaningful problems, the teacher helps shape his inquiry so that he draws on the academic disciplines that are applicable to the problems. Gradually, in this way, he learns the major ideas and ways of inquiry that are used in the disciplines. In the course of years of this activity, he will have encountered a great deal of the significant material that might have been prescribed for him, but he has done so in a way that has high value to him. Also, the skillful teacher will press him to encounter the significant areas of the disciplines that are relevant to his problems.

Contemporary advocates of this position include Herbert Thelen[4] and John Holt[5], who start from far different premises but

---

[4] Herbert A. Thelen, *Education and the Human Quest* (New York: Harper, 1961).

[5] John Holt, *How Children Fail* (New York: Pitman, 1964).

end up with much in common with respect to the selection of content.

They are joined by those who, like Davis, want the child to experience the imaginative, exciting aspects of inquiry in the disciplines, who see the important task of the school with respect to academic learning to be to help the child absorb the spirit of inquiry.[6]

Product of group inquiry

Another principle is to weld the students into inquiring groups and then permit the inquiry of the group to develop the content that will be treated. This principle operates in the same way as the one just described, except that it is the group that develops the ideas to be pursued. As in the case of the other principles, it need not operate alone. We can prescribe some content, leave some for development through personal inquiry, and allow room for group inquiry to supply more. Or, as in the case of personal inquiry, we can select the modes of inquiry or certain skills for emphasis and then permit the students to identify the problems through which teachers will lead them to the aspects of inquiry they are to learn.

Many exciting areas have traditionally received little attention in schools. The history of art, for example, and the history of music, are seldom treated. In both areas the *avant garde* feel slighted. Philosophy is not often used, although it could be. Ethics is taught infrequently, and logic is seldom included. Literature receives surprisingly little attention, except that children have increasing access to better libraries and more titles. But formal study is relatively rare. We could go on. Most of the people making decisions about the academic content of the schools — school faculties and administrators — do not have available to them the expert advice they need to analyze the academic disciplines properly, let alone make intelligent syntheses. Moreover, many of the possible principles of selection require that the faculty have the academic competence to carry them out. A faculty that does not know the modes of inquiry of the disciplines will have some difficulty teaching them, to put it mildly, whether the modes of inquiry are prescribed or taught

---

[6] Robert Davis, The Madison Project, Webster College, Missouri.

in the course of personal or group inquiry. In the same vein, a faculty that cannot handle individual and group inquiry would be foolish to use those as principles of selection of content. An educator's capability with means, obviously, has a bearing on the ends he should strive for.

Set of tasks — building curricular system

The first tasks, then, in the creation of curricular systems, are the development of the working objectives of the school and their translation, in turn, into the curriculum areas or segments of the school program, each with its own set of operating objectives.

Then, working within the curriculum areas, we can develop specific objectives, teaching strategies, patterns of content, and plans for continuity, sequence, and evaluation. Several alternatives are possible within each of these tasks.

Specific objectives

These may be spelled out and organized so that one follows another, defining a rather tight sequence for each level of the school. This tight sequence is necessary and appropriate when a highly-organized instructional system is to be developed (see pp. 160 ff.). It is not appropriate when much of the content and the processes to be used are developed cooperatively by learner and teacher. When much latitude is to be given to teacher and learner, objectives by "level" should be rather broad, to serve as guidelines rather than as specifications.

Teaching strategies

The essence of the teaching strategy is the induction of the kinds of behavior that are identified in the objectives. Hence, teaching strategies and objectives need to be closely matched, or the curriculum is not likely to have much coherence. In the example given above, the objective, "ability to write original stories" should be matched, hence, to a teaching strategy that induces the students to write stories of their own creation.

Teaching strategies range from the highly directive, where most of the material and ideas are identified beforehand and are presented to the learner, to the inductive and cooperative, where teacher and student work together to attack problems. Teaching strategies also range from mass methods to the highly personal or individual. Some are therapeutic, where the social climate is closely related to the kind of teaching that goes on, whereas others are matter-of-fact and the social climate is left to fend for itself.

The more open strategies permit the teacher to tailor the curricular system to meet the characteristics, interests, and needs of the students. The more closed systems specify what will be done, and they leave personal adaptation to improvisation.

For the achievement of some objectives, teaching strategies might be the same for younger children as for older ones. (For example, inductive teaching of science is frequently recommended for all levels.) In other cases the strategies may shift. To develop creative writing, for example, the system for the primary grades might emphasize language development through many directed activities, whereas, for older children, the emphasis might shift to creativity with dramatics and other expressive activities receiving greatest stress.

Teaching strategies also differ in the amount of technical support needed. Individualized self-instructing requires either a massive amount of self-administering learning material or a veritable army of teachers who can create personalized materials on the spot. Creative writing should draw on a good fiction library but requires few mechanical aids. Dramatics can be helped by videotape feedback facilities, and so on.

Let us examine a sample of teaching strategies, with possible technological support and the types of teacher and pupil roles that could be appropriate. They can be contrasted with the cooperative inquiry strategy that was explained earlier as an example of a strategy which works through the medium of the social system. Whereas the cooperative inquiry strategy was drawn from a model of society as a democratic process, we will turn now to teaching strategies developed from several other sources. Two of the strategies are developed from models of mental processes. Another comes from a theory of personality development. A fourth comes from a theory of learning. The fifth is developed from a view of therapy.[7]

These sources provide a good idea of the range of possibilities and of some of the more interesting developments now taking place.

The extension of the discussion into models from several sources is done deliberately. Our purpose in dealing with models drawn from so many different avenues is to illustrate the enormous range of possibilities that lie before us, and by implication to make clear the dangers inherent in assuming that curriculums or teaching, or instructional systems, should, as a matter of course, follow one or two or three of the more popular strategies being used today. For example, it seems to me that far too many instructional systems today are using the programmed strategy. My feeling comes, not from any antipathy to operant conditioning, which I feel is extremely valuable for certain purposes, but more from my concern that many instructional systems are using operant conditioning where a different strategy would, in fact, be more appropriate, had the manufacturers of the material considered it. Similarly, today as in the past, there is a craze for inductive teaching strategies. While inductive teaching is no doubt appropriate for many worthwhile ends, I would think it a pity if it came to dominate teaching. While inductive teaching is salutary for teaching inductive reasoning, there are alternative strategies available that can accomplish many other purposes at least as well, and perhaps much better, than inductive teaching can. In short, I have come to the belief that the educational menu for today's youngster should include curriculums, encounters with teachers, and encounters with instructional systems representing among them a range of strategies appropriate to the spectrum of educational ends which are necessary for a thorough and vigorous education.

Let us begin by looking at some of the dimensions along which teaching strategies can be analyzed and define some terms that we can use to make our discussion explicit.

---

[7] Much of this material has appeared, in somewhat different form, in Bruce R. Joyce, "Creating Teaching Strategies for Curriculums, Teachers, and Instructional Systems," *Audiovisual Instruction, 12,* No. 8 (October 1968).

Describing teaching strategies

Since the function of a teaching strategy is to provide a model or a paradigm around which an educational environment can be built, it has to establish a blueprint on which a curriculum, or a media package, can be built, or on which the teacher can model his behavior so as to achieve desired effects. It is important, then, that a teaching strategy be constructed so it can be *acted on*. Curriculum workers, teachers, and media specialists have to be able to do the things it asks, or it will not work for them.

We will look at several aspects of teaching strategies that provide us categories that can be acted on. In the first case, we will describe teaching strategies in terms of their *syntax*, or structure, by which we mean the phases of activity and the purpose of each phase, and the relationships between phases of activity. Second, we will describe the *social system, or social structure,* which is to be created. We will describe that in terms of the sharing of initiatory activity by teacher and learner, and the amount of control over the activities that emerges from the process of interaction. Third, we will describe the *principles which govern the reactions or responses by teachers or materials to the activity of the learner*. For example, in some strategies, the teacher attempts to respond to a learner's activity by being extremely supportive of what the learner does and attempting to reflect it back to the learner so that the student himself can be assisted in deciding what to do next. In other strategies, the teacher corrects the learner and reshapes his behavior along a predetermined line, or by following a set of prescriptions that have been prepared in advance. The principles, in short, tell the teacher or the materials-maker how to program his behavior as a learning activity or unit develops. A fourth aspect of a teaching strategy are the *optimal support systems* needed to facilitate the teacher's and learner's behavior. Strategies vary widely in the support they need, and some support systems are highly specific. For example, in history, one can construct an inductive teaching strategy which requires learners to reconstruct historical events by making inferences from original source documents. That strategy must be supported with sets of original documents in some kind of storage system where learners have access to them. Otherwise, obviously, the major activity cannot take place. Similarly, strategies which employ individualization of learner activity require appropriate materials by which many learners of differing capacities and achievement levels, perhaps even learning styles, can engage in activity which is suited to their particular needs and make-up. Yet other strategies need to be supported by teachers who have a high degree of subject-matter or pedagogical competence. For instance, some strategies for teaching foreign languages specify the need for teachers of virtually "native" fluency. Others do not, but they depend on teachers who have the skill to administer highly complex sets of self-instructional materials or "language laboratories." *It is worth noting that a great many attractive teaching strategies never come to fruition because support systems are not developed to back them up.*

Let us look at a teaching strategy drawn from each of our six sources, (models of thinking, models of social process, models of human development, systems from academic disciplines, models of skills, and models drawn from learning theory), and examine it in terms of the four concepts which have been briefly indicated above (syntax, social system, principles of reaction, and support systems).

Let us look first at a strategy derived from an analysis of how people think — from a model of a mental process.

Taba's inductive strategies: a model derived from analysis of a mental process

The late Hilda Taba was probably more responsible than anyone else for the popularization of the term "teaching strategy," and in her work with the Contra Costa school district in California, she provided a first-rate example of the development of a teaching strategy from a model of an intellectual process. The strategy formed the backbone of a social studies curriculum.[8]

---

[8] Hilda Taba, *Teaching Strategies and Cognitive Functioning in Elementary School Children* (San Francisco: San Francisco State College, 1966). Final report of United States Office of Education Cooperative Research Project No. 2404.

Taba analyzed thinking from a psychological and logical point of view, and came to the following conclusion: "While the processes of thought are psychological and hence subject to psychological analysis, the product and the content of thought must be assessed by logical criteria and evaluated by the rules of logic."[9] She identified several postulates about thinking, beginning with the notion that thinking can be taught; second, that thinking is an "active transaction between the individual and the data in the program."

"This means that in the classroom setting the materials of instruction become available to the individual mainly through his performing certain cognitive operations upon them: organizing facts into conceptual systems, relating points in data to each other and generalizing upon these relationships, making inferences and using known facts in generalization to hypothesize, predict, and explain unfamiliar phenomena. From this it follows that the conceptual schema and the mental operations which an individual acquires cannot be taught in the sense of being 'given by a teacher' or of being acquired by absorbing someone else's thought products. The teacher can only assist the processes of internalization and conceptualization by stimulating the students to perform their requisite processes while offering progressively less and less direct support from the external stimulator.[10] "Taba's third idea was that the processes of thought evolve by a sequence which is "lawful." She postulated that, in order to master certain thinking skills, you had to master certain others earlier and that the sequence could not be reversed. Therefore, "this concept of lawful sequences requires teaching strategies that observe the sequences."[11] In other words, Taba concluded that specific teaching strategies needed to be designed for specific thinking skills and that, furthermore, these strategies needed to be applied sequentially because thinking skills arise sequentially.

She developed a set of cognitive tasks, or thinking tasks, and then developed sets of teaching moves, called teaching strategies, which would induce those tasks. To illustrate this, let us look at one of

[9] *Ibid.*, p. 36
[10] *Ibid.*, p. 34
[11] *Ibid.*, p. 35

these — the task of concept formation. This cognitive task involves grouping those items according to some basis of similarity. It also involves the development of categories and labels for the groups. In order to cause students to engage in one each of these activities within the tasks, Taba identified teaching moves in the form of questions which she called "eliciting questions" which would be likely to cause the student to engage in the appropriate type of activity. For example, the question, "What did you see?" might induce the student to enumerate a list. The question, "What belongs together?" is likely to cause people to group those things which have been enumerated or listed. The question, "What would you call these groups?" would be likely to induce people to develop labels or categories.

Thus, the syntax, or structure, of the concept-formation strategy is designed around the process of concept formation which serves as the model for the strategy. The first phase is "enumeration," the second is "grouping," and the third is "developing categories." The teacher guides the development by the use of the appropriate eliciting questions. The *social system* is cooperative, with much pupil activity, but the teacher initiates phases and controls information flow. The teacher's *principles for reacting and responding* must be certain to match his moves or eliciting questions to the specific cognitive tasks, and must ensure that the cognitive tasks occur in order. That is, the teacher should not direct a grouping question to a person who has not yet enumerated or listed; and if the teacher is operating with a group, he must be sure that the enumeration and listing is completed and understood by everyone before proceeding to the grouping questions. The prominent moves by the teachers are questions, and they are questions, modeled after the cognitive functions, which elicit response. The support systems which are necessary are sources of raw data which can be organized. For example, statistics about economic factors in various nations of the world could provide the raw data for concept formation lessons which induce children to build categories of economic comparison and contrast among the nations.

Taba developed strategies to function in curricular systems and also to guide teachers as they developed and carried out units and lessons. In all probability, the same strategies could be adapted to structure media-based instructional systems. For example, television-mediated lessons could follow the concept-formation paradigm which Taba described. However, because teacher and learner would not be in direct contact, the strategy would have to be modified to employ, in certain roles, teachers who work directly with the learners. A fascinating example of Taba's use of this and other strategies in a social studies curriculum in Contra Costa, California, is described in the report cited here.

Concept attainment: a model of teaching drawn from a description of the cognitive process

In recent years, many psychologists have begun to turn their attention to the study of the ways in which human beings acquire and process information about their environment. In this section we will concentrate on the work reported by Bruner, Goodnow and Austin in 1956.[12]

Bruner, Goodnow and Austin studied the process by which human beings form concepts of categories which enable them to describe similarities and relationships among things in the environment. They begin[13] with the assertion that the environment is so tremendously diverse and man is able to discriminate so many different objects that "were we to utilize fully our capacity for registering the differences in things and respond to each event encountered as unique, we would soon be overwhelmed by the complexity of our environment." In order to cope with the environment, therefore, we engage in the process of categorizing, which means that we "render discriminately different things equivalent, . . . group the objects and events and people around us into classes, and . . . respond to them in terms of their class membership rather than their unique-

---

[12] Jerome S. Bruner, Jacqueline J. Goodnow, and George A. Austin, *A Study of Thinking* (New York: Science Editions, Inc., 1967). Originally published in 1956.

[13] *Ibid.*, p. 1

ness."[14] In other words, we invent categories. We use these categories to manipulate our confusing world. This process of categorizing or forming concepts benefits us in five ways. First, it "reduces the complexity of the environment."[15] Second, it gives us the means by which we identify objects in the world. Third, it reduces the necessity of constant learning. For example, once we have learned what an automobile is, we do not have to discover, at each encounter with an automobile, that it is an automobile. We simply need to find out whether or not it has certain identifying properties. In the fourth case, it gives us direction for activity. If we know that we've liked eggs before and that they are nutritious, it helps us select eggs rather than some other substances that we might eat for breakfast. In the last case, it helps us to organize and relate classes of events, for example, the subject disciplines, or cognitive maps, or sets of interacting categories that we use for rendering the world comprehensible, ordering it, and making decisions about investigations and their meaning.[16]

Bruner, Goodnow, and Austin devote their major work to the description of a process called concept attainment, a method by which we discriminate the attributes of things, people, and events and place them into categories. In the discussion, they identify three types of concepts. One is conjunctive, which means that the category is defined by the joint presence of several attributes, or characteristics. For example, red-haired boys is an example of a conjunctive category. When we find a boy who is also red-haired, we have an example of the concept. We also describe disjunctive categories and relational concepts (those in which there is a certain relationship between defining attributes). A relational category, for example, is that there are more accidents when people drive at higher speeds on narrow roads. Holding narrowness of road constant, drivers at higher speeds will have more accidents.

Concept attainment, according to Bruner, Goodnow, and Austin, occurs by making decisions about what attributes belong in what categories. The process of attaining a concept which has been invented by someone else is the process of determining the criteria

---

[14] *Ibid.*

[15] *Ibid.*, p. 12

[16] *Ibid.*, pp. 12, 13

by which they have placed certain attributes into certain categories. For example, let us suppose that a college senior is trying to describe (to someone who is trying to get him a blind date) the kind of girl that he would like to be matched up with. In order to do this, he is trying to *communicate* his concept and his friend is trying to *attain* the concept. Our senior communicates by identifying to his friend several girls both students know, who fit his concept of a desirable date, and several who do not. In the middle of his description, his friend interrupts him and says, "Ah, I see. You like girls who are shorter than you are, and you prefer blondes. You also like girls who laugh a lot, and you tend to avoid girls who are very good students and are very intelligent."

"You've got it, but how did you know?"

"All the time you were talking, I kept thinking about why you had put each girl on the preferred and not-preferred lists. Gradually, I began to get the idea that those were the reasons why you did it. For example, most of the preferred girls were short and only one was a good student."

The above process by the matchmaker was one of concept attainment. His friend has the concept of the girls he liked to date, and they could be defined by several attributes. As soon as his friend began to see by what concepts the girls were being discriminated into the two classes, he had attained the concept and was able to act.

Teaching the concept of a concept

Quite frequently students have difficulty developing concepts. A promising approach is to teach them, as closely as possible, what a concept is. An interesting approach is to provide the students with samples of information, some of which contain examples of a concept and some of which do not. The students know only which samples example the concept and which do not. Gradually, they are presented with more samples until everyone has developed an opinion about the concept. Then, by analyzing the process each student went through, one may be able to help them understand the nature of a concept and strategies for forming them. Let us try an example of this procedure. Each of the following passages is labelled "yes" or "no" depending on whether it represents a concept that I have in mind. As you read the passages, think of the concepts that the "yes" passages might represent: the principle by which they are designated "yes" and the others that were designated "no."

> A group of children are playing on the playground. One of the students makes an error that lets the other side win a point. The other children crowd around him, shouting at him. Some take his side. Gradually, the hubbub subsides, and they all return to the game.

YES

The above passage *does* provide an example of the concept. What concept? Is it playground, or games, or punishment, or children? What are the other possibilities? Let us turn to another passage in which the concept is *not* contained.

> Four children are sitting on the floor of a room. There is a rug, and they are shooting marbles. At one point there is a dispute over a shot. However, the problem is settled, and the game resumes.

NO

This passage contained a game, so we have to eliminate that concept. There was an argument, so we have to eliminate *that* possibility. What are some of the other concepts that are and are not exemplified in this passage and the previous one? Let us look now to another example in which our concept *is* represented.

> It is bedtime. A harried mother is putting the children to bed. It is discovered that one of the children has not scrubbed his teeth. The mother berates the child, sending her back to the bathroom and her toothbrush. When she returns, the mother smiles, the children crawl into bed, and the lights are put out.

YES

What is our concept? Is it punishment? Is it, possibly, simply children? Let us look at one more passage in which the concept is present.

> It is a track meet. One boy crosses the finish line in the one mile race far ahead of his competition. Yet, the next two runners cross the line, straining all the way as they vie for second place. As they slow down after the race, their parents and friends crowd around them, praising them for their effort.

YES

Now, we must rule out punishment. However, if we develop a larger concept, such as "things people do to influence one another's behavior" or "sanctions," or some concept that includes, "approval and disapproval," then we have one that could describe the principle on which the selections were made.

This "game" could continue through several more passages. However, we have included enough to illustrate its principle. It focuses attention on the basis on which we have made a categorization. Because that basis is not revealed clearly at first, we have to keep several possibilities in mind. Gradually we receive more information that enables us to eliminate some possibilities and think of some new ones. Hence, we are involved in a search for the concept on which the division was made, a search that helps throw light on the nature of concepts that provide a basis for categorizing events. It helps us identify the mental process that we must go through if we are to make categories.

Before turning to the usefulness of this "concept of a concept," let us look at a more difficult example of the exercise. The following list of nations is marked "yes" or "no" beside each nation. The task is to determine the principle on which the yesses and no's were assigned.

Ghana	yes
France	no
Kenya	yes
Germany	no

Chad	yes
Denmark	no
Egypt	no

At this point, if "African" was thought to be the basis for the division, it has to be discarded. What possibilities remain?

Peru	yes
Japan	no
England	no
Ecuador	yes

Have you arrived at a concept? Are the nations being divided on a basis of the extent of their economic development? Is it their voting patterns in the United Nations? What possibilities remain?

Russia	no
Polynesia	yes
Indonesia	yes
Canada	no

And on and on we might go, developing and discarding principles. Students who begin to get the idea can begin to make their own categories and examples and try them out on each other.

However, the real payoff of this concept game occurs when we begin to apply it to materials which are not arranged so as to help us be conscious of the categories that are being employed, when, for example, we turn to the analysis of passages in which authors have grouped material without a complete explanation of the basis for the grouping. For example, consider the following passage:

"Despite the ceremonial talk about the common destinies of the peoples of the Western Hemisphere, and the shared blessings of representative government and democratic ideals, and so forth, there never had been any real rapport between Anglo-Americans and Latin Americans. Anglo-American culture was derived from the British Isles and the European Countries of the North Atlantic, and it was Protestant, commercial, middle-class, prosaic and static.

"Latin American culture was derived from Spain, Portugal, and

Rome, and it was Catholic, non-commercial, caste-ridden, humanistic, colorful, and passionate."[17]

Let us see what principles Carleton has used for identifying Anglo-American (United States and Canadian) culture:

Protestant	yes
Catholic	no
Commercial	yes
Single class	yes
Prosaic	yes
Passionate	no
Colorful	no

But, we say immediately, there are many Catholics in Anglo-America, there are many classes and castes! His stereotype doesn't hold up very well, although there may be some truth in it. Whereas his prose is interesting and persuasive, a careful analysis of the concept he is using bids us take caution and, equally, helps us see more precisely just what he is saying.

The following passage from a fifth grade social studies text will bear the same kind of analysis:

"Cuba is the world's largest producer and exporter of sugar. The United States has been one of the largest consumers of Cuba's sugar. Would Haiti and the Dominican Republic import Cuban Sugar? Why or why not? Tobacco is Cuba's second most important crop.

"We have had many links with Cuba. The United States helped Cubans win their independence from Spain. We enjoy Cuban music and we like the rumba and other Cuban dances. Cuban baseball players play on our big league teams. Thousands of people from the United States have spent their vacations in Cuba. Many of our nation's businessmen have invested money in Cuban enterprises.

"Cuba has been a free nation less than a hundred years. Its people have not had a long time to learn to govern themselves. Several times dictators have gained control of the government. Each time, the

---

[17] William G. Carleton, *The Revolution in American Foreign Policy* (New York: Random House, 1965), p. 100.

people of Cuba have overthrown the dictators and attempted to establish a government 'of the people.' "[18]

It seems that this passage has as its intent to create (or avoid creating) an attitude toward the Cuban people. Let us examine the concept that the authors had toward the friendliness of the relations between the United States and Cuba.

United States has been a customer of Cuba with respect to sugar
(Implies at least working relations.)

United States helped Cuba win their independence
(Implies that relations were very close.)

"We" enjoy Cuban music and dances
(Implies that we are favorably disposed toward their leisure culture.)

Cuban baseball players play professional baseball in the United States
(Implies that they have imported and are successful at one of the games that originated in the United States.)

United States citizens have spent many vacations in Cuba
(Implies friendship again, since one hardly vacations where he is not wanted.)

United States businessmen have invested much money in Cuban enterprises
(Again implies stable relations.)

Cuban politics are a struggle between democracy and tyranny
(Again implies kinship with United States aspirations.)

Now, we may note that many of the statements in these paragraphs were put in the past tense — the unwary reader might not notice this — and nowhere is there an outright statement about Cuban–United States relations. The concept, however, that the reader is allowed to reach, if he is not careful, is that extremely cordial relations exist between Cuba and the United States. Yet, as we

---

[18] Paul R. Hanna, Clyde F. Kohn, and Robert A. Lively, *In the Americas* (Chicago: Scott, Foresman, 1962), p. 310.

all know, that is not quite the picture of reality. We need a good bit more information before our concept will fit the case as it is.

It is worthwhile for a teacher, early in the year, to include some lessons intended to establish an understanding between himself and his students of what a concept is and then to apply this as they analyze resources, whether books, films, or visitors.

Students also can develop their own categories, as we have illustrated — and concept-building activity probably should be one of the major activities in any social studies unit.

Describing the concept-attainment teaching model

Syntax or structure

The first phase of the model involves presenting data to the learner. The data may be events or people or any other discriminable unit. The units of information are delineated to the learner as belonging or not belonging as examples of the concept. The learner is encouraged to speculate about the concept or principle or discriminatory concept which is being used as the basis of selection of units of data. In the next phase, students may be encouraged to compare their hypotheses concerning the concepts and their reasons for their choices. In succeeding phases, further units of data may be presented as before, and the above procedure may be repeated until there is consensus about the concepts. In succeeding phases, learners begin to analyze their strategy for attaining concepts. For example, some learners initially try very broad constructs and then gradually narrow the field or become more specific in their statement of the concept. Others move rather quickly to specific concepts and combinations of them. Concept attainment strategies are particularly interesting when relational concepts are being considered. Suppose that units of data are presented which compares countries by agricultural productivity in relation to technological level (use of fertilizer, for example), climate, general level of development of the country, and so on, and the students are attempting to attain concepts of relationship among the several factors. In such a complex case the strategies students will use will be varied and interesting. (See Bruner, Goodnow and Austin's *A Study of Thinking* for examples of different strategies.)

Social system or structure

In the initial phase the teacher presents data and designates it as belonging or not belonging as an exemplar of the concept. (This designation is in sharp contrast to the typical move of the teacher when he tells people what a concept is.) In the latter stages, when students are beginning to analyze and compare their strategies for attaining the concept, the teacher shifts to an analytic role, but again draws the students into analysis, being exceedingly careful not to provide them with the criteria by which they can judge their strategies. If it is desired to improve students' efficiency in attaining concept, successive concept attainment lessons are necessary with subsequent analyses of the effectiveness of various strategies. The teacher is the controller, then, but the atmosphere is cooperative and the procedures of the lesson stay closely in tune with the learners.

Principles of teacher reaction and response

During the flow of the lesson, the teacher wants to be supportive of the students' hypotheses about concepts, but to emphasize that they are hypothetical in nature and to create a dialogue in which the major content is a balancing of one person's hypotheses against another's. In the later phases of the model, the teacher wishes to turn the attention of the students toward analysis of their concepts and strategies, again being very supportive. He should encourage analysis of the merits of various strategies rather than attempt to seek the one best strategy for all people in all situations.

Optimal support systems

Concept attainment lessons are extremely difficult unless data sources are available and have been classified according to concept. It should be stressed that the student's job in a concept attainment strategy is not to invent new concepts, but to attain the ones that have been previously attained by the teacher or teaching agent. Hence, the data sources need to be known beforehand.

Utility of the model

The concept attainment model is widely useful. In many senses, much of language learning can be viewed as concept attainment inasmuch as the society has already devised categories of things and labels for those categories, and the language learner attains those concepts and learns those labels. The same is true in the learning of the vocabulary of a foreign language. It is even true in terms of the grammar or the syntactic structure of every language in that the linguistic structure consists of relational concepts of various kinds that need to be attained. To learn the structure of the disciplines is to attain the concepts of that discipline. In mathematics, for example, the basic properties of integers, the commutative, the associative, and distributive properties, are existing concepts which become attained by the mathematics student. Whenever students seem not to be understanding something, the concept attainment strategy can be brought into a play in an effort to establish the fundamental ideas which are at the root of the difficulty. Because of its great flexibility, the concept attainment model can be adapted to entire curriculums in the various disciplines and it can be the basis for extensive man-machine systems. It can function as a model for television teaching, both when the teacher is seen and when the medium is used to carry an instructional sequence without a visible teacher.

An advance organizer strategy: a model derived from a theory of verbal learning

The psychologist David Ausubel tends to accept the view expressed in Bruner's *Process of Education*[19] that each of the academic disciplines has a structure of concepts which can be identified and taught to the learner and which provide an intellectual map

---

[19] Jerome S. Bruner, *The Process of Education* (Cambridge, Massachusetts: Harvard University Press, 1961).

which can be used to analyze particular domains and solve problems in those domains. For example, Bruner would assume that political science contains sets of concepts that can be used to analyze political events and that these can be taught to learners in such a way that they can function so that when he tries to analyze political behavior and to solve political problems, this structure will be available to him. For a complete view of this position, the reader should familiarize himself with Bruner's *Process of Education* and Heath's *The New Curricula*[20] in which various authors apply the Brunerian hypotheses to the specific subject disciplines. It is worth noting that nearly all of the curriculum projects of the late 1950's and 1960's which are described as the new math, the new science, the new social studies, the new English and so on, have made the same assumption and have attempted to organize their materials accordingly.

Ausubel accepts this view, but attempts to extend it in terms of two principles which he says should govern the programming of content in the subject fields. The first is the idea of progressive differentiation. "The most general and inclusive ideas of the discipline are presented first, and are then progressively differentiated in terms of detail and specificity."[21] "The assumption we are making here, in other words, is that an individual's organization of the content of a particular subject matter discipline in his own mind, consists of a hierarchical structure in which the most inclusive concepts occupy a position at the apex of the structure and subsume progressively less inclusive and more highly differentiated subconcepts and factual data."[22]

Ausubel feels that "optimal learning and retention occur when teachers *deliberately* order the organization and sequential arrangement of subject matter along similar lines."[23] By similar lines he means the type of hierarchical organization of concepts that has been described earlier.

---

[20] Robert W. Heath (ed.), *The New Curricula* (New York: Harper, 1963).

[21] David P. Ausubel, *The Psychology of Meaningful Verbal Learning* (New York: Grune and Stratton, 1963), p. 79

[22] *Ibid.*

[23] *Ibid.*

The second principle Ausubel operates on is that of "integrative reconciliation" which means that new ideas are reconciled and integrated with previsously learned content. In other words, the sequence of a curriculum is organized so that successive learning builds on what has gone before.[24]

The essence of the model

The salient feature of Ausubel's "Organizer Technique of Didactic Exposition," as he puts it, is to program sequences of content for learners so that each segment of learning material is preceded by a conceptual "organizer" which we can think of as an advance organizer. The organizer has a higher level of "abstraction, generality and inclusiveness of" the material and is selected on the basis of its "suitability for explaining, integrating, and interrelating the material."[25] An organizer is not to be confused with an overview or summary which is ordinarily at the same level of abstraction as the material which is to be learned. An organizer is an idea, a general idea, which is fairly abstract relative to the material and which precedes the material. It functions cognitively to organize the material. It functions cognitively to organize the material as it is presented; that is, it provides a kind of conceptual framework into which the learner will integrate the material. Ausubel recommends that in terms of material unfamiliar to the learner that a general "expository" organizer should be used to provide a wholistic conceptual structure to which the learner can relate the new material. The organizer provides "ideational anchorage in terms that are already familiar to the learner."[26]

When relatively familiar material is being presented to the learner, Ausubel recommends a "comparative" organizer which will help the learner integrate new concepts with "basically similar concepts in cognitive structure, as well as to increase discriminability

---

[24] See Ralph W. Tyler, *Basic Principles of Curriculum and Instruction* (Chicago: University of Chicago Press, 1950) for a thorough exposition of principles of sequence and the way they function in curriculum and instruction.

[25] *Ibid.*, p. 81.

[26] *Ibid.*, p. 83.

between new and existing ideas which are essentially different but confusable."[27]

Let us look at an example of this. Suppose that the material that is to be presented to learners is a matrix of multiplication facts. This matrix might be preceded by the commutative property with respect to multiplication (that is that $A \times B = B \times A$). Then the exposition of the material in the multiplication matrix can be at least partly organized by the learner in terms of commutation; that is, he will be prepared for ideas like $3 \times 2 = 2 \times 3$, and his memory task will be considerably reduced. The organizer, the commutative property, is more abstract than the multiplication facts themselves, but they are explainable in terms of it. In fact, they could be presented in commutative pairs. Later on, when the learner is being introduced to long division, a comparative organizer might be introduced that would stress the similarity and yet differentness of the division facts from the multiplication facts. For example, whereas in a multiplication fact, the mulitplier and multiplicand can be reversed without changing the product, that is 3×4 can be changed to 4×3, the divisor and dividend cannot be reversed in division without affecting the quotient, that is, 6 divided by 2 is not the same as 2 divided by 6. This comparative organizer can help the learner see the relationship between multiplication and division and therefore anchor the new learnings about division in the old ones about multiplication, but at the same time can help him discriminate the new learnings so that he does not carry over the concept of commutativity to a place where it does not belong.

Let us look at the advance organizer model in terms of our four dimensions of a teaching model or strategy.

Syntax or structure

The first phase of the activity is the presentation of the organizer which must be at a more general level than the material that is to follow. The second phase is the presentation of the material itself. In a sequence of learning activities, the first organizer and its materials should be hierarchically more abstract than the succeeding

---

[27] *Ibid.*

ones which get more and more specific and elaborate than the original one. For example, in English, if the content were to deal with metaphors, the first organizer would deal with the general idea of methaphor and the content would illustrate that general idea. The next lessons would go into more and more specific kinds of metaphors and the ways they are used, so that the first unit of work with its organizer would intellectually anchor the material that was to come in the successive unit activities.

The social system of the model

Many people at first find startling Ausubel's proposition that an abstract idea should precede material rather than being discovered by learners who have analyzed the material. Ausubel is not an advocate of discovery learning, to put it mildly, and the really striking feature of the model is the presentation of that abstract idea ahead of the content which is to be learned. The social system, then, is controlled entirely by the teacher.

Principles of reaction or response by the training agent

In the flow of the lesson, the training agent can function to point out the conceptual anchorages for the material and to help learners see the relationship between the material that is being presented and the organizer. The teacher or the instructional material is the controller in the situation. The content has been selected for the learner, and the teacher should function to hem the discussion in around the material at hand.

Optimal support systems

Well-organized material is critical. The advance organizer depends on an integral relationship between the conceptual organizer and the rest of the content. It may be that it works best as a paradigm around which to build instructional materials so that the time can be taken to insure complete relevance of content and organizer. *However,* the model was designed for use by the face-to-face teacher and can be used, if the time is given to prepare lectures or other types of material carefully.

Applicability of the model

The advance organizer is another extremely versatile model in the sense that it can be applied to any material that can be organized intellectually. It can be used in nearly every subject area, although it was designed for use with verbal material rather than with skills and the mastery of problem-solving paradigms. However, Ausubel assumes that it will be useful in the transfer of materials to new problem settings, and he presents some evidence to that effect.

As a model it provides very good discipline for lectures for reasons which were outlined above, especially because the content of the lectures would have to be very carefully related to the organizer, and the lecturer would not be permitted to ramble or digress without cause. Also, it can serve very well in the analysis of expository materials in textbooks and other instructional materials where abstractions and information alternate in various patterns. It is worthwhile to examine lessons and units in several of the disciplines and look for the ways in which organizers are handled either consciously of unconsciously, for, it should be obvious by now, a teacher who is not careful can unwittingly present a poor organizer that will actually confuse the learner.

A differential training model: example of a teaching strategy derived from a developmental theory

Let us now turn to a very different kind of teaching strategy which comes from a very different source. David E. Hunt describes a teaching strategy which is derived from a theory of personality development.[28] This theory describes personality in terms of the complexity and flexibility of an individual's conceptual linkages to his environment and postulates the kinds of conditions which

---

[28] David E. Hunt, "A Model for Analyzing the Training of Training Agents." *Merrill-Palmer Quarterly, 12,* No. 2 (1966), pp. 138–156.

would be likely to induce a person to develop along the continuum towards greater flexibility and complexity.

According to the developmental theory of Harvey, Hunt, and Schroder, the optimal procedure for inducing individuals to progress toward complexity and flexibility is to match their present stage of personality development to the training environment, tailored to the characteristics of that stage of development. The following table indicates how personality stages and training environments can be matched in this way.

Characteristics of Stage

1. This stage is characterized by extremely fixed patterns of response. The individual tends to see things evaluatively, that is, in terms of rights and wrongs, and he tends to categorize the world in terms of stereotypes. He prefers unilateral social relationships, that is, those which are hierarchical and in which some people are on top and others on the bottom. He tends to reject information which does not fit in with his present belief system or to distort the information in order to store it in his existing categories.

Optimal Training Environment

In order to produce development from this stage, the training environment needs to be reasonably well-structured, because this kind of person will become even more concrete and rigid under an overly open social system. At the same time, however, the environment has to stress delineation of the personality in such a way that the individual begins to see himself as distinct from his beliefs and begins to recognize that different people, including himself, have different vantage points from which they look at the world, and that the rights and wrongs in a situation, and the rules in a situation, can be negotiated. In summary, the optimal environment for him is supportive, structured, fairly controlling, but with a stress on self-delineation and negotiation.

2. In this stage the individual is characterized by a breaking away from the rigid rules and beliefs which characterized his former stage. He is in a state of active resistance to authority and tends to resist control from all sources, even non-authoritative ones. He still tends to dichotomize the environment. He has difficulty seeing the points of view of others, and difficulty in maintaining a balance between task orientation and interpersonal relations.

The delineation of self which is suggested above is now taking place, and the individual needs to begin to reestablish ties with others, and to begin to take on the points of view of others, and to see how they operate in situations. Consequently, the training environment needs to emphasize negotiation in interpersonal relations and divergence in the development of rules and concepts.

Characteristics of Stage	*Optimal Training Environment*
3. At this stage, the individual is beginning to reestablish easy ties with other people, beginning to take on the point of view of the other, and in his new-found relationships with other people has some difficulty maintaining a task orientation because of his concern with the development of interpersonal relations. He is, however, beginning to balance alternatives and to build concepts which bridge differing points of view and ideas which apparently contradict each other.	The training environment at this point should strengthen the reestablished interpersonal relations, but an emphasis should also be placed on tasks in which the individual as a member of the group has to proceed toward a goal as well as maintaining himself with other individuals. If the environment is too protective at this point, the individual could be arrested at this stage and, while he might continue to develop skill in interpersonal relations, would be unlikely to develop further skill in conceptualization or to maintain himself in task-oriented situations.
4. The individual is able to maintain a balanced perspective with respect to task orientation and the maintenance of interpersonal relations. He can build new constructs and beliefs, or belief systems, as these are necessary to accommodate to changing situations and new information. In addition, he is able to negotiate with others the rules or conventions that will govern behavior under certain situations, and he can work with others to set out programs of action and to negotiate with them conceptual systems for approaching abstract problems.	While this individual is adaptable, he no doubt operates best in an interdependent, information-oriented, complex environment.

Now in the table above, the training environments are matched with each state in such a way as to pull the person toward the next stage of development. A teacher or a therapist, or another trainer, who is operating from such a theoretical position can develop teaching strategies which enable him to create the training environments which are postulated for learners of each category. One person who did exactly this with Hunt's strategy is Marguerite Warren who works in San Francisco with programs for the rehabilitation of delinquent boys and girls.[29] Warren has developed out of Harvey,

---

[29] Marguerite Warren, "The Classification of Offenders as an Aid to Efficient Management and Effective Treatment." Prepared for the President's Commission on Law Enforcement and Administration of Justice, Task Force on Corrections, 1966.

Hunt, and Schroder's developmental theory a set of teaching strategies which are taught to probation officers who then endeavor to match those strategies to the type of youngster they are working with. For example, if a delinquent is categorized within stage two, as a person who engages in severe resistance to authority, but who is delineating himself and discovering who he is, and who is in a process of rejecting his former belief systems and trying to establish a core of beliefs that will be his own, then the probation officer attempts to maneuver his own behavior in such a way that the optimal training environment is produced. That is, he tries not to impose authority directly on the trainee, but works to help him establish the rules for his own behavior, and to make agreements that they will both abide by the rules that they negotiate together. Further, he attempts to help the delinquent establish relationships with other people which are not hierarchical and where neither one attempts to impose his will on the other person.

Hunt's teaching strategy is aimed at the curricular level — it describes how to shape major aspects of an educational environment so they are tailored to the characteristics of the learner.

The *syntax* of the strategy consists of the sequence of environmental types which are to be matched to the learner. Each type has a different *social system,* ranging from a high degree of teacher structure in the optimal environment for stage one to great interdependence at stages three and four. The *principles for responding to the learner* vary with each type of environment that is prescribed, as indicated above, and the differences are very important, for the essence of the strategy lies in the interpersonal relations that are developed. The *support systems* for such a strategy lie entirely in the trained teacher personnel. In such a strategy, the syntax or structure is not predetermined. The trainer must be able to radiate a wide variety of behaviors, or, in other words, must be able to produce the proper environment for each learner. If trainers are not flexible enough to do this, then there must be more than one trainer who can produce the teaching behaviors which are indicated at the proper times.

There have been several sets of interesting research studies which have explored the effectiveness of the teaching strategy derived from Hunt's developmental theory. In addition to Warren's use of the model for the rehabilitation of juvenile offenders, Hunt has used the structure to analyze the effectiveness of the Upward Bound programs. While the sample of Upward Bound youngsters did not run the gamut of the developmental stages, Hunt demonstrated that the interactions between training environment and personality were significant in terms of the kinds of growth that the Upward Bound programs were trying to achieve.[30]

Hunt has also taught the strategy to teachers of the inner city, who attempted to match environments to the kinds of culturally-deprived children they were teaching, and I have used it in teacher education programs.[31] The model is interesting precisely because it provides a framework for analyzing learners and adjusting the school to their personality needs.

At present, there are a number of attempts to build differential (individualized) teaching strategies from developmental theories that pertain to cognitive development. For example and for criticisms, see the work of Edmund Sullivan of the Ontario Institute for Studies in Education.[32] The essence of these attempts is that we take the descriptions of intellectual development which are described by Piaget and then attempt to produce teaching strategies calculated to induce the learner to engage in the intellectual operations appropriate to a stage slightly ahead of his present level of development. The work of Wallach and Kogan is interesting because of implications for teaching strategies based on conceptions of creativity and intelligence, looked at simultaneously.

---

[30] David E. Hunt and Robert H. Hardt, "The Role of Conceptual Level and Program Structure in Summer Upward Bound Programs." Paper presented to the Eastern Psychological Association, April, 1967.

[31] See, for example, Clark Brown, "The Relationship of Initial Teaching Styles and Selected Variables in Student Teaching" Unpublished doctoral dissertation, Teachers College, Columbia University, 1967).

[32] Edmund Sullivan, "Piaget and the School Curriculum: A Critical Appraisal." Bulletin No. 2 of the Ontario Institute for Studies in Education, 1967.

Selecting from among alternative teaching strategies

When a teaching strategy is formulated or adopted to structure a curriculum, it provides theoretical underpinnings for the selection and creation of activities, materials, and evaluation procedures. Some strategies have been constructed to accomplish specific ends. All strategies are distinguished by the stance they take about what increases learning. Taba, for example, believed that if mental operations are to be taught, the curriculum must lead the children through the operations.

A curriculum that does not have a teaching strategy is like a ship without a rudder. It is without criteria to guide the development of activities, the construction of materials, and the behavior of teachers.

The intelligent selection of teaching strategies requires that the faculty have knowledge of the alternative strategies that are available (and we have described only a small proportion above) and that the best prospects for given curricular ends be identified and refined for the specific needs of the children who are concerned.

Patterns of content

In curriculum, sequence refers to the progression of events. Continuity refers to the major ideas, values, issues, and ways of thinking that are repeated again and again, providing organizers that hold the program together in the mind and emotions of the learner.[33]

Some curricular systems specify the content to be covered. For example, many social studies curriculums recommend a sequence of content that begins with the learner's immediate environment in the nursery and primary school and proceeds to the study of state, nation, and world, in the upper grades. Some curriculum guides specify sequence of content very rigidly (study *this* nation in *that* way during *that* year) while others leave much choice to the teacher

---

[33] For expanded definitions of these terms, see Ralph W. Tyler, *Basic Principles of Curriculum and Instruction* (Chicago: University of Chicago Press, 1950).

who, in his turn, may pass along much of that freedom to the students.

Many possible principles of sequence can be developed. Sequence can be permitted to emerge from the problem-solving activity of the children. It may be developed logically from the subject matter (many mathematics curriculums are). Sequence may be based on the maturity of the learner (study the concrete things first, the abstract later on). It may be based on learner interest (read what you like, but *read*!) It can come from a task analysis of skills that are to be developed (many reading and writing curriculums follow this pattern).

Let us compare some of the kinds of patterns of sequence that can be employed:

(1) Sequence can be created through individual learner selection, with the teacher serving as guide, reflector, counselor, or tutor.

(2) Sequence can be created through selection by groups of learners, with the teacher carrying out the role in (1) above, and a role as group leader or facilitator.

(3) Sequence can follow the structure of a discipline or an amalgamation of structures. Teacher and pupil latitude may vary greatly. Self-instructional programs and multi-media systems may or may not be used.

(4) Sequence can be created by a task-analysis of skills. (Reading is often done this way.) Again, teacher and pupil roles and technological support systems may vary widely.

(5) Sequence may follow historical chronology, again with all possible roles and technological systems.

Where a curriculum system is based on a discipline with a clear structure, the structure is frequently followed, as in the case of mathematics or science. Where skills seem to have a logical progression, they tend to be followed in order, as in music, art, physical education, and reading. Where a curriculum is based on an amalgamation of disciplines, as in the case of the social studies, humanities, or language arts, then the progression tends to be more loose. In the case of creative arts, usually the sequence is barely identified, because development is assumed to be idiosyncratic. In areas involving emergent processes, such as the study of current events, sequence has to develop as events unfold.

Instructional sequences: "bite-size chunks"

To make manageable the job of creating actual instructional activities, the curriculum system needs not only to be divided into curriculum areas or longitudinal subsystems but also into short time-segments or units, For instance, planning all the details of a mathematics curriculum for children from ages three to eleven would be an overwhelming task. So one obvious solution is to use the principles of sequence as guidelines for identifying instructional sequences or segments of study that, when assembled, make up the larger sequence.

Here again, one encounters many alternatives. The progression of units can be fixed or optional. Units can be assigned to age levels or made available when needed. They can all be prepared with the same teaching strategies or they can represent a variety of them.

In any case, to the materials maker, the teacher, and the child, units represent series of "bite-size chunks" of work around which their activities can be organized.

There is a tendency for sequence to be much more vaguely defined in the nursery and kindergarten levels than in the primary levels, which in turn tends to be looser than the intermediate and upper grades. Similarly, one finds that the more critical an area is assumed to be, the more tight will be the organization. Hence there is a tendency to be tighter about specifications for reading and arithmetic than for literature, whose practical utility is not as clearly felt.

The tendencies identified in the above paragraph are well ingrained in the habits of school people and in the minds of the public. Stating principles of sequence clearly and tightly in some areas and vaguely in others operates indirectly to make it difficult to build a school around a unique mission. For example, many schools have as a *nominal* objective the development of productive thinkers. To develop productive thinking probably requires leisurely, reflective learning situations in which students have time to develop and explore different solutions to problems and ways of doing things. However, when it comes to the development of many curriculum areas (arithmetic is a good example), a tight sequence is developed, with many minute objectives carefully building on one another to add up to sure achievement of skills and knowledge. The fear that some child won't learn the traditional mathematical fare is often stronger than the desire to help him become a productive thinker.

Because of this resistance — this tendency to perpetuate the normal or traditional means of the school, it has been extremely difficult to develop curricular systems that implement missions which are substantially different from the "normal" ones. Traditionally, textbooks have determined much of the content and teaching strategies and patterns of teaching strategies that have been employed in the schools. Mass socializing activities have dominated the preschool and the kindergarten. It is awfully easy for the Responsible Parties to develop a new potential mission for the school and then leave the development of means to a staff unable to create an appropriate social system which is not backed by appropriate technical support systems, and which permits the textbook and the traditional teaching methods to create the curricular systems. The result is our old friend, THE SCHOOL AROUND THE CORNER all over again.

Assessment and feedback systems

To find out what is going on as a result of the application of the curricular system, a program of assessment and evaluation has to be carried on. If this program is carefully constructed it can:

(1) Provide a "tracking" of the progress of the students,

(2) Permit regular assessment and feedback to teachers and students about progress and possible future courses of action,

(3) Contribute to research on teaching and learning and factors affecting them, and

(4) As a result of (3), provide guidelines for the revision of the curricular system.

In today's public schools there are so few personnel competent to develop and carry on adequate assessment and feedback that I see no chance of improving the situation until specialists are trained and are made available to the schools. In nearly all schools, tests standardized on national samples are now used with teacher-made tests for assessment. Standard tests are valid only when the objectives of the local school approximate those of schools across the land and when the social, technological, and curricular systems of the school are nearly "average." Teacher-made tests are adapted to local systems but teachers are quick to admit that competence and time stand in their way. (For an example of the time problem, imagine the information-processing required to track the progress of twenty students who complete an average of one hundred mathematics exercises in one week. The possible permutations and combinations of error in 2,000 mathematics exercises is staggering, even if all pupils work the same exercises. What happens if the students are working with individually-prescribed materials is really awesome!)

Despite the obstacles, the development of adequate assessment systems can be accomplished. We are able to suggest a few guidelines to their development:

(1) Assessment should be continuous. When an instructional sequence is developed, assessment should be embedded in it.

(2) Assessment should be emergent. As objectives are developed in the course of events, the assessment system should respond.

(3) Assessment should involve practice of the behavior being focused on. Pencil-and-paper tests are very limited. For example, to find out if a student can build a theory, we have to observe him as he tries to build a theory. To see a four-year-old's capacity to direct his own activities, we have to watch him try to do this.

(4) Assessment needs to be multivariate in nature. We need to try to learn not only *how* the learner is doing, but what complex of factors is operating.

(5) Assessment needs to look at many sides of progress. Emotional and social learning are as important and complex and just as much the business of the school as is cognitive learning.

(6) Assessment should be viewed as diagnosis. The response to

indications of progress should be, "What shall we do next?" rather than the usual question, "What grade will we give?"

The alternatives in assessment and feedback systems are many and complex. Many of the processes are so technical that specialists should be consulted continuously if the system is to be effective.

Creating curricular systems

The development of curricular systems for a school, then, involves the completion of a set of tasks:

The development of working objectives for the schools, and
The identification of curriculum areas in which curricular subsystems can be developed.

Then, within the curricular areas several tasks have to be carried out:

The specification of operating objectives for the area,
The development of plans of continuity and sequence,
The identification of instructional sequences or units,
The development of teaching strategies for the entire area and specifically for the instructional sequences, and
The preparation of assessment and feedback systems.

At this point the curricular plan becomes ready for the development of appropriate technical support systems and for the development of teacher training systems preparatory for the implementation of the curricular plan. *In general practice,* the implementation of the curricular plan is left to the teacher, who is highly autonomous in his activity. Clearly, however, the teacher responsibility for making and carrying out instructional decisions[34] can vary greatly.

---

[34] For a discussion of the processes involved in making *and carrying out* instructional decisions, see Bruce R. Joyce and Berj Harootunian, *The Structure of Teaching* (Chicago: Science Research Associates, 1967).

He can have absolute autonomy in his clsssroom. He can work as the cooperative member of a teacher team that has curriculum guidelines to follow. He can serve as "facilitator" of children who make the real decisions. He can work as a cog in a complex man-machine system with his role tightly defined. We will look a little more closely at teacher freedom a few pages farther on, when we examine what we will call curricular modes. Before doing so, however, let us examine a curricular plan that is intended as a general guideline for the teachers who are to implement it. We will look within the social studies curriculum area for our example, simply because that is the area of my greatest competence.

Curricular systems in the social studies

The social studies are as broad as the school itself. Like the school, the social studies have three sources: the individual student, the society (including the student society), and the social sciences. Within the framework of the mission of the school, these sources will vary in their influence. Where the mission is highly personal, the personal sources will receive most emphasis, and so on.

In the following pages we will look at three curricular outlines, each of which emphasizes one of the sources of the social studies. To simplify interpretation, we will make the assumption that these curricular systems are for rather typical middle-class suburban children. (Let us tolerate a stereotype for the sake of an example!) Also, we will not assume any specific mission for the school. By emphasizing first the person, then the society, and then the social sciences, we can illustrate, hopefully, how a curricular system might emerge from missions that emphasized one of those areas more than others.

Consequently, the following pages are intended as an illustration only. They represent three wholly fictional guides for curricular systems. All three systems are loose, flexible ones in which much latitude is given to instructional sequence segments, and, moreover, much decision-making includes the children.

A person-centered curriculum

We will now examine the first of three curriculum plans. The first focuses on personal development, the second focuses on citizenship education, and the third focuses on the teaching of the social sciences. As we have indicated earlier, these three focuses are not incompatible, but it will help us to see what happens when one or the other receives greatest emphasis.

We will begin with illustrations from a curricular plan developed primarily to help each individual student find himself and prepare to live a coherent, meaningful life.

Objectives

Each of the illustrative objectives has been numbered so that it can be referred to easily when teaching strategies and the other curricular essentials are discussed. The objectives are:

(1) Willingness to examine his purposes and his relations with others,

(2) Knowledge of his heritage and his interdependence with others in his society,

(3) Skill in analyzing his social relations and the structure of his society,

(4) Attitude of inquiry and examination of societal values,

(5) Habit of examining his values and those of others,

(6) Desire to participate in the development of purposes in groups of which he is a part, and

(7) Willingness to participate in the development of human values.

Each of the seven objectives gives prominence to the learner. His relations with others are approached from *his* frame of reference.

The social sciences are not specifically mentioned but, as we will see, they are useful for achieving these objectives which originate to help the student acquire the knowledge, skills, and attitudes that will help him in his quest for personal understanding and meaning.

The content and methods of the social sciences are necessary for analyzing self, society, social relations, and values, rather than being taught for their own sake.

Teaching strategy

Any twelve- or thirteen-year-long curriculum needs a variety of teaching strategies that are good for different purposes. However, the primary goals of the curriculum and the beliefs of the faculty who design the curriculum frequently result in the identification of one or two strategies that characterize the core of the approach.

In this case the chief element in the teaching strategy is to handle instruction so that the student participates in the development of objectives for each unit of work and so that there is ample opportunity for him to explore personal interests. Because this kind of instruction demands that a teacher have a close and insightful relationship with the student, the school is organized to provide for "cycling" of teachers of social studies. That is, each teacher follows a group of students for a period of three years. Over twelve years, then, each student has four social studies teachers, one for each three-year cycle of the curriculum. This enables the teacher to use his knowledge of the student so that instruction is closely geared to the needs and problems of the student. For example, as adolescents begin to be disturbed by the alienating factors in modern society, they can examine and learn to cope with these factors. Similarly, if they begin to act in an alienated fashion, the teacher can make *that* a part of their study. Again, when values and controversial issues are at hand, the students can express their real feelings and endeavor to make their own quest for meaning a part of their study, under the guidance of a teacher they know well enough to be open with.

Sequence

In such a curriculum, many topics cannot be predicted in advance. The important basis for sequence is to lead the student progressively to the examination of his society and the development of personal values. The older student can be led to study social movements and issues that are shaping the world in which he has to delineate himself and find a meaningful existence.

Thus, the sequential plan can provide for some topics and ideas, but may permit many to be introduced by the teacher and his students. The following sequential plan illustrates this with reference to just a few of the sequential items that would have to be included in a complete plan.

Level	Topic	Approach
Primary	Cultural universals	Comparative study of families, communities, including the home scene
		Anthropological concepts emphasized to build base for later study
	Interdependence	Study of factories, communities, own groups; also basis for later study
Intermediate years	American politics	Inductive study of the local political process
	American values	Inductive study of beliefs: from documents and from study of the local community
Junior high years	What is a person?	Attempt to define what makes a human and what makes an individual
Junior high years	How we are different	A study of the ways individuals and cultures develop particular frames of reference
Senior high years	Ideas that change the world	Historical studies of communism, democracy, religions, and other movements
	The world to come	Study of movements that are shaping the future and their impact on individuals

The entire plan for sequential study would need to include many more topics. However, the above show one characteristic approach and indicate how sequence can include a progression of topics, ideas, and approaches to teaching.

Continuity

Three sources of continuity might be employed.

Personal Quest ● The responsibility for the learner's education would continually be thrust on him. Many individual projects would take place. Also, the issues and problems that concern the learner would be the starting point for much of his education.

Social Context ● The student would see himself continually shaped by social influences and as a person who has the reciprocal opportunity to affect his social groups and participate in the shaping of his society.

Social Sciences ● Critical social issues and methods for analyzing social influences are introduced to the student. Ideas such as "cultural universal" are repreated throughout the curriculum. Our third illustrative curricular plan, on the following pages, will demonstrate the cumulative use of social science ideas.

Assessment and feedback

When, as in a curriculum such as this, many topics and approaches to teaching are created in the teaching-learning situation, an overall testing program is probably not appropriate. Rather, each teacher has to be responsible for identifying the specific objectives of each unit of study and devising ways of determining whether they are accomplished. Specific performance levels for all students are probably not appropriate either.

We have sketched a plan representing one approach to building a curriculum in which the personal quest for meaning is given greatest emphasis and the other sources for social study are given secondary roles. As we turn now to a curricular plan in which the requirements of citizenship education are made most prominent, we will find that the shift in emphasis from person to society changes what is taught and how it is taught; but the most striking change is the shift in point of view.

A citizen-centered curriculum

The society expects the schools to prepare *citizens,* people I find it comfortable to define as "prepared to participate in *and* enhance the society." Sometimes this has been interpreted to mean that the school should indoctrinate the student with patriotic values and teach him the evils of communism, socialism, and other movements that challenge the existing social order. In other cases, it has been interpreted to mean the development of an aggressively revisionist citizen, aware of counter systems and prepared to revise and redevelop the present society. We will see a moderate position here, neither avoiding the responsibility of acquainting students with the movements that shape other societies nor shaping a citizenry of active revisionists.

Objectives

As before, we will look at the curriculum in terms of objectives, overall teaching strategy, sequence, continuity, and assessment and feedback.

(1) Skill in democratic action, in large and small groups,

(2) Ability to diagnose and improve group performance,

(3) Understanding of the development of democratic society,

(4) Values of the fundamental ideals of liberty, government by consent and representation, and responsibility for the welfare of all,

(5) Skill in analyzing social forces, and

(6) Ability to think productively about the improvement of the society.

These objectives emphasize the societal processes. The intellectual is not neglected — numbers (2), (3), and (5) — but is subordinated to the social purposes of the curriculum. The teaching strategies also do not neglect the intellect but emphasize group inquiry and other tactics whereby social process and intellectual development are made compatible.

Teaching strategy

Cooperative group inquiry is the byword. Each class is organized into a group responsible for developing objectives and plans for attaining the goals. Instruction begins with mutual interests. The processes of the inquiring groups are to be studied — each class learns to analyze itself as a social system and develops skill in improving social dynamics. The social sciences are learned by practicing them; hypotheses are developed and checked out using social science methods, then results are checked against those of contemporary behavioral sciences.

This strategy requires teachers who are highly skilled in group process, who can handle students deftly to see that significant issues are studied with vigor and efficiency. The strategy has to be modulated depending on the character of the group. Young children and socially immature students require greater amounts of structure and strong leadership. Units have to be evolved which can help students develop greater group skills.

Sequence

As in the case of a person-centered curriculum, the citizenship-centered curriculum allows for many topics to be selected by the teacher and learner, working together. However, many topics can be identified that help the young child develop basic understandings and skills and lead the older student directly into preparation for citizenship.

Level	Illustrative Topics	Approach
Primary school years	The classroom and the school	The functional analysis of groups
	Families around the world	Interdependence and division of labor
	A study of games	Provides a gentle basis for the introduction to both conflict and co-operation

Level	Illustrative Topics	Approach
Intermediate school years	Analyzing group behavior	Introduction to social science methodology
		Emphasis on ways of establishing facts, drawing inferences, making value judgments
	Our social heritage	Study of the evolution of democratic institutions and values
	Government in action	Study of contemporary social action
Junior high years	Organizing a group	Strategies for analyzing and improving group activity (More sophisticated versions can be introduced each year.)
	The history of the United States Senate	A depth study of the practices and history of the Senate
	A social problem	Depth study of a contemporary social problem and what can be done about it
Senior high centers	Today's isms	The study of communism, totalitarianism, socialism, authoritarianism, democracy
	Group processes	An advanced inquiry into group dynamics
	Social movements and world government	Selected social movements and issues in world government
	Conflict and cooperation in America	The study of public controversy

The sequence provides for early introduction of group dynamic skills and social science concepts that are useful for the later study of democratic and other social institutions. In all curricular plans, depth studies are preferable to the superficial coverage of broad topics.

Continuity

The group inquiry process and the constant analysis of group dynamics provide one thread of continuity in this program. The analysis of democratic institutions provides another element that is reiterated. The use of the analytic tools from social science provides a third basis for continuity. Last, but no less important, the revisitation of values and controversial issues provides the lively sense of reality throughout.

Evaluation and feedback

Each person's acquisition of democratic skills and social science methodology can easily be evaluated. The group analysis of group process builds into this curriculum a constant evaluative device and puts much responsibility for the determination of progress on the group.

Although self-perpetuating once it is begun, the assessment of group dynamic skills requires special training for its inception. As presented here, the citizen-centered curriculum has much in common with the person-centered curriculum, with the major differences occurring in emphasis and amount of reiteration. It is hard to understand people without paying attention to personal meanings, and it is hard to understand the individual without giving much attention to *his* social environment and interaction.

A social science-centered curriculum

At first, a social science-centered curriculum may seem much different than these first two patterns — a person-centered curriculum and a citizen-centered curriculum. However, if one grants certain views of the social sciences, they are most relevant to personal meaning and the production of citizens.

The social sciences have several sides to them, and we had best identify these facets before proceeding further. First of all, a serious problem in the social studies has arisen because there are so many social sciences. Mathematics curricula have only one source discipline, and the sciences draw from only three or four. English, French, and German language curricula each have but one parent discipline. But the social studies have history, political science, economics, geography, sociology, anthropology, social psychology, psychology, and the social studies draw from philosophy and religion as well. Many scholars from these disciplines do not like to see their discipline merged with others. Consequently, it is frequently difficult to get their help when we try to develop common approaches.

We can examine the important question, "How much do the social sciences have in common?" by considering several different aspects of each discipline. In some aspects we will find that the disciplines have a great deal in common; in other aspects they are quite different. Before we look at a social science-oriented curriculum, we will find it useful to address ourselves to the task of identifying some of the important characteristics of the social sciences.

Scientific method

The social sciences share the attempt to develop and apply increasingly scientific procedures. Social scientists give constant attention, for example, to the development of techniques that enable *observation,* or the collection of data, to be more precise and thorough. Sociologists try to improve sampling techniques by interview and observation schedules. Historians seek more effective devices for obtaining accurate and balanced information about past events. Political scientists seek more reliable means of ascertaining the sources and uses of power.

Social scientists also seek more precise and valid ways of making *inferences* that explain human behavior more fully and honestly. Psychologists *infer* general principles of learning and development. Economists *infer* theories that explain the interplay of economic forces. Anthropologists *infer* the existence of mechanisms by which culture is transmitted. Because it is such a long jump from describing the behavior of individuals to the development of generalizations that take into account variations in human behavior, and because it is an even greater leap to making general theories that explain what is going on, the process of making inferences is extremely difficult, but important.

While there are substantial differences in specific technologies among the social sciences, common to all are the general attention to objective observation and measurement of human behavior and the making of inferences. Much resemblance to methodological considerations of the physical and biological sciences is apparent.

Frame of reference

In one sense, all of the social sciences study the same general landscape — the interaction of human beings. However, each of the social sciences employs a frame of reference that emphasizes certain features of the landscape and deemphasizes others. Now social scientists frequently shift points of view (for example, sociologists often use a psychological view and vice versa). Also, there are wide differences among members of the same discipline. However, each field tends to work on certain kinds of problems and theories. For example, geographers tend to focus on the interaction between culture and natural environment, whereas the political scientist emphasizes power relationships, and anthropologists study the development and transmission of culture.

Organizing concepts, or "structure"

The social scientist endeavors to collect facts that describe and explain relationships among the facts. The system of concepts that organizes and explains data is frequently, after Bruner,[35] referred to as the structure of the discipline. Each discipline uses sets of organizing concepts, although there is overlapping. For example, sociologists and anthropologists describe prestige relationships in terms of "caste" and "class." Economists use concepts such as "scarcity," "supply and demand," "division of labor." Psychologists have invented terms such as "manifest anxiety," "belief system," and

---

[35] Jerome S. Bruner, *The Process of Education* (Cambridge, Massachusetts: Harvard University Press, 1961).

"dyadic relationship" to refer to relationships they study. The organizing concepts of a discipline form a kind of map that represents the codified knowledge of that area.

Using social science in developing a curriculum

To achieve full scholarly control over a discipline, we need to master its methodology, its frame of reference, and its organizing concepts. For the purposes of general education we have several choices.

(1) We can simply teach those parts of the social sciences that apply naturally as the students study social problems and prepare to be citizens and understand themselves.

(2) We can emphasize *one* discipline, teaching it well and letting it be an illustration.

(3) We can develop an integrated social science approach, teaching the general elements of methodology, the frame of reference of several disciplines, and some of the more important organizing ideas of each.

(4) We can teach the more general methods and concepts in the early years, and provide opportunity for depth exploration of some of the specific disciplines during the high school years.

We will illustrate an integrated social science approach — number (3) above — in the next pages.

A social science curriculum

Objectives

(1) Knowledge of the general elements of social science methodology,

(2) Skill in collecting data, making inferences, and organizing hypothecated experiments,

(3) Knowledge of the general frame of reference of each social science,

(4) Skill in analyzing small-group interaction, using social science techniques and concepts,

(5) Flexibility in using social science knowledge to analyze social problems,

(6) Acquaintance with the social movements now operating to change the present world and bring about a new one, and

(7) Awareness of personal values and commitment to developing a philosophy of personal and social life.

These objectives give prominence to the social sciences, but they also give attention to the requirements of face-to-face social life, citizenship, and the quest for personal meaning. As in the cases above, this curriculum reflects the emphasis on one curriculum source rather than the complete neglect of the others.

Teaching strategy

Several strategies will be used as they are appropriate to the different objectives.

First, depth studies which emphasize the methods of the social sciences will be developed. For each depth study, a core of materials that facilitates cooperative inquiries using the social science methods will be put together. To introduce the frames of reference of the different social sciences, certain of the studies will emphasize specific disciplines.

Second, some of the depth studies each year will focus on contemporary social problems, so that the methodologies and ideas learned are applied to contemporary problems.

Third, a group-dynamics laboratory method will be used to teach students to analyze and improve their group process skills.

Fourth, self-instructional units will be developed to teach many skills and acquaint students with basic information from several of the social sciences.

Fifth, independent study units will facilitate depth inquiry by individuals into social problems.

Some of these strategies, such as group inquiry, are extremely inductive. Others, as the self-instructional units, are prepackaged for the students and use sets of readings or programmed instructional techniques. In addition, "concept units" will be available.

These are self-instructional units that can be used to review, or catch up on work missed, or as preparation for group units. Each concept unit is built around an important concept (such as "latitude," "power," "culture") and provides materials for self-teaching.

Sequence

The pattern of units provides for the progressive development of the methodology and philosophy of social science. Second, it provides for the systematic introduction of the frames of reference of each social science and *repeats* that frame of reference several times in the twelve years. Third, it provides for early introduction of two or three social science concepts and for continual reiteration and deepening of them. Fourth, it provides systematic development of group dynamic skills.

Continuity

The methodology of social sciences and the improvement of interpersonal understanding and skills are repeated throughout. At every opportunity, students are asked to examine assumptions, to build and test hypotheses, to weigh values. The idea of frame of reference is stressed throughout — the fact that each of us has one and that each discipline has one is used to help each student to assess his own and the frames of reference of people with whom he interacts. In other words, a world of alternatives is developed — alternative views of human interaction, alternative solutions to problems, alternative ways of seeing things.

The spread of topics results from the plans for sequence and for continuity as they work together.

Level	Topic	Approach
Primary years	What is a family? An anthropological approach	In depth and at leisure, a study of a primitive family (Trobriand Islanders) a western family (France), and an African family (Bantu)

Level	Topic	Approach
Primary years	What is a community? An anthropological approach	In depth and at leisure, a study of cultural universals in several communities (Trobriand, France, Bantu, Sweden, Thailand)
	What are tools?	An indirect beginning to the study of civilization; tools, technologies, ideas used by several peoples throughout the development of civilization
	Our group	The study of ways of having amicable and business like groups — study modulated to the character of the group
	Things to believe in	A study of human interdependence; can relate to culture groups previously studied, family, community, and face-to-face group
	Basic map and chart skills	An elementary self-instructional unit; teaches map- and chart-making and decoding
Upper grade years	Our political world	A study of decision-making in families, communities, and nations
	Our economic world	A study of economic processes in families and communities; follows "What are tools"
	The beliefs of man	Follows "Things to believe in"; studies values in primitive and modern communities
	The political and economic history of the United States	A self-instructional survey course; readings, films, programs

Level	Topic	Approach
	Groups at work	A depth study of group dynamics, including one's own groups
	The social sciences at work	Observing methods of validating inferences; the concept of causation, fallacies in reasoning
	Frames of reference	A study of perception experiments showing how preconception affects perception
Junior high years	What is a society?	A study of two small, well-defined societies such as Israel and Ceylon
	A study of law	Freedom and authority in Greece (Athens and Sparta), Rome, and twelfth century England
	Urbanization in America	Economic and political factors
	The political and economic history of Brazil	A self-instructional unit
	The political and economic history of Japan	A self-instructional unit
	My community	Political, social, and economic aspects; an inductive study
	Group dynamics and perception	Laboratory techniques; advanced course
Senior high years	International relations	Using internation simulation — several units
	World law	A study of international organizations, including NATO, SEATO, the UN; using original sources
Senior high years	Demography	A study of population distribution and dynamics
	Political belief systems	Communism, democracy, etc.

Level	Topic	Approach
	Macroeconomics	An emerging nation (such as Nigeria); a small, well-developed one (such as Sweden); a huge one (such as India)
	Group dynamics, caste, and class	The study of the relation between the internation system of a group and its external system or social matrix
	Collecting and organizing data	Self-instructional units

This curricular plan leans so far toward the intellectual that severe modification would be necessary to adapt it for use with fairly nonverbal or culturally disadvantaged children. However, most of these units are reasonably easy to adapt, for they deal with real events that are easy to see and feel. Also, the use of depth studies enables long periods of data collection so that the students are less dependent on verbal learnings than is frequently the case in familiar curricula.

The limitations of curricular systems

Guides like the above can be followed in any curriculum area. Then, other tasks are necessary if the curricular systems are to be put into effect. Teachers are usually in need of special preparation, both for the teaching strategies and for subject matter. Instructional materials have to be developed — the technological backup systems, which enable the curricular system to come into being, have to be created. Then, the appropriate social system has to be identified and meshed with the curricular system so that the behaviors encouraged by the social organization are consonant with the kinds of learning implied by the curricular system.

In other words, the curricular system doesn't stand alone any more than the technological or social systems do. Perhaps the curricular system is more rational and intellectual than are the other dimensions of the educational environment; but it is not any more independent nor any more powerful. So let us look at the identification of special ends-means combinations that include social, technological, and curricular systems — let us turn to the consideration of curricular modes.

The means of education, 4:
the concept of curricular modes

There are many methods of teaching and, for all we really know, there may be just as many methods of learning. . . . The method of an inspirational lecturer is rarely confused with the method of teachers who work through projects and committees. Nevertheless, the search for the universal method goes on; educational research continues to scrutinize the teaching act in order to discover the essential steps, their articulation with one another, and to determine whether one method is more effective than another. *

7

A mode is a manner, a style, a particular distinctive way of doing things. Some people have style. Their manner is distinctive and inimitably their own. The way they are is *theirs*. No imitations are acceptable.

A curricular mode is a way or style of doing things that permeates all aspects of the environment. In a real sense it is the system of the system. Just as personal style belongs to the whole man, a curricular mode represents harmony among the dimensions of the environment. *The concept of mode suggests that it is possible to have the curricular, social, and technological systems working together to achieve a part or all of the missions of the school.*

Let us look at an example of this. Suppose that one of the missions of a school is to teach the modes of inquiry of the social sciences. Suppose further that the view is taken that we learn how scientists work by practicing what they do by "trying on" the methods of the sciences and seeing how they function to help us inquire into meaningful problems. Let us combine that mission and build a curricular mode.

In the social system, teachers would function as facilitators

---

* From Harry S. Broudy and John R. Palmer, *Exemplars of Teaching Method* (Chicago: Rand McNally, 1965), p. 9.

of the inquiry of groups of children. They would help the children learn how to operate as a miniature scientific society and help them identify meaningful problems that they could inquire into. Students would need to learn to function as cooperative inquirers, working with their peers to identify and solve problems and using their teachers and technological systems efficiently. The norms would have to encourage independence of ideas and a free give-and-take of views. The norms would also have to encourage industriousness on the part of the students and to regard exploratory behavior rather than the matching of external standards.

The technological system would have to support open-ended work. Information storage and retrieval systems would be needed as well as certain kinds of laboratory equipment. It would be desirable to have as consultants some experts on the modes of inquiry of the social sciences. Instructional systems designed to help students learn systems of inquiry might be desirable.

The curricular system could look like the example of a social science-oriented curricular system given on pp. 188 ff.

The result would be a *curricular mode*. The social, technological support, and curricular systems would be in harmony around a specific objective that was regarded as a part of the central mission of the school. The mode would be characterized by its unique content — the modes of inquiry of the social sciences, its prominent student roles as members of inquiring groups, the important but muted roles for the teachers, and the open-endedness of the technological and curricular systems.

Let us look closely at a number of other curricular modes.

Alternative curriculum modes: some samples

The modes that will be described here represent some of the more common and vigorous theories that are current in education and psychology. However, we begin with the disclaimer that when we begin thinking of possible combinations of the elements of the three dimensions of the environment, the number of alternative models for means becomes simply staggering. And of course they should not be generated simply for the pure intellectual joy of it. The modes that make up the life of the school represent the young lives of many children who are its captives, so we should look carefully toward established theoretical positions when we seek to develop modes of curriculum.

The child as a growing self: an indirect mode

The psychologist Carl Rogers has become famous as the leading advocate of client-centered therapy. His view is essentially that the therapist's role is to help the patient understand himself and his reactions to the world. He carefully avoids leading the patient in predetermined directions. Instead, he assists the patient in defining his own goals for rehabilitation and helps him to follow them. The therapist tries to be as passive as possible in the situation, trying to induce the student to undertake the active role and, thereby, to reorganize himself into a healthy organism.

Rogers has made a translation of this theory into educational terms.[1]

The translation takes the form of a set of hypotheses that are offered for testing.

The basis of the view is that a great part of teaching consists of helping the students develop their own educational purposes: the purpose of education is not imposed on the student but is formulated by him. Rogers states:

> We cannot teach another person directly; we can only facilitate his learning. . . .
>
> If instead of focusing all our interest on the teacher — What shall I teach? How can I prove that I taught it? How can I "cover" all that I should teach? — we focused our interest on the student, the questions and the issues would all be different. Suppose we asked, What are his purposes in the course, What does he wish to learn, How can we facilitate his learning and his growth? . . .

---

[1] Carl R. Rogers, *Client-Centered Therapy: Its Current Practice* (Boston: Houghton Mifflin, 1951) states the basic position on therapy. In Chapter Nine of Rogers's *On Becoming a Person* (Boston: Houghton Mifflin, 1961), he sets out his educational views.

This view is rooted in Rogers's conception of the nature of the personality. He goes on:

> A person learns significantly only those things which he perceives as being involved in the maintenance of, or enhancement of, the structure of self.[2]

Given this view, it follows that the student has to develop the aims of education, because the aims otherwise imposed on the learning situation would have little effect on him. (This aspect of Rogers's view shows how very much our goals for education are tied to the frame of reference or stance which we take when we examine the individual, or the society, or even the academic disciplines. Because Rogers believes that the self acquires the learnings that will enhance it, then the central educational task is to help that self develop the goals of education.)

Any significant learning is likely to require the organization of the self to be changed somewhat — a person becomes different when he learns. The learner is likely to resist changes — the self tends to protect itself against threat to its existing structure and to become more rigid when threat is increased. Consequently, a goal of education has to be the development of flexible, "relaxed," personal organization that is capable of expansion through learning.

> The structure and organization of self appears to become more rigid under threat; to relax its boundaries when completely free from threat. Experience which is perceived as inconsistent with the self can only be assimilated if the current organization of self is relaxed and expanded to include it.[3]

This position also flows from Rogers's concentration on the self and his giving self-organization and self-image positions of prominence in his theory of psychological functioning. Because self-organization is the central mechanism in human functioning, the goals of education (the Mission of the School) naturally become the

---

[2] Carl R. Rogers, *On Becoming a Person* (Boston: Houghton Mifflin, 1961), p. 389.
[3] *Ibid.*, p. 390.

enhancement of that self and the development of the kind of flexible, seeking organism that will find new knowledge, new problems to solve, new learning goals that will lead it to a better and more full level of function.

Let us translate Rogers's position into the dimensions of the school environment, into a unified curricular mode.

The social system would find the teachers fulfilling nondirective roles, carefully helping the students set purposes and teach themselves. The student's role would be that of initiator: he would participate as an equal in the development of the social system.

The technological system would emphasize open-ended access to information and resources. Possible self-instructional systems would be constructed so that once a student selected a goal he could employ the system he desired.

The curricular system would be completely emergent. The behavioral objectives would be entirely in terms of the content of the self, and no external content would be specified. Content and ideas would emerge as did the inquiry of the students. The teacher would be free to suggest ideas and resources to the students, but he would be expected to impose no curricular system of his own making.

Rogers's views provide an excellent example of a curricular mode based on an essentially therapeutic view of education. Not many people would accept this curricular mode as the sole approach of a school. It is a strong, unified position, however, and it illustrates the potential strength that lies in the creation of curricular modes from theoretical stances that speak to both the ends and the means of education.

Social sciencing in the elementary school: another curricular mode

In an earlier section we mentioned the development, by the author, of data banks for use by children as they explore their own and foreign cultures. Let us now examine, close up, a curricular mode using those data banks as support systems.

It is Monday, May 3.[4]

Nine year old Charles takes his seat in the small room on the second floor of the Broad River School in Norwalk, Connecticut.[5] The room is fairly dark, but its walls are covered with drawings of ceremonial articles from a certain New Mexico pueblo, and there are several pictures of the two from the 1880's to the present. Before him Charles has a tape recorder and a slide projector. Mrs. Green[6] shows him how to operate the tape recorder and gives him a tape, which he threads and begins to listen to.

"Welcome to La Stella," the voice on the tape begins. "La Stella is a small town in New Mexico. While it is not very large, it is very important to people who try to understand human beings. For La Stella has been where it is for a very long time, and many people have studied it and tried to understand it for almost four hundred years.

"And, you are now *in* La Stella. Oh, you are not really there, of course. But in this room there are over four thousand pictures and written pages and maps and charts that can tell you something about La Stella. And every picture and written page has a tape recording that goes with it, so that you can get information about La Stella by listening as well as by watching and reading.

"So in this room you can visit La Stella and learn about it by looking at pictures, reading, and listening to tapes. You can get these materials by asking questions. When you ask a question about La Stella, Mrs. Green will give you a number. You can take that number to the storage center across the room, and there you can get the slides and tapes you can use in order to try to answer your question.

"Before you begin, let's take a little trip to La Stella to give you some idea what it is like there. Turn on your slide projector and show yourself the first slide in the box in front of you, the one marked 'Orientation to La Stella.' —— In this slide you see a mountain. On your map of La Stella, do you see the number "one?" If you were living in La Stella, and you were to stand at the "one" and look toward the South, you would see this mountain looking about the way it does in the picture.

---

[4] A version of this account appeared as: Bruce R. Joyce, "Social Sciencing," *Instructor Magazine, LXXVIII*, No. 2 (October 1968), pp. 85–92. Copyright, The Instructor Publications, Inc. Reprinted with permission.

[5] Mr. Robert Bottomley, Principal.

[6] Mrs. Josephine Green, Research Assistant, Wilton, Connecticut.

"Now, show yourself the next slide. In *this* picture you can see ———."

And so on, the voice goes, leading Charles through a guided tour of the pueblo and showing him how to obtain the tapes and the slides that contain pictures or written descriptions of the various aspects of the pueblo. After the "tour," Charles is given another tape and group of slides, and these start him off on one of several "tasks" or assignments designed to help him explore this culture which is new to him and — to teach him to try on the methods of the social scientist as he explores. His first job is to "Learn all you can about La Stella until you think you are ready to teach someone else about it."

What questions does he ask?

"Do they play baseball in La Stella?" is his first question. Given the number for "Sports and Recreation," he retrieves twenty 35-millimeter slides and shows them to himself. He discovers that (among several other athletic games) baseball *is* played in La Stella. On a three-by-five file card on which his question has been written by Mrs. Green, he writes his answer. "Yes, they play baseball. And other things." He asks another question. "What kind of animals do they have in La Stella?" He gets two numbers for this one, and retrieves two batches of slides, for "Domesticated Animals" and for "Fauna." He finds out about domesticated cattle and horses, and begins to absorb information about desert animals of several kinds. The animals are so different from the ones he knows that he is prompted to ask: "What is the land like?" and "What is the weather like?" Again, he receives quantities of slides, some with pictures, some with graphs, and some with written passages on them. It takes him a long time to progress through this batch of slides, and he has trouble extracting meaning from some of the charts. He asks for tapes and, with the taped commentary, is able to use the charts comfortably.

At this point, his session comes to the end for Monday, and he returns to the normal activities of his class. Tuesday morning he resumes his questions:

"How do they get water?"

"What are their houses like?"

"How do people make a living in La Stella?"

"What is their religion?"

With the information he gets from the last question, Charles begins to grasp the fact that the pueblo reveals a very complex pattern of interaction among several cultures. (He would not articulate it that way, of course. More than likely, he thinks something like this. "Hey, they have their own religion and they are Catholics, too. The Spanish tried to make them stop their own religion, but they wouldn't do it, even when the soldiers killed some of them. Now lots of them work in the towns near there, where the people are just like us. That is, they're not Indians. But there is trouble between our people and the people from La Stella. I wonder if they have their own country.)

He asks, "What country are the people of La Stella from?"

He discovers that they are United States citizens, but that they were colonials of Mexico, and before that Spain. Before that, they governed themselves.

"Who makes their laws?" In return for this question he finds information about the internal political organization of the Pueblo and about its relation to the United States government and the government of New Mexico. Learning that some members of the La Stella tribe have political and religious duties entwined, he remembers an earlier question, triggered by information about the religions. "What are their religious stories like?" The result of asking this is that he receives all of the old myths, rewritten from notes made by the anthropologists who first visited La Stella around 1880.

The myths are very rich. To a sophisticated reader they can tell much about the feelings and thoughts of the people of La Stella. To Charles, however, they are beautiful and strange stories. He likes them, but he does not know what to make of them. He reads them curiously.

Charles asks a few more questions and then tells Mrs. Green that he is ready to teach another youngster about La Stella. She gives him a reel of magnetic tape, and he makes the following statement: "La Stella. In the town of La Stella which is in the United States there are many people. Those people are Indians. They have founded the town many many years ago. The families of La Stella are supported by usually the father. The most important income to the family is that what comes from the making of pottery. This pottery is used for many things in the home. Sometimes it's just decoration, sometimes it is used for things like carrying water, and holding corn and corn meal, and many other things. They also are farmers in La Stella. The men take care of the farms, and when a boy gets old enough he is able to help the parent. On the farm there are grown wheat and corn, and other things. This corn can be used as to making bread, and so can the wheat, and it can be sold to people from out of town for use. The education of the children of La Stella starts at the age of five — as the normal school here does. They go through until sixth grade, and if they want any more education they have to go out of town to boarding school. People have been leaving La Stella because the Indian ways are harder and old fashioned, and they have found out by leaving the town to go to school and for other things. The Indians do not believe in following the white man's ways. They do not like our ways because they have not been used by the ancestors of their town. The Indians do not like our ways but they participate in many of the things we do, such as playing baseball and other um events such as this. They also wear our kinds of clothes except for sometimes they wear headdress and beads and moccasins. In La Stella the weather is very humid. Due to the heat, sometimes they have many droughts. In the winter it is cold and sometimes it ain't very often (not clear) they have snow, but in the spring they have warm weather, and it's very dry. In the summer they have rain, which is usually a lot of rain, but they still have to use irrigation instead of um this rain water. Just depending on the rains that come. They have to be irrigated. The town itself is very small. The houses themselves are made of adobe, which is clay. And on the inside the floor is either made of wood or adobe, and in the middle of the house which is very curious they have a large pole. And on the pole they hang many things such as coats, and they hang — instead of having cradles they hang their children from the ceiling in like a basket. The pole is also used to help the ceiling hold up. On the ceiling instead of having like it painted they have like tar paper going across the ceiling. The normal home has a herd of horses to itself. It's not actually a herd, but it's like a group of horses that is owned by the family. The children play in many games, in events. Such as races and special relay games, and the children also play some doing the things we play such as hopscotch and jump rope, and even baseball. But baseball is mostly played on good events like Saint Days. If someone should get sick in La Stella, they would have as much care as they would here. There are no facilities that they have that we don't have and we don't have anything that they don't. It is very odd town because of the old ways and the houses and everything, but it is still part of the United States and the people have the right to vote and everything that we have a right to. And as I said there are no facilities such as um household appliances mostly. Some houses have them, but very few do. La Stella is a very interesting place because of the way that they live that is so different from us. Another source of income is selling pottery itself and making drums. Drums are made from animal hides and gourds. The drums are very colorful and they also bring a lot of money from tourists. Tourists are usually people just like you and I. They come just to see how the people live and festivals in La Stella. They have many events such as I have mentioned as the sports. And they also have dances. In these dances they wear special costumes such as very colorful hats and feathers and very religious clothing as to their faith used to be. The normal clothing is still like ours, but they still wear the clothes that they used to wear long ago —"

What kind of school is this where Charles is able to get so much information about one tiny pueblo?

Charles is one of the students who is studying in a small laboratory in the Broad River School. The backbone of the laboratory is a set of data banks for children. Each data bank is a random-access data storage and retrieval system on a particular culture. The ones available to Charles are the pueblo called La Stella and a small New England town which is named "Prestonport." In addition, several storage systems about small towns around the world are being added. Each town has been selected to represent a particular cultural pattern.

To make each data bank, a research team started with an index system which is used to store anthropological data. This index contains nearly 800 categories, each category referring to one aspect of a culture. For a sample, consider some of the chief categories and their subcategories:

Agriculture
   Village
   Agricultural science
   Cereal agriculture
   Vegetable production
   Arboriculture
   Forage crops
   Floriculture
   Textile agriculture
   Special crops

Structure
   Architecture
   Dwellings
   Outbuildings
   Public structures
   Recreational structures
   Religious and educational
     structures
   Business structures
   Industrial structures
   Miscellaneous structures

Exchange
  Gift giving
  Buying and selling
  Production and supply
  Income and demand
  Price and value
  Medium of exchange
  Exchange transactions
  Domestic trade
  Foreign trade

Social stratification
  Age stratification
  Sex status
  Ethnic stratification
  Castes
  Classes
  Serfdom and peonage
  Slavery

Interpersonal relations
  Friendships
  Cliques
  Visiting and hospitality
  Sodalities
  Etiquette
  Ethics
  Intergroup antagonisms
  Brawls and riots

Religious practices
  Religious experience
  Propitiation
  Purification and expiation
  Avoidance and taboo
  Asceticism
  Orgies
  Revelation and divination
  Ritual
  Magic

The major categories, of which there are seventy-eight, together with the subcategories (up to ten for each major category) provide a complete spectrum for any known culture. To make the data banks, the research team obtained from original sources all available information about each of the towns around which a bank was to be built.

In the case of the pueblo, the results of archaeological explorations were available, as were pictures and field notes made by anthropologists between 1850 and 1900, records from the Spanish and American governments, and the work of contemporaty anthropologists. In addition, we traveled to the pueblo, took hundreds of pictures, interviewed citizens, and collected much information from New Mexico state government sources and the United States Bureau of Indian Affairs. The team then rewrote information, put pictures together with written passages, and created charts and graphs, all in an attempt to fill all possible categories with information so packaged that, with the aid of tapes, an average second grader could have access to it. Every effort was made to build the systems *so that each child would have potentially available to him all known information about life in those towns.* Also, all items were developed to emphasize facts rather than interpretations, so that the children, as they worked, would get data they could interpret themselves rather than being led to conclusions. (The same developmental process was involved in building the bank around the New England town we call Prestonport.)

Then, tape-film-map orientation units were created so that the children would be maximally free from dependence on adults. Adults would play two roles. One, which has already been described, is to translate questions into index numbers. The other is to select tasks or assignments that will gradually increase the child's ability to apply the tactics of the social sciences to the study of human culture. Let us return to Charles and see how a teacher can combine assignments with self-instructional units of various kinds, but which have in common the purpose of teaching the systems of inquiry which are used by behavioral scientists.

Teaching social science: diagnosis as the first step

Charles, in his first excursion to the laboratory, has been an interested inquirer. He has learned many facts about La Stella. However, his search is raw and unsophisticated. He knows no systematic way to inquire into a society, whether his own or another one.

Mrs. Green, fortunately, has many available ways of helping Charles learn how to study society as the social scientist does. She can give him practice applying social science generalizations. She can give him material designed to teach him the methods of archaeology, anthropology, geography, sociology, economics, or social psychology. She has materials designed to teach him how the social scientist formulates questions, collects and organizes data, and builds theories. Last, she has tasks or assignments designed to confront Charles with the kinds of problems that social scientists study. Charles can carry on activities by himself or as part of a group of children who are trying to learn the methods of the social scientists.

After Mrs. Green looks at Charles's pattern of questions and his description of the pueblo, she decides that he should begin work with structured tasks that will help him learn about the kinds of generalizations that social scientists use. She attaches him to a group of three other children, all of whom have been studying La Stella also. Daily, they come to the laboratory and try to apply social science generalizations to La Stella and Prestonport.

The first day the group meets, they listen to a tape that organizes their tasks and then presents the generalizations. Excerpts from the tape, plus five of the generalizations, follow:

> Prestonport and La Stella are towns whose people belong to differ-ent societies. La Stella is an Indian society which has been influenced by the Spanish and by European society. Prestonport is an example of the North American version of Western Society.
>
> Social scientists who have studied different societies have come to believe certain things about human societies. For example, they believe that all socieites have religion, families, sports, and several other things.
>
> We want to give you several statements that social scientists make about societies and see if you can find out whether those statements are true with respect to La Stella and Prestonport. For example, if we gave you the statement, "All societies have religion," you might ask to see the information we have about religion in La Stella and Preston-port, and you would find that both places have religion — in fact, each has more than one form of religion.

Statement one

All societies divide people by age and give people of different ages different things to do. Children, for example, do different things from old people. *Find out if this is true in La Stella.* You may ask any questions you wish about La Stella to find this out. When you think you have the answer, please call one of us and tell us the answer. Then go on to the next question.

Statement two

Most adults (grown-ups) in all societies are married. *Find out if this is true in La Stella and in Prestonport.* Again, please call us before going on.

Statement three

In all societies, the father is more likely to have authority (be the boss) than is the mother. In other words, the leader of the family is likely to be the father. *Is this true in La Stella and Prestonport?*

Statement four

The closer you get to the center of a modern town, the less money the people who live there are likely to have. *Is this true in Prestonport?*

Statement five

If a society depends on industry (factories or places that make things) families under one roof are likely to be smaller (just father, mother, and children) than when a society depends on herding and farming. (Then families under one roof often include uncles, aunts, grandfather, grandmother, and so on.) *Is this true for La Stella and Prestonport?*

The children retrieve data from the storage centers and debate their answers to the questions. In all, they try to validate the generalizations. *The purpose of this exercise is to familiarize them with the types of concepts that social scientists use to guide their study of society.* Since they have an easy time with these exercises, Mrs. Green asks them to see if they can find out whether the statements are true for their own town. They return in a week with solutions to seven concepts, but have been unable to find information about three of them.

Mrs. Green then decides to lead the children to learn how to analyze the tangible aspects of cultures. She plans a two-step program for Charles and his little group. The first step involves administering to themselves two of the units from the University of Chicago Economics Program, which was developed for use in grades four to six. The units she selects are designed to introduce the children to concepts that are used to analyze trade and the use of capital investment.[7]

With occasional help from Mrs. Green, Charles and his two friends work their way through the economics units. While they work, they keep a careful list of the economics concepts they are learning.

Next, Mrs. Green presents them with another tape, labeled, "Orientation — the New Business Task." Listening to the tape, they find they are being asked to study La Stella and Prestonport once more, but this time in order to make a recommendation about the kinds of businesses that would be likely to thrive in the two towns.

Once again they begin to ask questions and to retrieve information about La Stella and Prestonport. At first their questions are awkward and unordered — they have no strategy. During their second hour Charles has an "aha" experience. "Hey," he says, "how about some of those ideas we just learned! Didn't some of them have something to do with starting a business?" They discussed this for a while, and eventually decided to try to identify products for which there would be a special demand within either of the towns, and products which "their" towns were in an especially good position to create.

They retrieved information on house furnishings, diet, and transportation and found that nearly all of these were well-satisfied by existing businesses in Prestonport, but not in La Stella, where nearly all furnishings and foodstuffs were purchased in stores outside the pueblo.

And so their search went. Altogether they explored the possibility of more than thirty businesses before arriving at a list of five which they felt they could defend.

When they discussed their list with Mrs. Green, she had some

---

[7] See The University of Chicago Economics Project. Industrial Relations Center, The University of Chicago. William Rader, director.

suggestions to make, but did not ask them to continue the task. Before she could say anything about next steps, however, one of the boys said, "Don't tell us, we've guessed. Now you want us to find some good businesses for our own town."

During the next weeks, while the boys studied their town and developed a list of possible businesses, Mrs. Green decided that they were ready to deal with more difficult concepts that pertain to the whole of a culture. To prepare them, she introduced them to a set of self-instructional units which were developed by the University of Georgia Anthropology Project. These units were designed to teach children how to analyze cultures using the cultural universals — a set of concepts that can be applied to the study of any culture.

Weeks later, when they were asking for another problem to solve, she gave them their last one for the year.

> One way that cultures change is by borrowing and trading with other cultures. See if you can find out how La Stella has changed over the years by borrowing things and ways of doing things that were originally developed by other people. You may find that life in La Stella changed in some ways, but not in others. If you think of the cultural universals, they may help you find places where La Stella has changed and where it has stayed the same.

Once again the boys began to retrieve information about La Stella. They worked for nearly two weeks, spending one hour each day in the laboratory. When they were finished, they made a tape recording which they gave to Mrs. Green. It was the end of the year's work, and they remade the recording several times before they let her listen to it. The transcript follows:

> La Stella is a small Indian Village in New Mexico. It is called a *pueblo* which is the Spanish name for town. When the Spanish first saw La Stella hundreds of years ago, that was the name they gave it.
>
> The Spanish gave La Stella pueblo many things besides its name. The Indians didn't have any horses or cattle until the Spanish came. They had fire, but the Spanish taught them how to build stoves out of adobe. They had their own religion, with their own gods, but the Spanish taught them the religion of Christianity. Up till then they had used the water from the river to flood their fields. The Spanish had the idea of making ditches.

The pueblo Indians didn't always like what the Spanish brought them. They really didn't like to be Christians. But the Spanish soldiers were strong and sometimes mean. The Indians pretended to be Christians and kept their old religion, too.

In that time, the Spanish and Indians were living close together. They borrowed and stole from one another. The Spanish took jewelry when they could, and Indian blankets. They like the Indian adobe for houses, and when they built their town, Santa Fe, they used adobe bricks for houses. I don't know how the Indians plowed their fields before the Spanish came, but afterwards they used horses and Spanish plows. And they learned to talk Spanish.

When New Mexico became part of our country, La Stella pueblo seemed like a Mexican town. The people spoke Spanish and wore some Mexican clothes. Their ovens and their plows were Spanish. They even had carts with big wooden wheels like the kind they have in Spain! But they weren't Spanish or Mexican — they were Indians.

Now the people who live in La Stella seem like other Americans. They dress like us, have schools like ours, and they all speak English (except the very old people, who don't). They have television and new machinery for their farms. Some of the young men from La Stella are fighting in Viet Nam. The fathers are working in the American towns. They want to be more American. They remember their old ways and their old religion, but they want to be more like Americans now.

This is about what the people of La Stella have borrowed from their neighbors. The End.

Social sciencing with children

What was going on in the little laboratory in the Broad River School? The answer is simple, but the execution is complex.

Charles, his friends, and Mrs. Green were part of an experiment in ways of teaching children to try on the concepts and methods of the social sciences. Its ultimate goal is to learn how to teach children to analyze their social life and that in other cultures with the tools of the social scientist. Although the story of Charles and his friends is an illustrative conglomerate of activities which were engaged in by several groups of children, all the elements of their experience are available in the little laboratory. (Charles's description of La Stella, for example, is a protocol that was not even edited.)

Although the children had an unusual resource in Mrs. Green and her repertoire of self-instructional units and tasks, what they were doing can be done in any classroom, and many of the materials, in fact, are the products of curriculum projects and are available to schools for very nominal costs. An annotated list follows at the end of this chapter. The data banks were produced by a contingent of the research team that was made up entirely of determined housewives and college drop-outs. Similar but less elaborate data banks could be produced by teams everywhere. In any event, a professional team will continue to develop data banks on many societies and these will become available to schools.

The basic teaching strategy which we have illustrated really involves two simple steps. The first is to identify the concepts and methods of the social sciences. The second is to apply them to new content. Preferably the concepts and methods should also be applied to the child's own life and community.

The methods of small-group sociology and social psychology, of course, are suited for the analyses of face-to-face interpersonal relations. Anthropology is directed at large-scale cultural analysis. Economics, political science, and geography are adaptable to a wide variety of different-sized institutions.

Some teachers may prefer, at first, to rely on instructional materials to introduce to the children ideas that are drawn from the social sciences. However, it is much more vital to help the kids to collect and analyze data and try to explain and evaluate human situations in one's own, spontaneous fashion. In so doing, the social sciences will become transformed — they may lose some of the formal quality of science — but they will become live and relevant, without which no science, however carefully it is contrived, lives for long. The raw data of the child's social life is always available for his own study, and he deserves to learn how he can use the processes of the social scientist to organize and comprehend his experiences.[8]

---

[8] In the last few years, several curriculum projects have developed ways of teaching the processes of the social scientists to children and in a number of cases instructional materials have been developed. For example:

Race and Culture. Drs. Joseph Grannis and John Gibson have experimented with ways children can be helped in their attempt to comprehend Race and Rac-

Alternative modes

The two examples above have been only hints of what is possible. For example, any of the teaching strategies described in the last chapter can structure a curricular mode. In the next chapter we will examine ways of building entire school programs around several curricular modes, each of which plays a certain role in the educational life of the child.

---

ism. See John S. Gibson, *Race and Culture in American Life* (Boston: Tufts University, 1967.)

Economics. The University of Chicago Economics Project has developed sets of units for teaching children concepts from economics. Department of Industrial Relations, University of Chicago, Chicago, Illinois, 60637.

Economics. Also, the well-known Elkhart program, Lawrence Senesh, director, is available commercially through Science Research Associates.

Anthropology. The University of Georgia Project is a very comprehensive course. (Department of Sociology and Anthropology, University of Georgia, Athens, Georgia, 30601).

Public Issues. Some interesting ideas, adaptable for use in the elementary school, can be found in Donald Oliver and James Shaver, *Teaching Public Issues in the High School.* (Boston: Houghton Mifflin, 1966).

Social Psychology. Ronald Lippitt and Robert Fox of the University of Michigan have developed a beautiful set of upper-grade units which teach the methods of social psychology.

Inductive Thinking. Hilda Taba guided the Contra Costa (California) school district to a curriculum built entirely around processes of thinking. (Write Contra Costa County for information).

General Social Science. Bruce R. Joyce, *Strategies for Elementary Social Science Education* (Chicago: Science Research Associates, 1965) provides a comprehensive treatment of the teaching of social science to young children.

Data Banks. The materials described in the article have been developed by a team at Teachers College, Columbia University. Bruce and Elizabeth Joyce direct the project.

The regeneration of education: a multiple-modes approach†

*Any activity, any program should be in the nature of a challenge to youth, requiring concerted planning and action. Involvement in the planning and execution affords, at the same time, the occasion for the individual to test his acceptance or rejection by others, and an occasion personally to excel in the process.**

8

This chapter is about staff utilization — the organizational patterns that generate and regulate the daily flow of activity in the school.

The last fifteen years have seen a healthy multiplication of the forms of organization of the elementary school. In 1950 nearly all schools used self-contained classrooms in which a single teacher taught nearly everything (with some specialists in art, music, and physical education); but now we see several forms of team-teaching and academic departmentalization. However, the multi-purpose teacher, working alone, still dominates the scene.

Whereas technical support was once limited to textbooks and a few library books, we now see television facilities and extensive instructional resource centers; and at least one

---

† Elements of this chapter appeared, in substance, in two publications: Bruce R. Joyce, *Man, Media, and Machines* (Washington, D.C.: National Education Association, Center for the Study of Instruction, 1967) and Bruce R. Joyce, "The Principal and His Staff" *The National Elementary Principal, XLVII,* No. 1 (September 1968), pp. 24–29. Copyright 1968, Department of Elementary School Principals, NEA, All rights reserved. Reprinted by permission.

* From Muzafer Sherif and Carolyn W. Sherif, *Reference Groups* (New York: Harper and Row, 1965), p. 315.

school now has a specialist in the creation of game-type simulations.

Even with this increase in types of organizational forms, we are only beginning to scratch the surface of possibility. In the next few years much should be learned about how to combine new teacher roles, new pupil roles, and new systems of technical support into very powerful organizational structures.

In this chapter we will take the view that the organizational structure of the school should be derived directly from the curricular modes that are generated to implement the mission of the school. Once the curricular modes have been developed, a determination can be made of the staff roles required by the social, technological, and curricular systems of the school, and these roles will constitute the structure for staff utilization within the school.

In other words, we do not set out to develop a school that will have a particular organizational structure (a school for "team-teaching," for example). Instead, we let the structure flow from the requirements of the entire instructional program.

Many existing schools are plagued by two problems that emanate directly from the fact that their organizational structure was developed before their means were formulated. The first problem is that they are unable to create effective sets of means because their structure does not permit it. The second is that they are unable to adapt to changing conditions because their organizational structure is not designed for flexibility. Let us dwell for a moment on both problems.

To avoid both problems — a structure that does not follow from or facilitate the desired educational means, and a structure that inhibits change and adjustment of means — let us identify some of the organizational needs of a growing, creative educational environment.

Structural forms that facilitate staff growth

Teachers need opportunity to master new instructional maneuvers and roles in the social system of the school. They also need help in doing research on the teaching and learning processes and on social conditions. They need opportunity to study academic subjects and the transformation of academic material for children. A wide variety of support systems could be developed to help teachers do these activities, and many organizational forms make more efficient use of teacher time and thereby help produce the necessary time.

Specialists of the social system

The creation of effective social systems requires knowledge and technical competence available on few school faculties. In addition to a training center for all faculty, a school that wishes to develop effective social systems will need to include several people for whom the social system is the major responsibility. These people will have to help think through the social aspects of curricular modes, help the other teachers create and prepare themselves for social roles, and take major direct "social teaching" responsibility as well.

Technological support staff

Various curricular modes require various kinds of technological support, most of which were identified in the preceding chapter. Two considerations are of greatest importance. First, the technological support system should have creative ability — that is, it needs to be able to *produce* materials and ideas as well as use those developed elsewhere. For example, the instructional resources center needs writers who can develop written materials in response to demands from the instructional system. Second, technical expertness is needed. Experts in academic subjects areas, in the development of multi-media instructional programs, and so on, should be available.

Because the range of desirable technical competence is so great, it would be necessary in many areas (as television, for example) for one support center to serve several schools. Imagine, then, a series of technical support centers like the following:

Computer support center[1]

The staff includes two teachers who are specialists in computer-assisted instruction, several paraprofessionals, including computer programmers, and personnel who are temporarily assigned to the center for various purposes. These people are specialists in the application of computer technology to problems of curriculum and instruction. They develop computer simulations, automate "canned" programmed instruction materials, adapt them for use in the local schools, and work with other support centers to automate other procedures. They automate the scoring of objective tests and help the direct-instruction teams use the computer to track student progress. One computer support center serves about twenty direct-instruction teams. For many applications, it uses a large computer which in turn is used by many computer support centers throughout the region.

Self-instruction center

This center serves five or six direct-instruction teams. It contains many programmed materials and many packets of self-instruction materials — some purchased from commercial firms, others made up by the staff in consultation with subject specialists and direct-instruction team members. For example, it has self-instruction programs in mathematics and science which were purchased from commercial firms, and homemade social studies materials developed jointly by the staff, the computer support centers, and the social science specialists of the district. It has constructed packets of readings on world history that are used by the social science team in the high school and similar materials for secondary school science and mathematics. Direct-instruction teams — served by the self-instruction center — may use its library of materials or request the develop-

---

[1] These examples of centers are drawn from Bruce R. Joyce, *Man, Media, and Machines* (Washington, D. C.: National Education Association Center for the Study of Instruction, 1967), pp. 12–14.

ment of special materials. Children sometimes go to the self-instruction center where there are carrels and a staff to help monitor pupil progress. At other times materials are taken from the center to the suite of the direct-instruction team and their students.

It is important that a self-instruction center have the capacity not only to adapt commerical materials but also to develop materials on its own. In that way it can serve the particular needs of direct-instruction teams and the children for which they are responsible.

Inquiry center

The inquiry center is a library in the most advanced sense of the word. Its collection of materials includes slides, records, tape recordings, and facilities for listening and viewing.[2] The staff of professionals and paraprofessionals help the children use the equipment and carry out their personal inquiry. The staff includes subject specialists who are responsible for determining that the materials are adequate in each subject, consulting with members of the direct-instruction teams in developing resource and instructional units, preparing with team members teaching units in which they participate, giving lectures and demonstrations to large groups, and working with team leaders on in-service training programs.

Materials creation center

The materials creation center is staffed by professional writers, artists, and audiovisual specialists. They work with both the direct-instruction teams and the staffs of the self-instruction and inquiry centers. For example, a direct-instruction team and a social studies expert may want materials created for a special instructional unit on one of the new nations of the world. They consult with the staff of the materials creation center to have new materials prepared

---

[2] For a complete description of the development of an instructional resource center with comparable capability, see the Education Facilities Laboratory publication, *The School Library*, (New York: Fund for the Advancement of Education, undated).

that would be appropriate for the children. Or a team may want materials especially for culturally disadvantaged children. The center can respond when no suitable commerical materials are available, and it might develop projects on its own.

The materials creation center frees the schools from overdependence on commercial firms. It enables the development of books and other materials about topics which do not attract commercial publishers.

Human relations center

The human relations center staff helps the direct-instruction team with diagnosing and correcting problems within the social climate. A human relations center expert might work with a small group of children for a period of time, helping them to organize themselves more efficiently and to work together more effectively. Children might be sent to the center for a period of time to work in a special program designed to increase their interpersonal capacity and flexibility. The human relations center, however, is not a "life adjustment factory," devoted to subordinating individuals to the interests of the group. On the contrary, it exists to help in human relations situations which occur among staff and children so that both group and individual learning needs are satisfied. In large-city school districts, such organization might work in inner-city schools for long periods of time, helping to improve the climate of the schools and to work out better social systems within those schools.

Guidance and evaluation center

This center works with both the computer support staff and the human relations staff to help the direct-instruction team diagnose and make prescriptions for individual progress. It creates special tests and special assessment devices. The counselors work with children to identify intellectual capacity and growth and to make prescriptions so that each child can grow according to his own capacity. The guidance and evaluation staff does the test-making for most direct-instruction teams, although some teams prefer to do their own and rely on the center for advice and technical assistance.

Curricular systems staff

A multitude of possibilities is available here. In a multiple-systems approach, a staff will need to be assembled and trained for several types of positions. Tutorial positions, cooperative inquiry leaders, academic curriculum area specialists, reading specialists, and other positions must be designed as the curricular systems are developed. This approach contrasts with the common present-day practice of hiring general-purpose teachers to work individually or in teams, creating the systems as they go along.

Staffing for curricular modes

Various members of the social, technical support, and curricular staffs will work together, of course, to implement the curricular modes. Leadership can come in several ways. Possibly a curriculum systems coordinator could provide leadership through the entire organization. Perhaps "curricular modes teams" would have leaders. Another alternative would be to organize the social, technological, and curricular staffs into centers and subcenters that have their own organizational structures.

Decision-making responsibility must be established in any organization that emerges. The possibilities range from complete decision-making responsibility for all functionaries to rather tight central control or a binding democratic organization. In a multiple-systems approach, the patterns for making decisions would probably vary widely. In some modes teachers and/or children might have complete latitude and responsibility. In others, staff and students might work within cooperatively-developed guidelines. In still others, staff and students might operate within a tightly-defined instructional program.

The important consideration, again, is to derive the decision-making roles as staff roles are defined within the total set of systems in the school. To create decision-making roles before staff roles are developed is to invite an organizational lock-step.

The personal and the technical in education

One of the dilemmas we face in trying to bring technological power and systematic thinking to the education of the young is that systems and techniques can be imposed in such a way as to reduce the personal and the immediate in learning. Our great challenge is to seize the horns of this dilemma and spring between them, gaining the advantages of system and expertise, and use them to increase the personal and exciting elements. One way to do this is to create an organization that gives to a few wise teachers the task of creating personal, relevant education, but an organization that supports them massively with scholars, human relations specialists, makers of instructional materials, and other factors.

The following hypothetical example has been constructed to explore some of these possibilities. It represents a structural model that illustrates combinations of many of the alternatives we have been discussing. This model is not presented in any hope that it will be followed. It is only one of countless alternatives that can spring from the demands of each unique situation.

Restructuring elementary education: a multiple-modes approach

When we talked about the mission of the school, it was easy to see that, while it is not practical for the school to try to serve a great many functions, neither can it find its mission in one purpose. None would argue, for example, that the school should try to create great scientists or artists but leave to chance the development of human values. Nor would very many people want to create fully-enculturated youths who are unable to think creatively.

Just as the mission of the school needs to be plural, so the means of the school need to be many.

Far too many of today's schools use only one mode. For example, textbook-recitation modes dominate some. Cooperative inquiry modes dominate a few others. There is much unexplored power in combination of modes — in arrays of means that serve the multiple ends of the schools.

At present an unfortunate void appears to separate several approaches to the reformation of schooling. For example, there seems to be a gulf between those who feel that the likeliest avenue for the improvement of schooling is through the education of teachers[3] and those who have so little faith in teachers that they are trying to fill the schools with "teacherproof" instructional materials.[4] One group of reformers is exploring computer-assisted instruction[5] while many educators shrink from it as dehumanizing. There are those who see instruction as a counseling behavior[6] or see the teacher as a leader of democratic groups,[7] while there are others who would reorganize the school to assure "continuous progress" along predetermined lines.[8]

Furthermore, discussion of educational reform frequently assumes an "either-or" character that inhibits productivity, to put it mildly. Arguments too often assume a negative character. It is easy to put computer-assisted instruction in a bad light by suggesting, for example, what would happen to the child whose *only* tutor was a magnetic tape. Equally, academic counseling comes off poorly when we imagine all education as a one-to-one tutelage. Cooperative group inquiry is at a disadvantage when it becomes the only mode of instruction, if we realize that the wisdom of a group of young children, even skillfully led, is not an adequate guide to the whole of their education. Teacherproof materials may accomplish

---

[3] This is a central, if implicit, assumption of the proposals of the Project on Instruction, Ole Sand, Director. For example, see National Education Association Project on Instruction, *Deciding What to Teach* (Washington, D. C.: National Education Association, 1963).

[4] Many of the curriculum projects in academic subjects have accepted this. See, for a summary and critique: Robert W. Heath (ed.), *The New Curricula* (New York: Harper, 1964).

[5] Richard Wing, of the Board of Cooperative Educational Services, Yorktown, New York, is experimenting with the teaching economic principles through computerized economics games.

[6] Carl Rogers, *On Becoming a Person* (Boston: Houghton Mifflin, 1961).

[7] Herbert A. Thelen, *Education and the Human Quest* (New York: Harper, 1961).

[8] George W. Stollard, *The Dual Progress Plan* (New York: Harper, 1961).

some function well but may become an absurdity when they require the average six-year-old to do things the teacher presumably can't or won't do. (As when the "processes" of sciencing are to be introduced to young children through instructional materials taught "by the numbers.")

The absence of dialogue on alternative approaches to curricular reform is especially disappointing because each of the reform movements has much to offer the child. The distinctive curricular mode each espouses is pertinent to certain kinds of educational objectives, although each mode has disadvantages when it becomes the entire educational strategy.

Let us examine, therefore, a structure for the reformulation of the elementary school — a structure that utilizes three curricular modes: a cybernetic systems mode, a personal discovery mode, and a group inquiry mode. Each of these curricular modes has advantages for some educational purposes, but severe limitations for others. Blended together in proper proportions, they can achieve a far greater and a more balanced educational result than can any one of them, taken alone.

However, before describing how we might restructure the school using these three kinds of curriculum modes, I want to enter one disclaimer: I am *not* advocating the system I am going to describe. My purpose is simply to indicate the kind of power inherent in the current reform movements *when they are used together to develop a humane and efficient educational program*. This is not to say that all of the would-be educational reformers of today have something to offer the school. Nothing could be less true. But we have passed the day when we should think undimensionally about curriculums and, if we can learn to think in terms of educational programs using several kinds of curriculums, we can develop a very potent program.

Three curricular modes

Briefly, we will discuss the three kinds of planned educational program. One kind can be called the cybernetic systems mode. It is characterized by being made up of preplanned materials, largely automated, and, usually, using self-instruction by individuals or groups for whom instructional activities have been prescribed, again by an automatic assessment system that also feeds back progress reports to the learner.

A second curricular mode involves individual counseling to help the learner structure his own educational goals and activities. Guidelines to continuity and sequence might be developed, and the learner might be led to encounter some kinds of preselected problem situations, but learning is seen as personal and continuity as psychological.

A third curricular mode involves group inquiry in which the scholarly endeavor of the group and its interpersonal processes are included as subjects for study. The disciplines are learned by practicing them. Democratic process is valued. Feedback is collective and emergent. Content may be partly preselected and partly produced by active inquiry and dialogue on the nature of society.

Each of these curricular modes can be adapted to perform unique and important functions in elementary education. Blended, they can offer a common general education, the development of personal talent, and the humanizing effects of cooperative inquiry into critical issues. Let us examine them individually and then see how they can be used together.

The cybernetic systems mode

We are more certain of some educational objectives than others. The cybernetic mode is appropriate in areas of curriculum where:

(1) We have relatively stable agreement about cognitive or skill objectives. That is, we are relatively sure that we want to accomplish the objectives and will want to accomplish them for some time to come. A good example is skill in the four fundamental operations integers and rational numbers. For the next few years (not forever!) it seems safe to say that we want all possible children to develop reasonable proficiency in this area. Reading skills are another area in which we are sure that in the foreseeable future all possible learners should be brought to a high level of competence. It is not necessary for elementary school faculties or individual teachers to decide annually that the arithmetic operations or reading skills will be

taught. We can stabilize these and certain other areas for a long period, so far as general objectives are concerned.

(2) We can construct adequate self-instructional devices for the vast majority of students. "Self-instructional" should be broadly defined here. One can learn many things by reading about them. Books are self-instructional devices. *Programmed instruction* should be included. Units using films, tapes, and other media have been developed. Computerized games can teach many things. Simulation techniques will expand self-instructional possibilities greatly.

(3) We can develop automated feedback systems for keeping the learners and responsible adults informed of progress. Programmed instruction has an edge here, because of the precision with which objectives are specified and ordered, and the easy amenability of the process to "embedded" tests. However, precise automated evaluation is possible nearly any time that objectives are clear and self-instruction is possible.

(4) The area can be learned as well alone as in a group. Many aspects of social dancing might be acquired in response to films and computer-controlled instructions, but much of the appeal would be gone. On a more serious side, controversial issues, drama, and improving social and socio-intellectual skills *require* group activity for a good bit (rarely all) of the instruction. Learning map skills, on the other hand, does not require group interaction or very much didactic presentation by a teacher.

(5) Pacing of instruction is important. For example, in any curricular mode, many arithmetic and reading skills are achieved at enormously different rates. In fact, teachers, working alone and with traditional materials and normal pupil-teacher ratios, have been unable to achieve adequate individualization of instruction in most skill areas.

With respect to the social system, the norms would stress independence and industriousness. Students would need to learn to judge their own progress and "reward themselves" for progress. An air of calm support and mutual help would be important, as well as openness about progress. Teachers would function as facilitators and troubleshooters.

To summarize, where we have curricular objectives that are very stable, but are achieved at varying rates, and where they can be achieved effectively by self-instruction that can be monitored by automated feedback systems, we can apply cybernetic principles to create instructional programs. *Such programs would not work for all students* (no curricular mode does), and effective diagnosis would result in placing some children with tutors, remedial specialists, and teachers of groups, but they could work effectively for many. Subprofessional technicians can be trained to work with the children and the feedback can be scrutinized constantly by a specialist who would sound the alarm for students for whom the program wasn't working.

Because of the negative reaction of so many teachers to automation, we must stress again that the cybernetic curriculum need not be a deadly array of sequenced "programs." It can be a rich multi-media program, diversely using film, games, books, programs, and other devices. Also, it would not be appropriate for all parts of any curricular area. For example, while much science instruction might be automated, the cooperative attack on original problems could not be accomplished this way. Yet the cooperative inquiry is important not only because it is an efficient way to learn scientific facts! The cybernetic mode would be under constant revision as objectives change and technology improves.

The personal discovery mode

The old story about Mark Hopkins and the log has long been the symbol for a delightful and wise teacher, the idea of having one's personal great teacher. We are always trying to find ways of giving students personal attention, whether by individualizing reading programs, providing guidance counselors, or offering the opportunity to learn the French horn. The ratio of pupils to teachers has been against us, however, and so has the idea that the "curriculum" must be "covered."

Well, the cybernetic curriculum mode puts books and machines to work, freeing manpower for the development of curriculums devoted not to the individualization of common learnings but to the development of personal talents and interests. The idiosyncratic curriculum is appropriate for those ends which:

(1) Are defined by the learner in his personal quest for understanding and self-development.

(2) Need personal counseling to assure definition and the availability of any special resources and advice which the learner needs.

(3) While they might be achieved in group activity, they are accomplished socially only through interest groups in the generic sense of that term. In other words, where personal interests are congruent enough, group inquiry serves idiosyncrasy.

An idiosyncratic curriculum can be achieved by assigning students to the kind of tutor whom we can name an academic counselor[9] who meets with each student regularly and helps him define personal educational goals and the means for achieving them. In some cases he might serve as tutor. In other cases he might help the student to locate a teacher, resource person, community resource, or whatever would help. If a student were studying justice, the counselor might help him find a court where he could watch cases. If the child were interested in the French horn, the counselor would help arrange a teacher.

The counselor would help the child develop a program of wide personal reading (we don't want him stopping with what we provide in the cybernetic curriculum). Also, the counselor would help him get together with others of similar interests (it's not much fun putting on plays or learning modern dance by yourself).

Our academic counselor would have overall charge of seeing that the child's life in school is a good one and that he receives help with out-of-school problems. If he shows talent or creativity, the counselor would see that it receives nourishment. If things aren't going well for the child in the cybernetic or group inquiry portions of the educational program, the counselor would be able to help — to intervene drastically if necessary.

---

[9] I am indebted to Charles Mansfield of Valley Winds School in Riverview Gardens, Missouri for pointing out to me this term and some of the concepts it represents.

We might envision some teachers whose sole function would be academic counselor, each with an assigned quota of students. Available to them would be subject specialists of many kinds. Developing the functions of the academic counselor for the six- and seven-year-old should provoke some interesting research, since relatively few people have tried this sort of relationship with the younger child. It should be evident that such a mode would emphasize rewards for initiative and exploration. Seeking, probing, questioning would be highly valued. The technical support systems would need to be responsive to the demands of a great many students seeking a great many ends.

The personal discovery curriculum belongs to the student. It can exist because of energy saved by the cybernetic curriculum. Both of these modes emphasize the learner as an individual. That is not all he is, however, so we need another curricular mode.

The group inquiry curricular mode

The inquiring group was at the core of the Progressive Movement's approach to education. The group of students, with their teachers, would learn democratic skills and scientific method simultaneously while they explored their world and developed commitment to the ideals of democracy. Until the academic curriculum projects began in the 1950's the chief thrust for school reform was provided by the legatees of the Progressives. An overwhelming proportion of curriculum supervisors in the schools of today was influenced by this tradition.

Its Achilles heel has always been its dependence on teachers with extraordinary skills. Given the supply of talent available to education, the demands made were simply too great for the average teacher. He could not know enough about enough things and handle groups well enough to cope with the range of educational objectives.

However, group inquiry as a mode is extremely useful when:

(1) Group skills and interdependence are to be acquired. The democratic way must be learned *in situ*.

(2) The learner should test himself against the ideas of others. Controversial issues and contemporary social movements, for example, need the interplay of diverse reactions to events. Many kinds of thinking can be learned if we have to balance our ideas against those of others.

(3) Group dynamics is an important learning agent. The power of the reference group, for example, can accomplish many things. The intellectual and social climate of the school is a consequence of group process. Students can teach each other a good deal about social life. Drama, debate, sciencing, are social and are dependent on social feedback as well. Internation games require groups.

(4) Individual differences are advantageous. A homogeneous group, studying its society, would probably develop much less vigor and heat than a heterogenous one.

A spinning of dreams

At this point, let us construct a design for a school (remembering that "school" means "pattern of education") in which the basic organization of the school consists of four teams of teachers and clusters of support systems built around each of the four curricular modes. One team will use the cybernetic mode, one the tutorial mode, and two will employ group inquiry.

(1) In the first case, let us build a self-instructional mode, using cybernetic principles and consisting of self-instructional units of many kinds which give to the learner the option of developing himself in a number of areas. First of all, in terms of reading skills, then also in terms of arithmetic, then in terms of world history, let us build a chronological course within this mode. Let us also make available courses in several foreign languages, in art history, music history, and literature. The staff of this team will need to learn how to build alternative routes for students who are unable to teach themselves by this mode. They will need to be experts in diagnosis and in the training of aides that will do much of the work in these realms. The support systems clearly will have to be massive self-

instructional systems employing many media, television tape, programmed instruction, conventional books, workbooks, language laboratories, activities packets that instruct people on projects to be carried out, and many other things.

(2) Second, let us build a tutorial mode of the kind that we described earlier. The team which will administer this mode will be skilled in training people to counsel with children and to facilitate their personal inquiry. Each youngster will need to contact his tutor several times a week and the tutors will need to call in consultants as the students develop interests in problem areas which are beyond their particular competencies. The support systems for this mode will need to include an enormous library, again utilizing many media, television tape, concept films, motion picture films, filmstrips, slides, books of many sorts will need to be developed, and arrangements will need to be made so that the students can reach out beyond the walls of the school for instruction and for information.

(3) Let us also include a scientific inquiry system. In this mode, skilled group leaders will lead groups of children to inquire into significant problems and in the course of that inquiry will teach them the modes of inquiry and the structures of the academic disciplines. Each child should be engaged in several groups during each year. Some of the groups should deal with literature, some with the social sciences. The support systems for this layer need to include the products of the academic reform movement, the systems for teaching the disciplines to the children. Since many of these teachers will be expert in their discipline, more important, probably, are laboratory facilities, excellent libraries, and aides who can construct materials when they are needed and help the youngsters get to data and to ideas when they have the need. In this mode, each group will identify problems and attack them at its relative leisure. Scientific inquiry should not be hurried, and it is in the dialogue and in the debate that the structures of the disciplines become clear and the modes of inquiry become explicated.

(4) The fourth layer of this school will be devoted to a dialogue on the nature of the society and on the future courses that it should

take. In this mode again, skilled group leaders will help groups of children identify and study serious social problems. Also television programs will bring to the youngsters on a weekly basis information and analysis about contemporary events. They will also expose the youngsters to experts on various aspects of the society and to controversial figures and figures who are important in the movement of contemporary events. At the present writing, activities in such a mode would deal with the problems of the cities, the problems of poverty, the problems of building an international community, and the like. The teachers need to be skilled in group inquiry and to be backed up by support systems and materials which include not only magnificent library facilities of the kind described for the layer preceding this, but also by people who can help construct materials when these are needed. Some aspects of this layer can be accomplished through the mass media, as indicated before. Television programs can bring to the students of an entire city information and opinion about certain events, and this should be done regularly. Other activities should be done at the group level where clusters of youngsters attack and try to solve problems that seem worthwhile to them.

The balance in a multi-layer school

In such a school, teachers work in teams. As a result, the student is not exposed simply to the personality and opinions at one person at a time, but is a constant participant in a dialogue about what to do next and how to do it. If one teacher cannot help him learn the skills he needs, then he can turn to others. If one teacher has strong opinions about some segment of academic inquiry, or about the society, then that person's opinions can be balanced by those of the other members of the team. Furthermore, such a school balances the possibilities in the life of the learner. He is not dominated by skills, nor by the dialogue on society. He has the opportunity to participate in all of these. Also because each teacher does not have to be responsible for all those kinds of learnings, it is possible for the teachers to become experts and to teach each other the skills which are needed to operate in their particular mode.

A major theme of this book has been that in today's schools too many teachers perform too many functions and students are clustered together in such a way that enormous effort has to be expended to treat them as individuals. In the multi-layered school, some activities would be organized for individualization, and others for group inquiry, and there would not need to be a conflict between the two. Furthermore, the mass media, instead of being argued about as an alternative to the classroom teacher, can be utilized to perform its natural function.

The political organization of such a school should provide places for students to share in steering committees that operate the support systems, create materials, and shape the ways that students select curriculum alternatives. For example, the library should be operated by a faculty, student, and teacher aide committee that keeps continuous touch with the needs of students, the needs of the faculty, and the demands that are made on the staff. All the other support systems, too, should have steering committees of this kind so that the governance of the daily life of the school is a cooperation among all the members of the community.

Sum

The school has many functions and it has to be organized in such a way as to permit the many kinds of necessary education to go on. In the past, too many of the pressure groups which have attempted to influence education have argued on an "either-or" basis about what they prefer. People who are concerned with skills and basic information have argued that it should dominate the elementary school to the exclusion of other kinds of education. Equally, persons concerned with child-centered education have argued against the imposition of skills or groups, or other concerns that arise outside of the life of the child. Still others have argued that scientific inquiry should dominate the school, that the modes of the scholars should be transmitted as the primary business of elementary education. Yet others (and I have belonged to this group) have argued that the primary purpose of elementary education is to induct students into the dialogue on the society that is essential if the school shall remain relevant to its society and a moving force in the reshaping of human events. If this last does not happen, then education will not be humane nor even worth having.

Yet none of these four purposes should dominate to the exclusion of the others. Students who can participate in the dialogue on society, but who cannot read, would not be an appropriate product of an educational system. Similarly, students well developed on their own terms, but who do not know the modes of the scholarly disciplines, would be deprived. And so it goes. We need to develop an education that is personal, and intellectual, and social, and to do so in a matrix of discourse about the society that makes humane values the central core of education. To do this, I believe, we must build educational systems, segments of which are devoted to each of those purposes. For the modes of operation of the youngster in accomplishing each of those purposes is different and should be served by different teachers and different systems of support.

It seems important to refer again to the purpose of this book, which is to add to the dialogue about school organization by suggesting some ways that teachers and technology can be brought together to create a myriad of personalized, creative educational programs. To this end, a structure was suggested in which the curricular decision-making task was invested in highly competent specialized staffs and technological support centers that could respond to their requirements and those of children.

The purpose is *not* to spread the idea that instructional teams, combined with support centers, comprise *the* desirable pattern for American public schools; there are countless desirable patterns. And the challenge is not to spread ideas about the use of teaching teams or programmed instruction or the use of paraprofessionals or any other old idea. It is to develop creative mixes of teachers, resources, and children.

For too many years uniformity of structure has characterized the American school. The self-contained elementary school teacher and the departmentalized secondary school teacher have served all functions for too many children. These teachers have been backed up by inadequate libraries and only those textbooks that publishers feel are commercially attractive and politically safe. *Now those patterns are breaking down.*

In the future there will be not just one nationwide organizational pattern; there will be many. Tomorrow will bring not one national curriculum; it will bring as many curriculums as there are curious children and exciting teachers.

Teachers and children will select together from what Ole Sand calls the "pharmacies of tested educational alternatives," and they will thus create the diverse education for the creative and varied Americans of the future.

The essence of the approach I am advocating is to consider a person's environment as a network of support systems which limit and extend the options he has for manipulating his environment. Both the teacher and the child are seriously affected by the network of support systems in a school setting or in a nonschool setting where they are endeavoring to carry on educational activities. One can almost say that the only reason for having special places for schooling is to provide specialized systems that enhance special kinds of behavior. For example, for many years information retrieval systems for libraries have been confined to rather large institutions. So one needed to go to school to have access to reasonable bodies of information about many kinds of things. We are now developing information systems which will be linked to the home by telephone, computer terminal, and television screen. And we are developing extensive microfilm systems so materials of many kinds can be transported almost anywhere one wants them. An outcome of this is that it will be less necessary to go to a school to have access to information.

In a similar vein, to have contact with teachers who are experts in many fields, a child had to go to school, whereas now television, videotape, audio tape and the motion picture provide portable contact with rather advanced scholars in many cases, making it much less necessary to think of school as a particular *place*. Let us look at the structure of the school in terms of the development of support systems that can affect the needs and options of the child and the teachers. In this way, we can see how the need structure of the school can be altered by the way one shapes the support systems provided for the teacher and his pupil. As we have reiterated throughout this book, this is a critical question for anyone who would change the school from what it is now. For change is dependent upon the generation of new sets of needs which will encourage different behaviors from the ones which are now manifested.

Postscript: alternative models

*Our perception of reality is highly conditioned. It is influenced
by our personal careers, our social location, the job we hold, and
the web of meanings arising from all of these by which the ideas
and experiences we encounter are screened and selected. Hence,
our perception of reality can be changed only as these conditions
themselves are changed.**

9

The state of the future

This postscript ends what has become a series of essays on the
creation of models for elementary schooling. Hopefully they
have explored enough combinations of ends and means
structures to open up a view of the myriad possibilities of the
future.

We have not really begun to develop the knowledge or
views of education that will surely develop in the years to
come. As knowledge and theoretical preferences grow, so
will the number of positive models multiply. Diversity will
appear in education for specific age levels. For instance, if
only one view dominates thinking about nursery education
(which was the case for many years) then only one type of
nursery education (curricular mode) will be recommended.
If nursery education is seen as many-sided and if several
theoretical positions flourish (as at present), then several nursery schools will develop, and these will use more than one
method for more than one goal. Diversity will also increase
within curriculum areas. In social studies, for example, a
single position dominated for many years, whereas now

---

* From Harvey Cox, *The Secular City* (New York: Macmillan, 1965), p.
104.

many positions compete, and the models of social studies education have multiplied accordingly.

Diversity, by itself, is not a blessing to all human activities. It is nice, for example, that the telephone company discourages idiosyncrasy among its affiliates in the matter of dialing. Otherwise, I should have trouble calling my home (Connecticut) from my office (New York), to mention one tiny example of the fantastic general problem that would ensue.

Diversity in education, however, is probably necessary to the development and survival of Western Civilization. *Educational methods will become more and more powerful as more is learned about how to shape the behavior of children. If this growth in strength is accompanied by a greater standardization of educational goals and means, then the vital human diversity, on which the human society depends for vitality and interest, will be truncated.* To build strength, we need an education that helps us explore our common humanity but which capitalizes on our uniquenesses. Alternate models will serve our society and our unique persons far better than one great model possibly could.

Because our schools have been so uniform they have lost much potential vitality. This same uniformity has cost much in knowledge *about* education, for we have learned much about the one or two dominant models and nothing, of course, about the dozens of feasible models we might have been trying. The big job in educational research is to design and try out educational alternatives. This job is not for a few intellectuals in an artificial atmosphere within a geodesic dome. Rather, the joyous spinning of possibilities and the careful, skeptical analysis of results is for every group of citizens who would be, or must be, the Responsible Parties of our story.

Bibliography

1. American Association for the Advancement of Science. *The New School Science; A Report to School Administrators on Regional Orientation Conferences in Science* (Washington, D. C.: American Association for the Advancement of Science, 1963).

2. ANDERSON, HAROLD H. and HELEN M. BREWER. "Domination and Social Integration in the Behavior of Kindergarten Children and Teachers," *Genetic Psychology Monograph, XXI* (1939), pp. 287–385.

3. BANDURA, ALBERT and RICHARD H. WALTERS. *Social Learning and Personality Development.* New York: Holt, Rinehart and Winston, 1963.

4. BARRON, FRANK. *Creativity and Psychological Health: Origins of Personal Vitality and Creative Freedom.* Princeton, New Jersey: Van Nostrand, 1963.

5. BELLACK, ARNO and others. *The Language of the Classroom.* New York: Teachers College Press, Columbia University, 1967.

6. BEREITER, CARL and SIEGFRIED ENGELMANN. *Teaching Disadvantaged Children in the Preschool.* Englewood Cliffs, New Jersey: Prentice-Hall, 1966.

7. BERELSON, BERNARD (ed). *The Social Studies and the Social Sciences.* New York: Harcourt, Brace and World, 1963.

8. BLOOM, BENJAMIN S., ALLISON DAVIS, and ROBERT HESS. *Compensatory Education for Cultural Deprivation.* New York: Holt, Rinehart and Winston, 1965.

9. BLOOM, BENJAMIN S. and others. *Taxonomy of Educational Objectives, Handbook I: Cognitive Domain.* New York: David McKay, 1956.

10. BROWN, CLARK. "The Relationship of Initial Teaching Styles and Selected Variables in Student Teaching." Unpublished doctoral dissertation (Teachers College, Columbia University, 1967).

11. BRUNER, JEROME S. *The Process of Education.* Cambridge, Massachusetts: Harvard University Press, 1961.

12. CAMPBELL, ROALD F., LUVERNE L. CUNNINGHAM, and RODERICK F. MCPHEE. *The Organization and Control of American Schools.* Columbus, Ohio: C. E. Merrill, 1965.

13. CANTOR, NATHANIEL. *The Dynamics of Learning.* Buffalo, New York: Henry Stewart, 1956.

14. CARLETON, WILLIAM G. *The Revolution in American Foreign Policy.* New York: Random House, 1965, p. 100.

15. CHAMBERLIN, CHARLES DEAN and ENID STRAW CHAMBERLIN, *Did They Succeed in College?* New York: Harper, 1942.

16. COLEMAN, JAMES S. *The Adolescent Society.* Glencoe, Illinois: The Free Press, 1963.

17. CONGREVE, WILLARD J. "Independent Learning." *North Central Association Quarterly, XL* (Fall 1965), p. 233.

18. COOK, LLOYD and ELAINE. *Intergroup Education.* New York: McGraw-Hill, 1954.

19. COOK, LLOYD and ELAINE. *School Problems in Human Relations.* New York: McGraw-Hill, 1957.

20. CREMIN, LAWRENCE. *The Transformation of the School.* New York: Knopf, 1961.

21. CROSBY, MURIEL. *An Adventure in Human Relations.* Chicago: Follett, 1965.

22. CUMMING, JOHN and ELAINE. *Ego and Milieu.* New York: Atherton, 1962.

23. DEWEY, JOHN. *Democracy and Education: An Introduction to the Philosophy of Education.* New York: Macmillan, 1916.

24. DEWEY, JOHN. *The Child and the Curriculum.* Chicago: University of Chicago Press, 1960, 1956.

25. DEWEY, JOHN. *How We Think.* Boston: Heath, 1910.

26. DEWEY, JOHN. *Reconstruction in Philosophy*. New York: Henry Holt, 1920.

27. DOWNEY, LAWRENCE. *The Secondary Phase of Education*. Waltham, Massachusetts: Blaisdell, 1966.

28. FRIEDENBERG, EDGAR B. *Coming of Age in America: Conformity and Acquiescence*. New York: Random House, 1965.

29. FROMM, ERICH. *The Art of Loving*. New York: Harper, 1956.

30. FROMM, ERICH. *Escape from Freedom*. New York: Farrar and Rinehart, 1941.

31. FROMM, ERICH. *The Sane Society*. New York: Rinehart, 1955.

32. Fund for the Advancement of Education. *Profiles of Significant Schools*. New York: The Ford Foundation, 1967.

33. GOFFMAN, ERVING. *Asylums*. Garden City, New York: Doubleday Anchor Books, 1961.

34. GOODLAD, JOHN I. *School Curriculum Reform*. New York: The Fund for the Advancement of Education, 1967.

35. GOODLAD, JOHN I. and ROBERT A. ANDERSON. *The Nongraded Elementary School*. New York: Harcourt, Brace and World, 1965.

36. HANNA, PAUL R., CLYDE F. KOHN and ROBERT A. LIVELY. *In the Americas*. Chicago: Scott, Foresman, 1962, p. 310.

37. HANSEN, CARL. *Amidon*. Englewood Cliffs, New Jersey: Prentice-Hall, 1962.

38. HARVEY, O. J., DAVID E. HUNT, and HAROLD N. SCHRODER. *Conceptual Systems and Personality Organization*. New York: Wiley, 1961.

39. HEATH, ROBERT W. (ed.) *The New Curricula*. New York: Harper, 1964.

40. HOFSTADTER, RICHARD. *Anti-Intellectualism in America*. New York: Knopf, 1963.

41. HOLT, JOHN. *How Children Fail*. New York: Pitman, 1964.

42. HOMANS, GEORGE C. *The Human Group*. New York: Harcourt, Brace and World, 1950.

3. HULLFISH, HENRY G. and PHILIP G. SMITH. *Reflective Thinking: The Method of Education*. New York: Dodd, Mead, 1961.

44. HUNT, J. McVEY. *Intelligence and Experience*. New York: Ronald Press, 1963.

45. HUNT, MAURICE P. and LAWRENCE E. METCALF. *High School Social Studies: Problems in Reflective Thinking and Social Understanding.* New York: Harper, 1955.

46. JACOB, PHILIP. *Changing Values in College.* New York: Harper, 1956.

47. JOYCE, BRUCE R. "Staff Utilization," *Review of Educational Research, XXXVII,* No. 3 (June 1967), pp. 323–336.

48. JOYCE, BRUCE R. *Strategies for Elementary Social Science Education.* Chicago: Science Research Associates, 1965.

49. JOYCE, BRUCE R. and BERJ HAROOTUNIAN. *The Structure of Teaching.* Chicago: Science Research Associates, 1967.

50. KENWORTHY, LEONARD S. *Introducing Children to the World.* New York: Harper, 1955.

51. KILPATRICK, WILLIAM HEARD. *The Philosophy of Education.* New York: Macmillan, 1951.

52. KIMBALL, SOLON T. and JAMES E. McCLELLAN, JR. *Education and the New America.* New York: Vintage, 1964.

53. KING, ARTHUR R., Jr. and JOHN A. BROWNELL. *The Curriculum and the Disciplines of Knowledge.* New York: Wiley, 1966.

54. KOZOL, JONATHAN. *Death at an Early Age.* Boston: Houghton Mifflin, 1967.

55. LEONARD, GEORGE B. "California: A New Game with New Rules," *Look, 30,* No. 13 (June 28, 1966), pp. 28–33.

56. LINDNER, ROBERT. *Rebel Without a Cause.* New York: Grune and Stratton, 1944.

57. LIPPITT, RONALD and ROBERT FOX (directors). *Social Studies in the Elementary School.* Ann Arbor: University of Michigan, project supported by the United States Office of Education.

58. MAGER, ROBERT F. *Preparing Objectives for Programmed Instruction.* Palo Alto, California: Fearon, 1962.

59. MICHAELIS, JOHN U. *Social Studies for Children in a Democracy.* Englewood Cliffs, New Jersey: Prentice-Hall, 1963.

60. MIEL, ALICE and PEGGY BROGAN. *More Than Social Studies: A View of Social Learning in the Elementary School.* Englewood Cliffs, New Jersey: Prentice-Hall, 1957.

61. MILES, MATTHEW (ed.) *Innovation in Education.* New York: Teachers College Press, Columbia University, 1963.

62. MITCHELL, LUCY SPRAGUE. *Our Children and Our Schools.* New York: Simon and Schuster, 1950.

63. National Education Association Project on the Instructional Program of the Public Schools, Ole Sand, Director. *Deciding What to Teach.* Washington, D. C.: National Education Association, 1963.

64. National Education Association Project on the Instructional Program of the Public Schools, Ole Sand, Director. *Planning and Organizing for Teaching.* Washington, D. C.: National Education Association, 1963.

65. NEILL, A. S. *Summerhill.* New York: Holt, Rinehart and Winston, 1960.

66. NEWCOMB, THEODORE. *Personality and Social Change.* New York: Harper, 1947.

67. PHENIX, PHILIP. *Education and the Common Good.* New York: Harper, 1961.

68. PHENIX, PHILIP. *Realms of Meaning.* New York: McGraw-Hill, 1964.

69. POPHAM, W. JAMES and JOHN D. MCNEIL. "The Influence of Taped Instructional Programs on Certain Cognitive and Affective Behavior of Teachers" (Paper presented to the Annual Meeting of the American Educational Research Association, Chicago, February 1965).

70. PRESTON, RALPH C. *Improving the Teaching of World Affairs.* Englewood Cliffs, New Jersey: Prentice-Hall, 1956.

71. ROGERS, CARL R. *Client-Centered Therapy.* Boston: Houghton Mifflin, 1950.

72. ROGERS, CARL R. *Client-Centered Therapy: Its Current Practice.* Boston: Houghton Mifflin, 1951.

73. ROGERS, CARL R. *On Becoming a Person.* Boston: Houghton Mifflin, 1961.

74. ROSENTHAL, ROBERT and L. JACOBSON. *Pygmalion in the Classroom.* New York: Holt, Rinehart and Winston, 1968.

75. SAMPSON, ANTHONY. *Anatomy of Britain Today.* New York: Harper and Row, 1965.

77. SCHAEFER, ROBERT J. *The School as a Center of Inquiry.* New York: Harper and Row, 1967.

78. SCHWAB, JOSEPH J. and PAUL BRANDWEIN. *The Teaching of Science.* Cambridge, Massachusetts: Harvard University Press, 1962.

79. SHAFTEL, FANNIE R. and GEORGE. *Role-Playing for Social Values: Deci-*

sion-Making in the Social Studies. Englewood Cliffs, New Jersey: Prentice-Hall, 1967.

80. SHIRER, WILLIAM L. *The Rise and Fall of the Third Reich.* New York: Simon and Schuster, 1960.

81. SMITH, KARL U. and MARGARET FOLTZ SMITH. *Cybernetic Principles of Learning and Educational Design.* New York: Holt, Rinehart and Winston, 1966.

82. SMITH, LOUIS and WILLIAM GEOFFREY. *The Complexities of the Urban Classroom.* New York: Wiley, 1968.

83. SMITH, LOUIS. *Social Psychological Aspects of School Building Design.* St. Louis, Missouri: Washington University, 1967. A report to the United States Office of Education.

84. STOLLARD, GEORGE W. *The Dual Progress Plan.* New York: Harper, 1961.

85. TABA, HILDA. *Intergroup Education in Public Schools.* Washington, D. C.: American Council on Education, 1952.

86. TABA, HILDA. *Thinking in Elementary School Children.* San Francisco: San Francisco State College, 1964.

87. TAYLOR, CALVIN (ed.) *Creativity: Progress and Potential.* New York: McGraw-Hill, 1964.

88. THELEN, HERBERT A. *Classroom Grouping for Teachability.* New York: Wiley, 1967.

89. THELEN, HERBERT A. *Education and the Human Quest.* New York: Harper, 1961.

90. TORRANCE, E. PAUL. *Gifted Children in the Classroom.* New York: Macmillan, 1965.

91. TYLER, RALPH W. *Basic Principles of Curriculum and Instruction.* Chicago: University of Chicago Press, 1950.

92. WALLER, WILLARD. *The Sociology of Teaching.* New York: Wiley, 1965. Originally published in 1932.

93. WERTHEIMER, MAX. *Productive Thinking.* New York: Harper, 1945.

Index

Academic domain, 57
Academic reform movement, 61
Academic structure, 59
Aesthetic capacity, 69
Alternative academic missions, 66
Amidon plan, 91
Anderson, Robert, 5
Assessment systems, 174 ff.
Ausubel, David, 161 ff.

Bandura, Albert, 106
Bellack, Arno, 20, 21, 99
Bereiter, Carl, 88
Berelsen, Bernard, 141
Bloom, Benjamin, 83
Boguslaw, Robert, 121
Broad fields approach to curriculum, 59
Broudy, Harry, 195
Brown, Clark, 105
Brownell, John A., 62
Bruner, Jerome, 59, 151, 187
Bureaucratic nature of school, 10

Campbell, Roald, 8

Canton, Nathaniel, 22
Chamberlin, Charles and Enid, 53
Child-centered education, 197
Citizen-centered curriculum, 182
Coleman, James, 2, 98
Community attitudes, 26
Community pressures on schools, 32 ff.
Compensatory education, 34, 36
Competency needs of teachers, 19 ff.
Computer assists, 6, 12, 127 ff., 138, 218
Concept attainment, 151 ff.
Congreve, Willard, 23
Controversial issues, 27, 28
Cox, Harvey, 237
Cremin, Lawrence, 53
Crosby, Muriel, 27, 73
Cumming, John and Elaine, 13, 103
Cunningham, Luverne, 8
Curricular mode, 5, 195
Curricular systems, 137 ff.
Curriculum, multiple mode, 215
Curriculum reform movement, 28
Cybernetic systems mode, 225

Data storage and retrieval systems, 6
as support systems, 124, 200 ff.
Dewey, John, 69, 90, 115
Disciplines, structure of 60, 61, 139, 187
Domains of educational function, 56, 138
Downey, Lawrence, 137

Educational objectives, 75 ff.
Educational purposes, 51
Ends–means relationship, 52

Feedback systems, 174 ff.

Geoffrey, William, 17
Goffman, Erving, 97
Goodlad, John, 5
Goodman, Paul, 137
Grading standards as controlling, 17
Group inquiry mode, 229

Harootunian, Berj, 19, 97, 125
Heath, Robert W., 61, 127
Hofstadter, Richard, 57
Holt, John, 19, 142
Homans, George C., 95, 97
Human relations, 72
Hunt, David E., 166 ff.

Individual differences and instruction, 167
Inductive teaching, 148 ff.
Information processing, 127
Innovations, institutional rejection of, 20 ff.
Institutional leadership, 98
Instructional systems, 124

Jacob, Philip, 100
Jacobson, L., 102
Joyce, Bruce, 3, 19, 23, 60, 81, 89, 97, 112 ff., 123, 125, 146, 176, 200, 213, 215, 218

Kilpatrick, William Heard, 95
Kimball, Solon T., 54
King, Arthur R., Jr., 62
Kozol, Jonathan, 16

Latent functions, 54
Leonard, George B., 51

McClellan, James E., Jr. 54
McPhee, Roderick, 8
Michaelis, John U., 115
Miles, Matthew, 118
Missions of the school, 55 ff.
Mission of school, sample 92–94
Modes of inquiry, 62
Moger, Robert F., 82
Multi-media systems, 126

National curriculum bank, 130 ff.
Needs of institutions, 13 ff.
Neill, A. S., 22
Non-graded schools, 5

Objectives, operational, 78, 144

Palmer, John R., 195
Personal discovery mode, 227
Personal domain, 66 ff.
Personal meaning, 69
Personalizing instruction, 166 ff.
Person-centered curriculum, 178 ff.
Phenix, Philip, 6, 140
Pressure groups, 38 ff.
Problem-solving capacity, 69

Productive thinking, 68
Programmed instruction, 125
Progressive movement, 53

Responsible parties, 44, 46 ff., 75, 76 ff., 85 ff.
Responsive technology, 129
Rogers, Carl, 22, 197
Rosenthal, Robert, 102

Sand, Ole, 1
Schaefer, Robert J., 29
Scopes trial, 39
Segregation, *de facto*, 46
Sequence in curriculum, 171 ff.
Sherif, Muzafer and Carolyn, 215
Simulation as educational service, 125
Smith, Louis, 17
Social forces and education, 8 ff.
Social influence as educational means, 101
Social missions of education, 70 ff.
Social science curriculum center, 185 ff., 188 ff.
Social sciencing as curricular mode, 199 ff.

Social studies, 177 ff.
Social system of school, 95, 102, 104 ff., 118
Socialization, 33
Student roles, 108 ff.
Support systems in education, 112 ff.
Symbolic purposes of school, 58

Taba, Hilda, 73, 148 ff.
Teacher, world of, 29
Teacher roles, 111
Teaching methods as controlling, 17
Teaching strategies, 99, 144, 147 ff.
Team teaching, 5
Technical means of education, 121
Technology and educational objectives, 42
Television courses, 125
Thelen, Herbert, 11, 72, 115 ff.
Tyler, Ralph, 76, 82, 92

University of Chicago Laboratory School, 23

Waller, Willard, 98
Walters, Richard H., 106